AF291220

CONCORDE

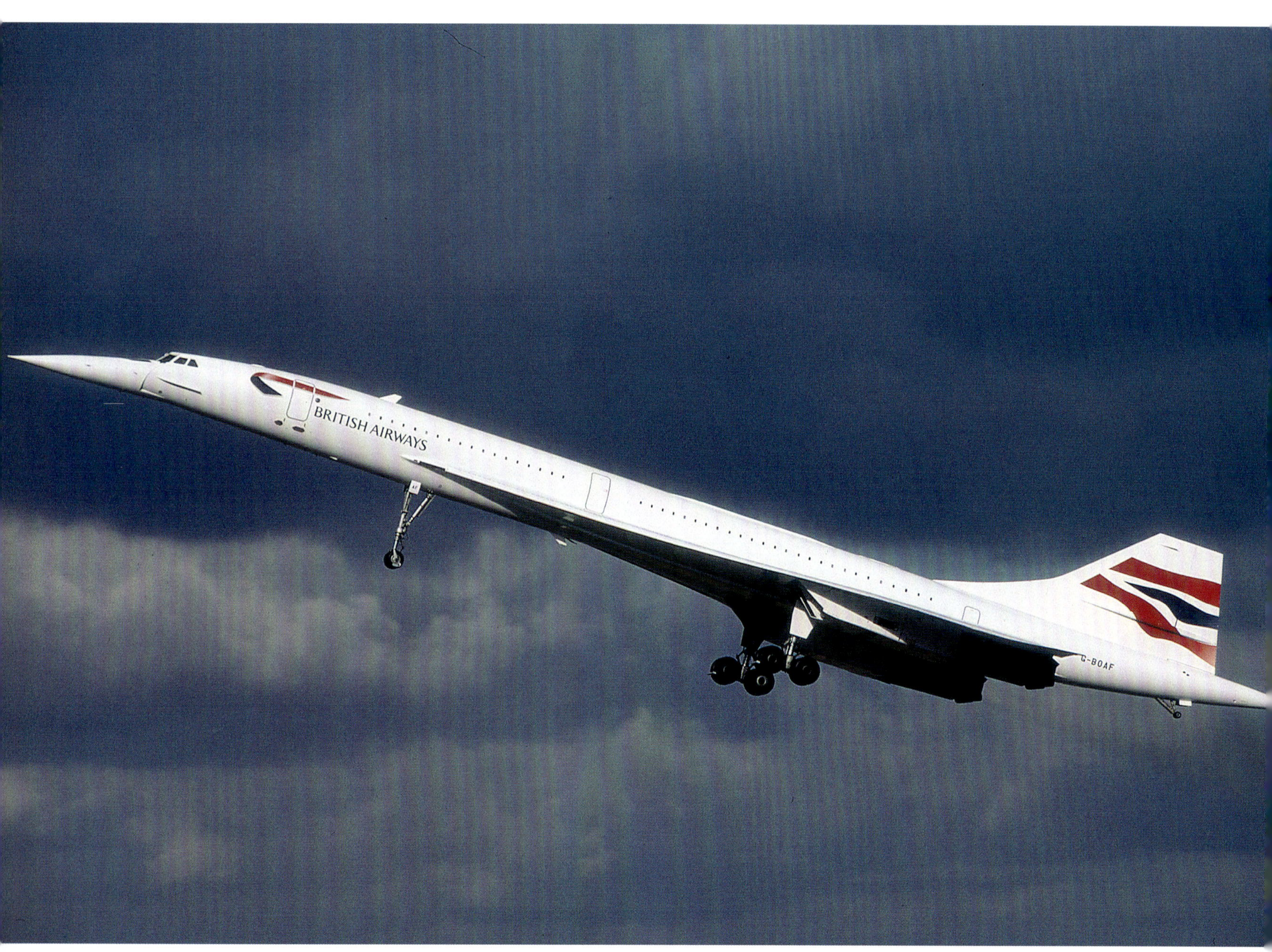

G-BOAF departs Heathrow with staff on board for a tour around the Bay of Biscay, which included a supersonic run.

A COLLECTION IN PHOTOGRAPHS
CONCORDE

ROBBIE SHAW

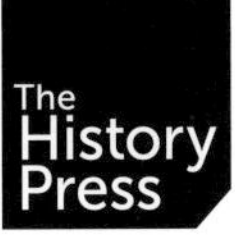

The History Press

Cover illustrations
Front: G-BOAG taxiing out from Terminal 4 at Heathrow, next stop New York. (Author)
Back: The Pepsi Blue Concorde bound for Dublin on 3 April 1996. (Author)
Author Photo: The author in cockpit of G-BOAE, 19 October 2003. (Author)

First published 2025

The History Press
97 St George's Place, Cheltenham,
Gloucestershire, GL50 3QB
www.thehistorypress.co.uk

British Library Cataloguing in Publication Data.
A catalogue record for this book is available from the British Library.

ISBN 978 1 80399 846 6

Typesetting and origination by The History Press
Printed in Turkey by IMAK

EU Authorised Representative: Easy Access System Europe
Mustamäe tee 50, 10621 Tallinn, Estonia
gpst.request@easproject.com

CONTENTS

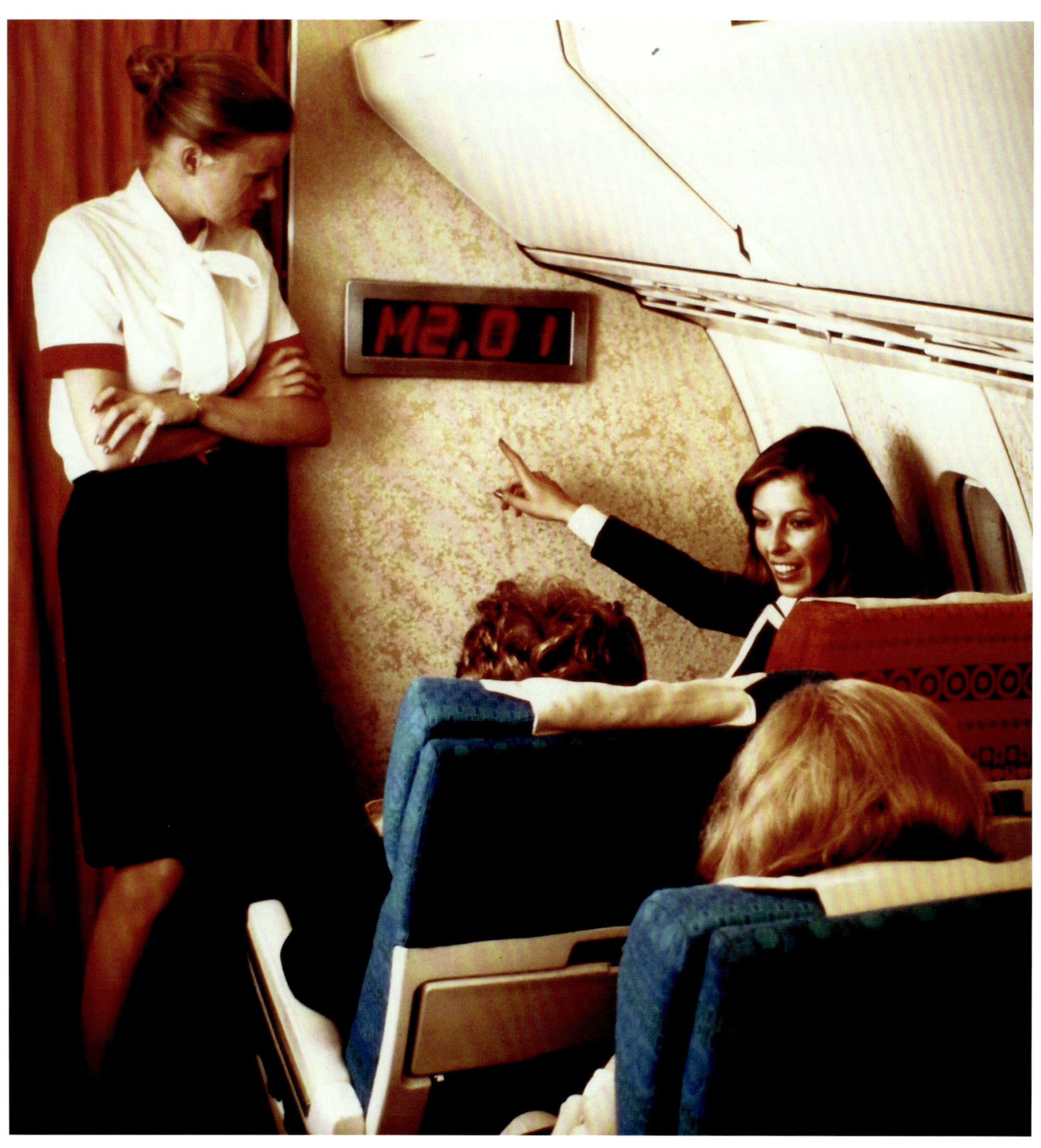

Look – we are flying at over twice the speed of sound! The Machmeter on the bulkhead was a brilliant marketing idea and proved very popular with the passengers. In this shot the female passenger seems very pleased to be flying at Mach 2.01, whilst the stewardess looks on as if to say 'seen it all before'. (BA Speedbird Heritage Centre)

ABOUT THE AUTHOR

Educated at Govan High School in Glasgow, I became an aircraft enthusiast at the age of 12, after attending the last ever air show at Royal Naval Air Station Abbotsinch (HMS *Sanderling*), which is now Glasgow International Airport. I was hooked. In my teenage years I would sometimes take a train to Leuchars Junction Railway Station in Fife, a short walk from the end of the runway at RAF Leuchars, where I would spend hours watching the base's Lightnings.

After school I joined British Rail on a two-year supply course, but after nine months my love of aircraft proved too strong and in March 1969 I joined the Royal Air Force as an assistant air traffic controller. Three of my first five postings were disappointing as they were not at airfields, namely Preston Air Traffic Control Centre at Barton Hall, Border Radar at Boulmer and Eastern Radar at Watton. Then there was Muharraq, Wyton (twice) and Bruggen.

Following training as an air traffic controller there were tours at Brawdy, Scampton, when it became the base for the Central Flying School (CFS) after its move from Leeming, Sek Kong (Hong Kong) and Benson, before I left the RAF in 1991 and embarked on a ten-month course to get my civil licences. In 1992 I went to Gatwick, where I spent the next nineteen years before retiring in 2011.

My interest was always in military aviation, until I spent a couple of years in Hong Kong. This coincided with the USAF painting everything, including the C-5 Galaxy, 'grot' green. At the same time the US Navy were dispensing with their colourful markings and aircraft like the P-3 were being painted overall grey. While in Hong Kong I thought I should go to Kai Tak to photograph the Chinese Tridents, which were regular visitors. I realised that there were lots of colourful liveries around, and I got more and more into the airline scene.

Once I was based at Gatwick I really became a civil aviation enthusiast, at the same time losing interest in military aviation. The current crop of fast jets like the Typhoon, Rafale, Gripen and F-35 do nothing for me, and I call them grey plastic aircraft. I am just glad that I grew up in an era of classic jets like the Lightning, Phantom, Buccaneer, Victor and Vulcan. Outside those, my favourites are the F-101 Voodoo, the Saab Draken and Viggen.

My wife has no interest in aviation, but she does like Concorde. So, I hope you will enjoy this selection of Concorde photographs. Unless otherwise stated, all photographs were taken by myself. Enjoy!

Robbie Shaw, 2025

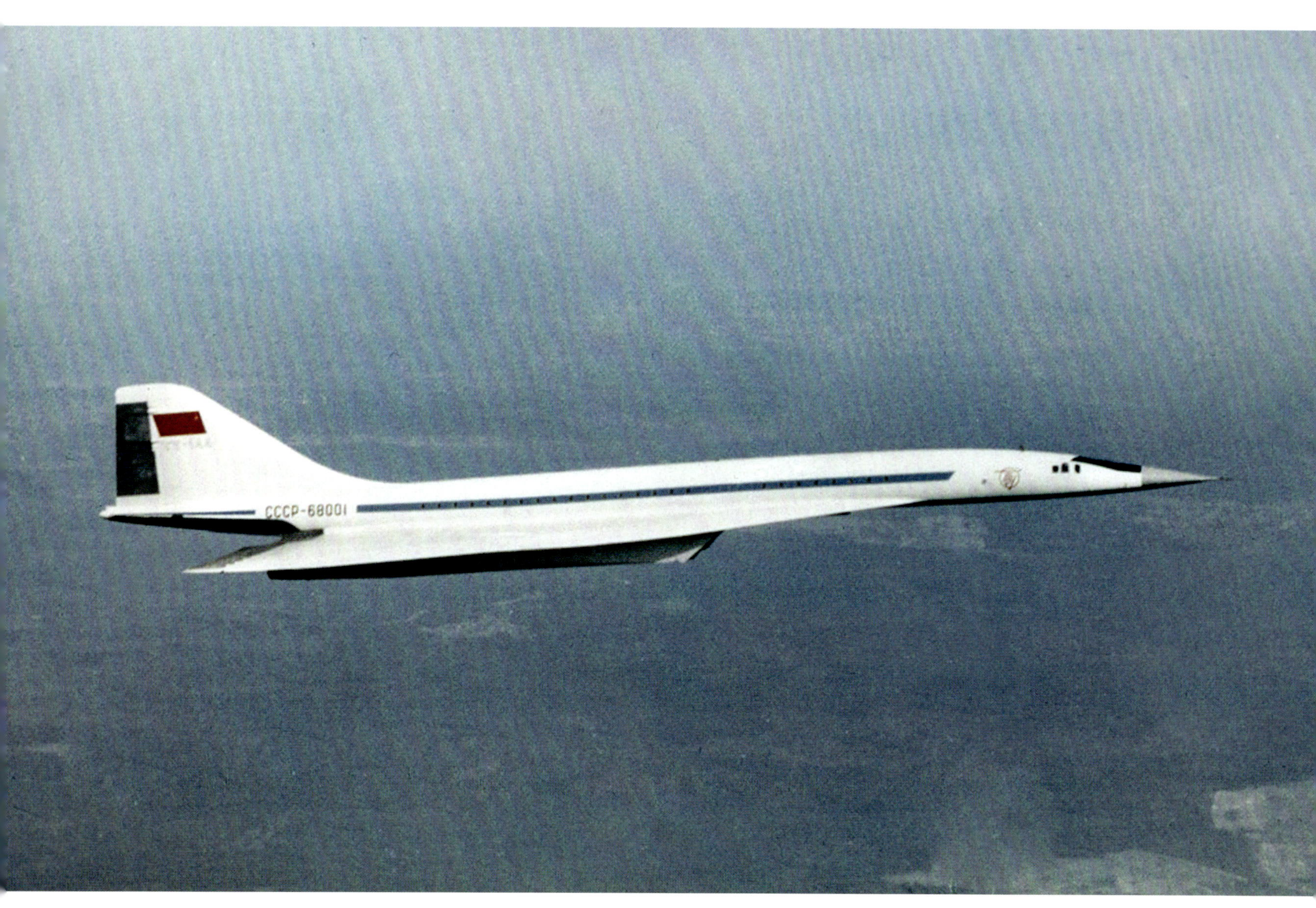

A Tupolev Tu-144 supersonic passenger airliner. (RIA Novosti archive, image #566221/Lev Polikashin/CC-BY-SA 3.0 via Wikimedia Commons)

INTRODUCTION

The British Aerospace/Sud Aviation Concorde was one of two supersonic airliners built, but it is the only commercially successful one. The other was the Soviet-built Tupolev Tu-144, which was popularly known as 'Concordski' in the West, despite its NATO codename being 'Charger'. The US Government did plan to build a third, the Boeing 2707 SST (Super-Sonic Transport), but withdrew funds when costs began to spiral. The US type was designed to fly faster than Concorde, at speeds up to Mach 3, and was to be larger, carrying between 250 and 300 passengers. Initially it was designed to have swing wings, but this made the aircraft too heavy and the designers defaulted to a delta. The size was also reduced to about 150 passengers and aimed at the transatlantic market. However, rising costs, environmental concerns, noise and the lack of a clear market led to its cancellation in 1971.

Although the Tupolev Tu-144 and Concorde looked very similar, many people were surprised to note that they differed structurally. The most obvious difference was the Tupolev's retractable canards in the nose, but it also did not have vortices over the wing to help provide extra lift at low speeds. It is believed that the engines were not flight tested on other aircraft before the prototype first flew on 31 December 1968 – two months ahead of Concorde. The Tu-144 flew only from 1968 until 1983, but it would seem it was an abject failure. Its limited Aeroflot career lasted from 1977 to the following year, when it was in regular use between Moscow and Vladivostok in the far east of the country, often carrying just mail and freight. It also flew services to Alma-Ata (now Almaty in Kazakhstan) but the loads were very poor and the service discontinued after just six months. However, because it flew over remote regions it often went supersonic on these routes. Those who have flown in the Tu-144 say it was extremely crude and uncomfortable inside, basic amenities like toilets and interior lights often failed to work, and it also had very limited baggage space. Amazingly, it only flew fifty-five times carrying passengers. In comparison, Concorde carried out 83,977 passenger flights.

The Tu-144 suffered two crashes, with the first at the Paris Air Show on 3 June 1973 shocking many. A Concorde had displayed first, and later came CCCP-77102, which was the second Tu-144 built. The aircraft made an approach to the runway with the canards extended, gear down and engines at or close to full power. It then pulled up steeply and pitched over, possibly stalling. As the pilot tried to pull out of the dive, the aircraft broke up and disintegrated, killing all six on board and eight on the ground, as well as destroying fifteen houses. Basically, the aircraft suffered a structural failure.

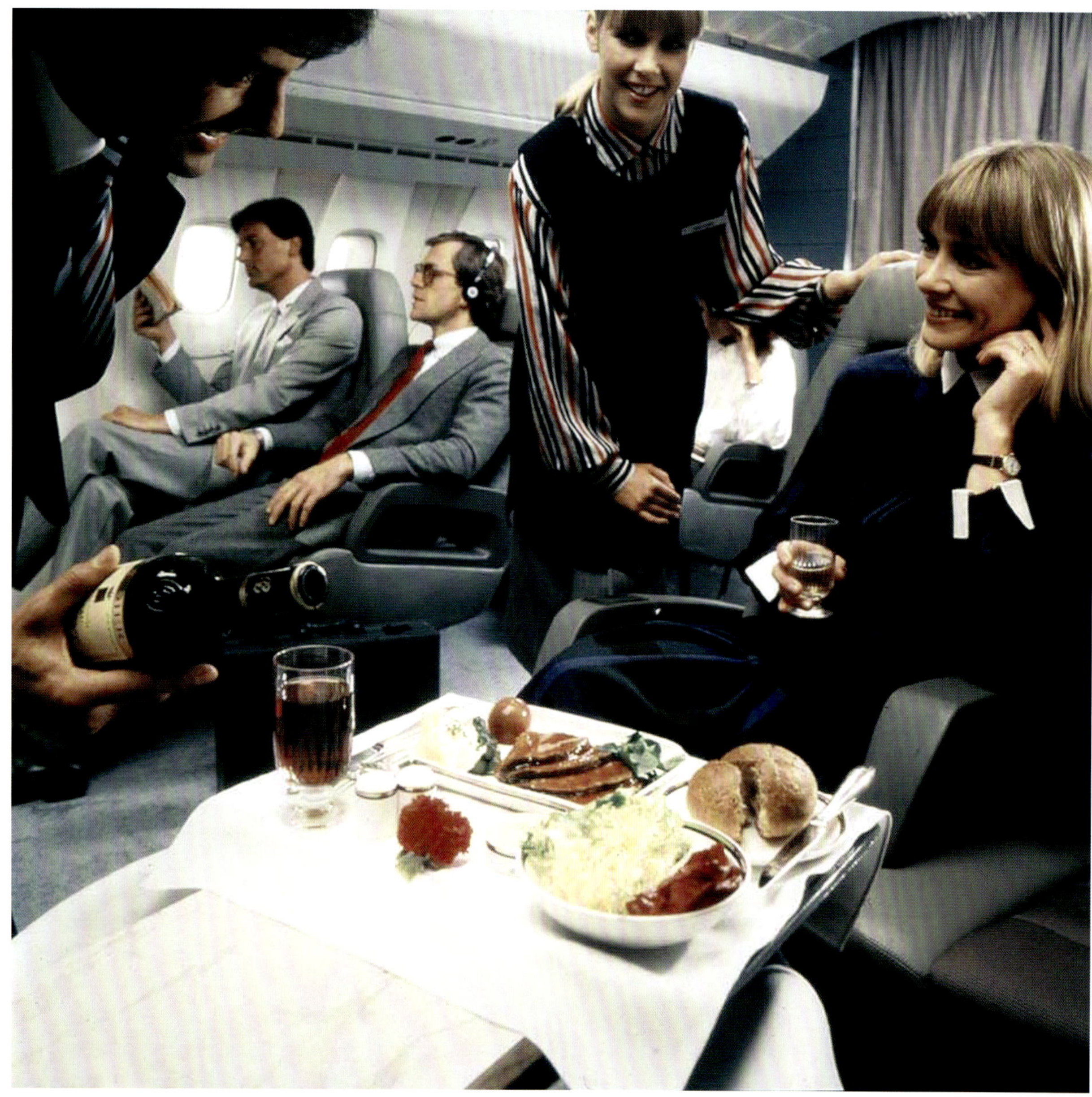

Meal time. The food and wine on board was of the highest quality. (BA Speedbird Heritage Centre)

The board of inquiry was never able to give a satisfactory reason for the crash. One test pilot who witnessed the display thought that the aircraft was trying a manoeuvre that it was not capable of recovering from in a bid to outdo Concorde's performance.[*]

In the second incident, during flight testing on 23 May 1978, two engineers were killed during a crash landing in a field that had been necessitated by an in-flight fire and subsequent engine failure.

A few years ago, I saw a very interesting television documentary that highlighted the incredible amount of espionage the Russians engaged in regarding Concorde.[**] I am pretty sure that the Tu-144 was rushed into flight just to beat Concorde. That could explain why the aircraft was anything but a commercial success. Surprisingly, though, Tupolev produced sixteen aircraft at Voronezh, with the prototype taking to the air on 31 December 1968 at Zhukovsky. The aircraft was retired from passenger service in 1978 after the second crash and from commercial service in 1983. The type sometimes used in research roles until it was finally retired in 1999, with several examples being given to museums.

Now we can turn to Concorde, an aircraft all enthusiasts, and many of its passengers, miss, and which many say was ahead of its time.

Like many, I have always had a soft spot for this inspirational aircraft. At the time it entered service I was in the Royal Air Force and therefore primarily interested in military aviation, not the airliner scene. However, I started working at Gatwick after leaving the air force, where I became really into photographing airliners, and substantial travel allowed me to photograph Concorde at Heathrow, Gatwick, Paris Charles de Gaulle and New York/John F. Kennedy. During numerous visits to Heathrow, I thankfully had plenty of opportunities to photograph the type. Seeing the many hundreds, if not thousands, of people on the roads around Heathrow on the final day of operations gives an idea of just how popular the aircraft was. In this book you will see chapters dedicated firstly to prototype and development aircraft. This is followed by chapters containing many photographs of the aircraft flown by British Airways and Air France, including a feature on the short-lived Pepsi Blue Concorde.

---

[*] Bureau of Aircraft Accidents Archives; Tu-144 SST Accidents, www.baaa-acro.com/crash/crash-tupolev-tu-144s-goussainville-14-killed.

[**] Channel 4 documentary, 25 November 2023, *The Race for Supersonic*; Dr Calder Walton interview, *The Times*, 25 November 2023.

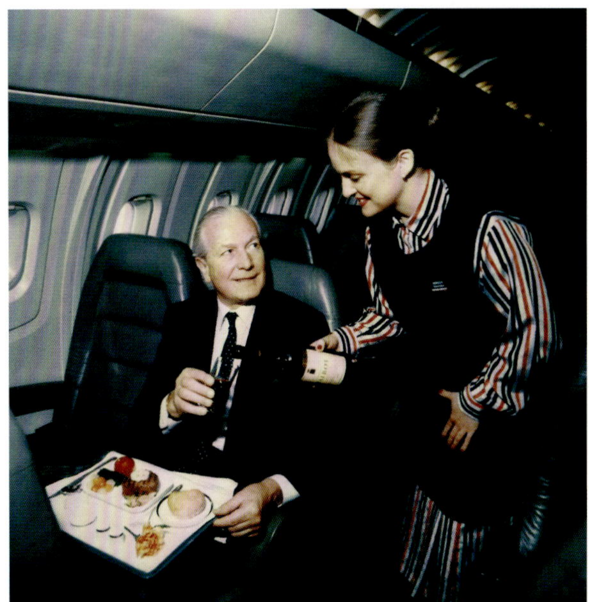

A passenger being served wine – does it taste any better at over 50,000ft? In the early years of British Airways, Concorde operations' passenger loads were low due to the high cost of tickets. That is noticeable in this shot showing many empty seats; one could almost ask, 'Where are the passengers?' (BA Speedbird Heritage Centre)

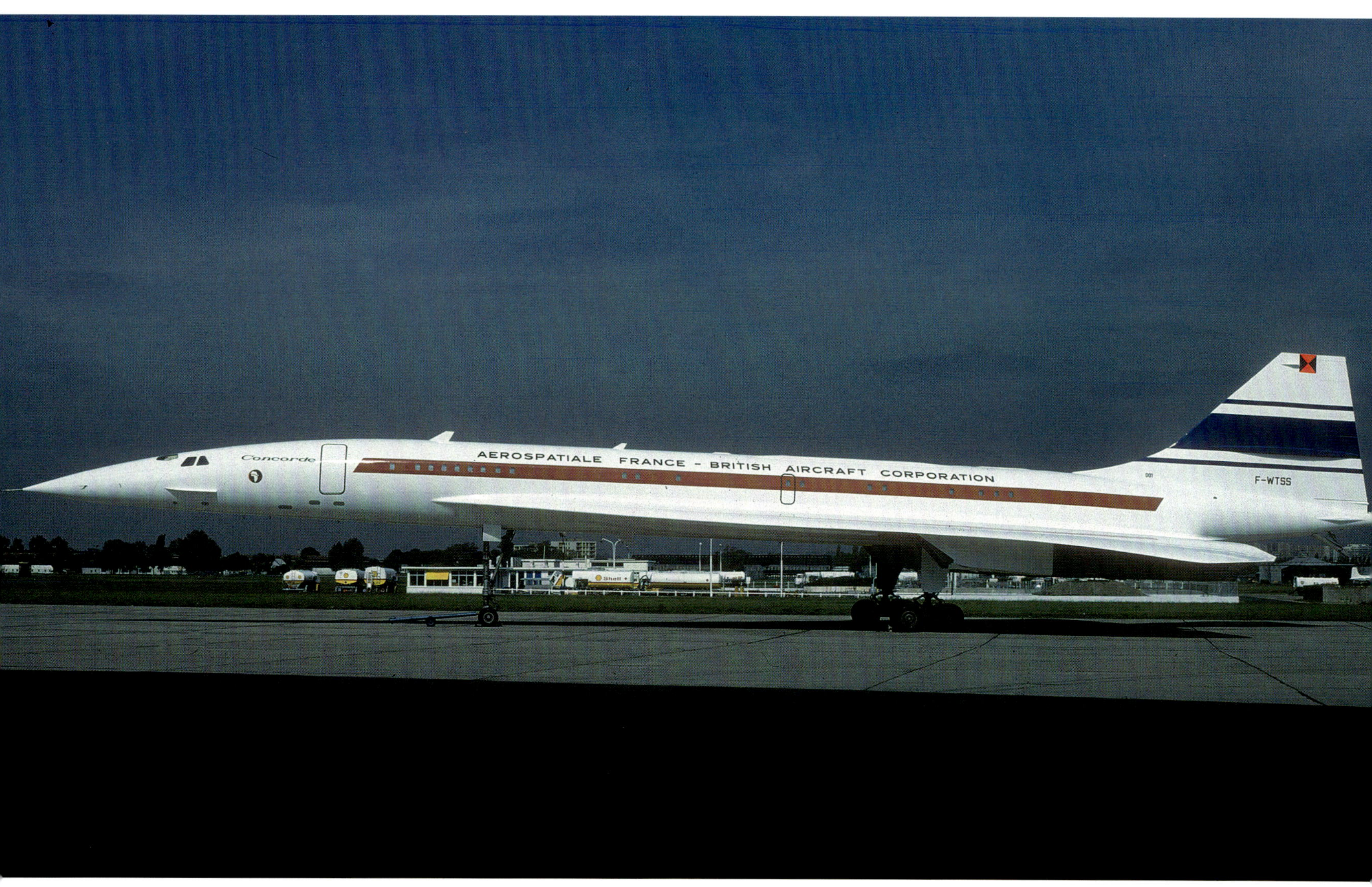

Concorde prototype F-WTSS under tow prior to the Paris Air Show at Le Bourget in June 1979.
(Tom Singfield collection)

1

CONCORDE

The only successful supersonic airliner can trace its history back to the late 1950s. Bristol Aircraft (later part of British Aerospace) in the United Kingdom and Sud Aviation (later Aérospatiale) in France had plans that were broadly similar: a supersonic airliner that would help the European manufacturers catch up with the Americans, whose Boeing 707 and Douglas DC-8 were looking to be bestsellers.

Both companies had plans for similar types, although the French design was slightly smaller with less range. It soon became obvious to both manufacturers that this would be a prohibitively expensive undertaking on their own. The answer was a joint venture between both companies, with a deal signed in November 1962 by both the British and French governments called the Anglo-French Supersonic Aircraft Agreement. This was quite an undertaking by companies in two different countries, and there were many potential problems, particularly for the engineers and designers. This was not just because of language difficulties: remember, both countries used differing systems for weights and measures – imperial in the UK and metric in France. Some of the engineers in both countries were given reciprocal language lessons.

The agreement stated that both countries agreed to jointly develop, finance and construct such an airliner to be built by BAC and Sud. Engine development was between Bristol Siddeley (later Rolls-Royce) and Snecma Motors. The chosen engine would be the Olympus 593, which powered the Vulcan bomber. However, it was redesigned to increase thrust from 20,000lb to 38,050lb with reheat capability, and even the fuel system was changed.

The futuristic-looking design of the aircraft featured a four-engined, tailless, delta-wing shape with the engines encased within the wing close to the fuselage. Needless to say, there were many problems for the designers and engineers to overcome. The thin fuselage and delta wing design would be needed to attain speeds of Mach 2.2 and heights of up to 60,000ft (18,288m), yet be slow enough to be able to land at regular airports. To enable the pilots to see properly during take-off and landing, the nose was hinged so it could be lowered. As part of the 'droop snoot' there was a retractable heat shield in front of the cockpit. For high angle of attack landings there was a pair of tailwheels to act as a bumper in case of over-rotation and a possible tail contact with the runway (the Ilyushin Il-62 had the same type of tail-wheels). The main undercarriage comprised eight wheels in two bogies of four wheels each. In front of the leading wheels on each bogie was a horizontal bar known as a deflector, whose function was to prevent water on the runway from entering the engine air intakes. Weighing around 4kg, these were made of composite materials and fibreglass to make them more frangible. There was also a pair of nosewheels on a very long undercarriage leg.

Without a doubt, Concorde was the most tested aircraft in history, and the flight programme lasted six years. In fact, even before it was built the British aircraft industry built two aircraft specifically for Concorde research. One was the Handley Page HP.115 testbed, which would examine low-speed performance of the slender delta wing layout; the other was the BAC 221 single-engined, delta-wing aircraft powered by a single Rolls-Royce Avon engine with afterburner. This aircraft originated in the 1950s as the Fairey Delta 2, built for research into flight at transonic and supersonic speeds. In 1956 the FD2 set a new world speed record when it became the first aircraft to exceed 1,000mph in level flight. Just like Concorde, the FD2 had a droop nose to aid pilot view both on the ground and on approach. The project was taken over by the British Aircraft Corporation (BAC) and one of the two FD2s was extensively modified as the BAC 221 specifically to assist Concorde development. It received a new ogival wing like Concorde's and first flew in this guise in 1964. Like the British prototype Concorde, it is now preserved at the Fleet Air Arm Museum at Royal Naval Air Station (RNAS) Yeovilton. Perhaps not so well known is the fact that in the United States NASA privately assisted Concorde development by using a Douglas F5D Skylancer aircraft with a modified wing.

A total of twenty Concordes were built, including one prototype, one pre-production and one development aircraft in each of the two countries. The production run totalled fourteen aircraft, seven each for Air France and British Airways, the national carriers of each country. It should be remembered that the British Airways aircraft were actually ordered for British Overseas Airways Corporation (BOAC), whose 1974 amalgamation with British European Airways (BEA) saw it become the state-owned British Airways.

The roll-out of the prototype (F-WTSS) at Toulouse in December 1967 showed that the name Concorde, spelled with an 'e', had been officially adopted. Previously there had been much discussion about this, with the British wanting it as 'Concord' without the 'e'. Already many adjectives

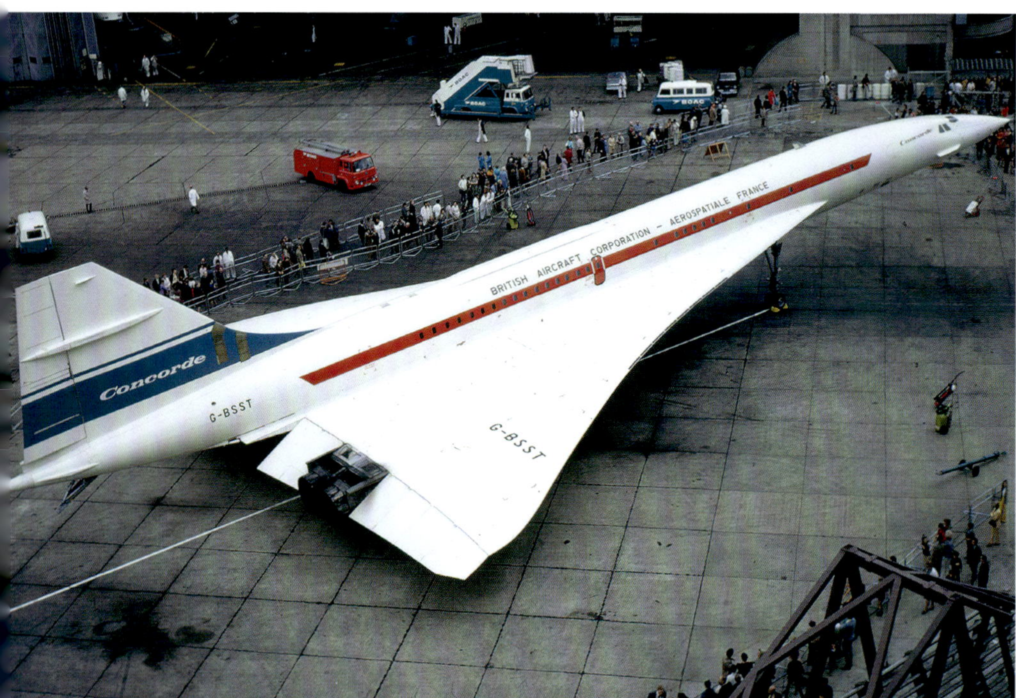

British prototype Concorde G-BSST at a press event at London Heathrow on 2 July 1972. This 'look down' shot shows the classic lines of Concorde. (Peter Elliott via Stewart Davidson)

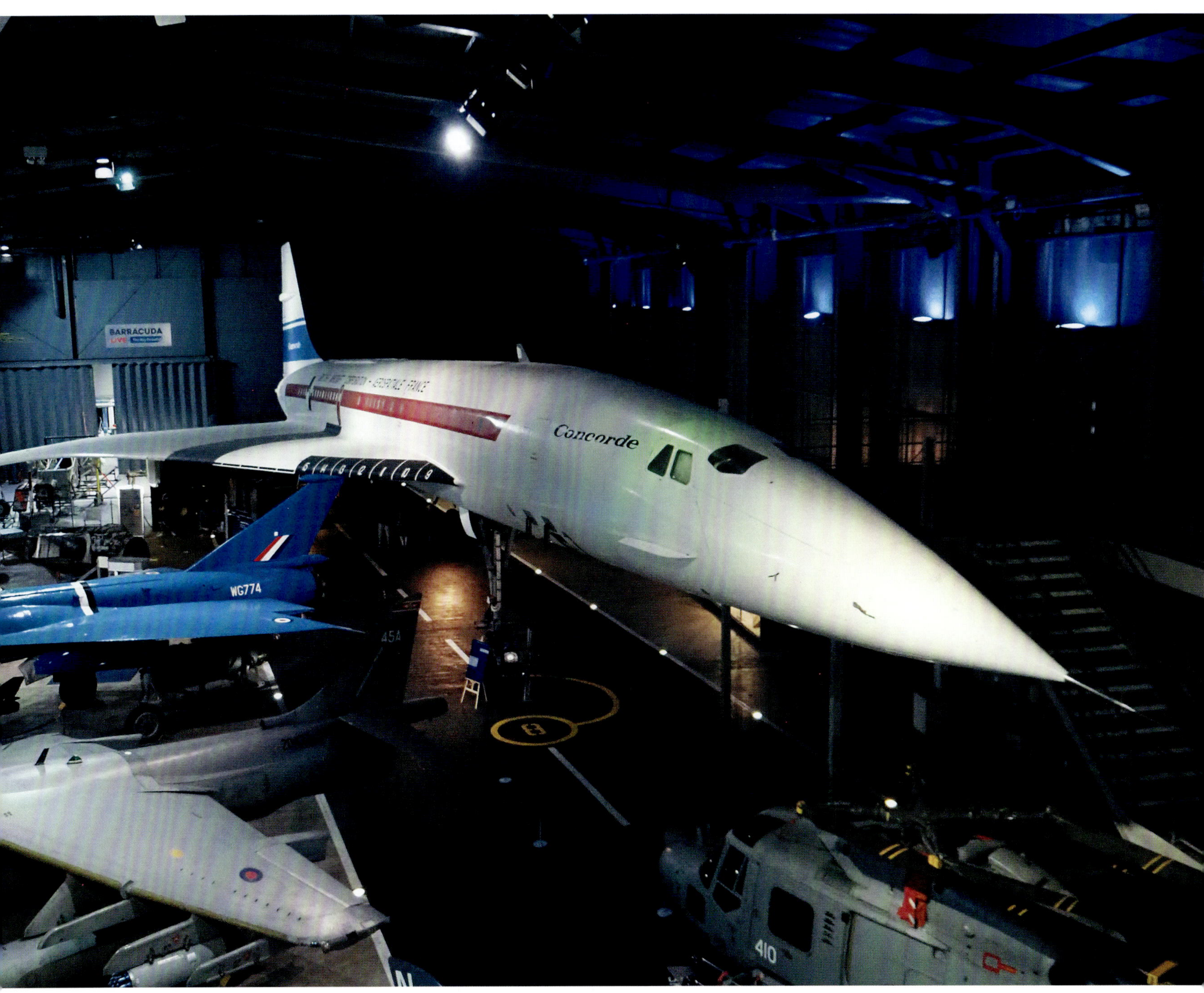

British prototype G-BSST is now preserved at the Fleet Air Arm Museum at RNAS Yeovilton. (Jon West/G-BSST from Science Museum Group collection)

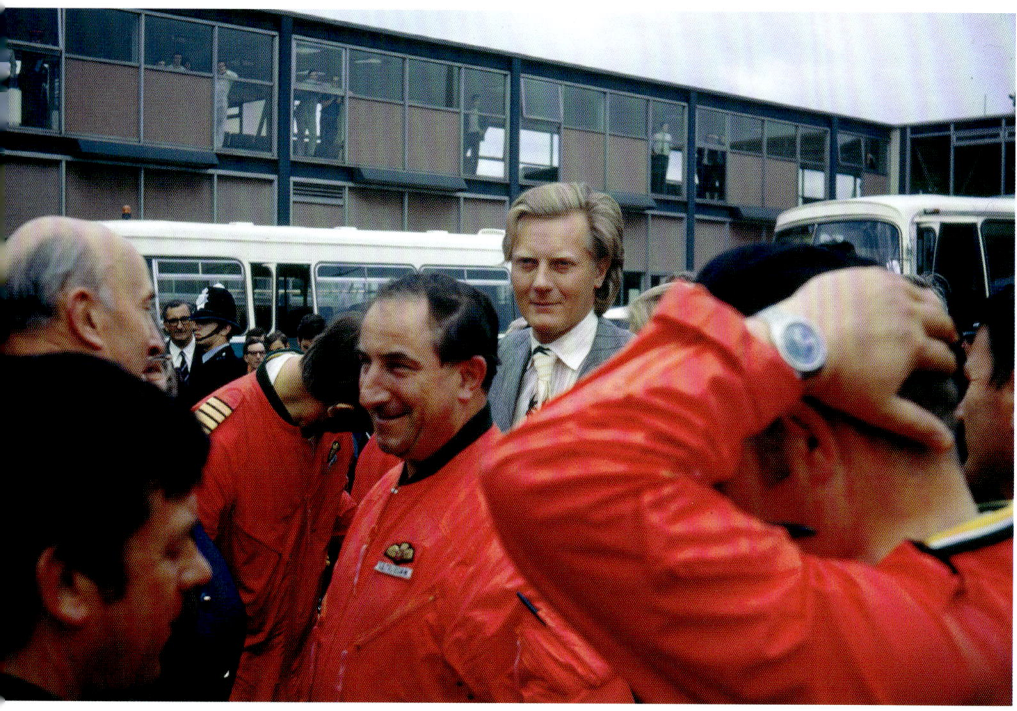

This shot, taken at a Heathrow press event in July 1972, shows Concorde test pilot Brian Trubshaw. Clearly visible behind him is a youthful-looking Michael Heseltine, who was Minister of State for Aerospace and Shipping in the Conservative Government at the time. Heseltine was a strong supporter of Concorde. (Peter Elliott via Stewart Davidson)

were being used to describe Concorde – beautiful, sleek, elegant and futuristic-looking, to name just a few.

The maiden flight with André Turcat at the controls took place from Toulouse on 12 March 1969, seven years later than originally planned. By then, the projected £170 million costs were spiralling. After its flight test programme was complete, this aircraft was preserved at the Musée de l'Air et de l'Espace at Le Bourget.

The British prototype carried the appropriate registration G-BSST (British Super-Sonic Transport) and made its maiden flight from Bristol Filton on 9 April 1969. I remember as a teenager watching the event live on television. The aircraft took off from Filton under the command of test pilot Brian Trubshaw, and after twenty-two minutes it landed 50 miles away at RAF Fairford in

Gloucestershire, from where it carried on with its test programme. Its flying career over, this aircraft is now in the Fleet Air Arm Museum at RNAS Yeovilton.

While the manufacturers had hopes for as many as 400 orders for Concorde, to me this looked a bit optimistic. By the time of the aircraft's world sales tour the management of both Air France and BOAC had shown no interest whatsoever in purchasing the aircraft. By the time the aircraft was in production the costs were five times the initial estimates, and it is no secret that on several occasions the British Government wanted to cancel the programme. However, an earlier agreement between the two countries meant that neither could cancel the project without incurring significant penalties. In the UK the aircraft were bought by the government and were given to British Airways under a profit-sharing scheme.

The initial plans were for Air France and BOAC to have six aircraft each, but orders from US airlines certainly helped swell the order book. Pan American was an early customer with an order for six. Other US airlines to commit to the type were American Airlines (four), Braniff (three), Continental (three), Eastern (two), Trans World (four) and United (six). Sadly, United cancelled its order in 1972, and the following year all the other US carriers did likewise, which was a major blow to the manufacturers. There were other orders from Air Canada (four), Air India (two), Japan Airlines (three), Lufthansa (three), Middle East Airlines (two), Qantas (six) and Sabena (two). However, in the space of two years all of them had sadly cancelled their orders. For Qantas it would have been an ideal aircraft, as to get anywhere from Australia you have to go over water where there is no one to complain about noise – perfect for a supersonic aircraft. The last two airlines to cancel orders kept their faith for much longer, and are perhaps companies that might have been least expected to buy the aircraft. These were the Civil Aviation Authority of China (CAAC) and Iran Air. Both airlines ordered two aircraft each, but cancelled in 1979 and 1980 respectively.

Of the development aircraft, G-BBDG (construction number 202) of British Aerospace was based at Filton, where it flew many hours in a seven-year-long test and research programme. Retired in 1981, the aircraft was stored in a hangar at Filton and bought by British Airways in 1984. It is said to have sometimes been used as a spares source. It was moved by road to Brooklands Museum in 2004 where, after restoration, it was displayed in British Airways colours.

Concorde entered both British and French service on 21 January 1976: British Airways London–Bahrain and Air France Paris–Rio de Janeiro with a technical stop in Dakar. However, as fuel costs began to rise significantly, it seemed that Concorde had entered the aviation market at exactly the wrong time.

Due to significant cost overruns, the British Government was often looking for excuses to cancel the programme. The British-built aircraft were paid for and owned by the government but, in 1983, British Airways convinced the government to sell the aircraft to the airline. That is what happened, though some say the sale was a virtual steal, or the sale of the century. State-owned British Airways was privatised in 1987.

After the tragic crash of the Air France Concorde at Gonesse on 25 July 2000, all Concordes were grounded for seventeen months. The investigation work seemed to drag on interminably, with some saying that the French judiciary system was part

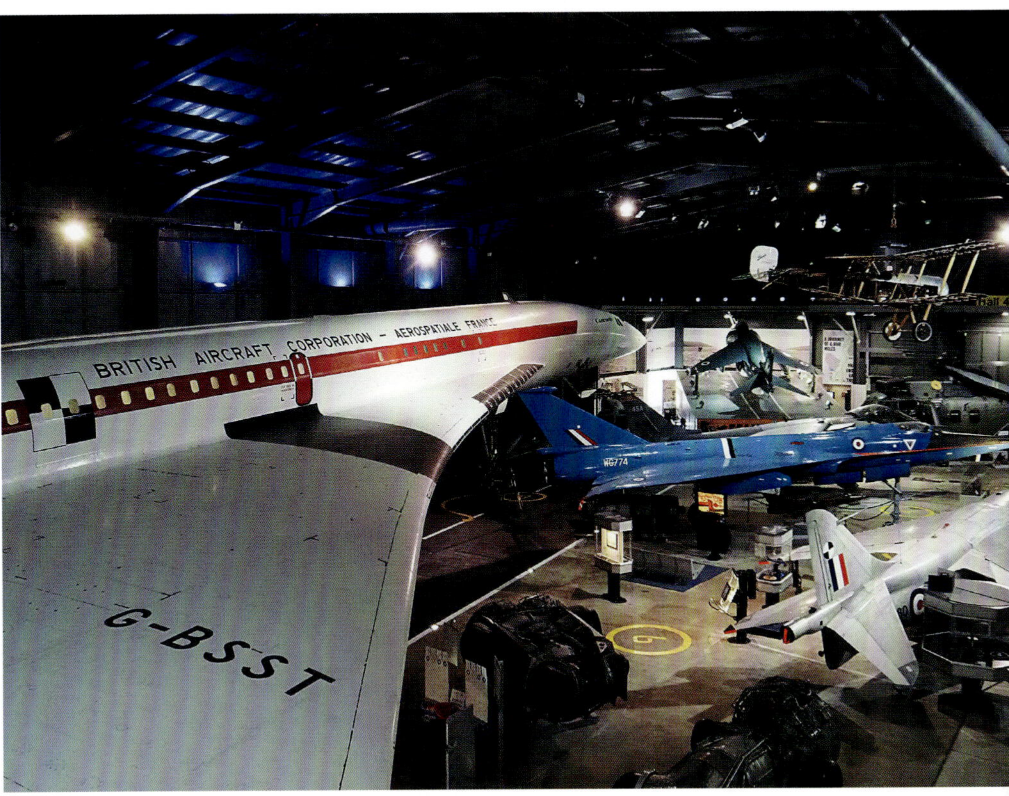

British prototype G-BSST with the BAC 221 alongside it at Yeovilton. (Jon West/G-BSST from Science Museum Group collection)

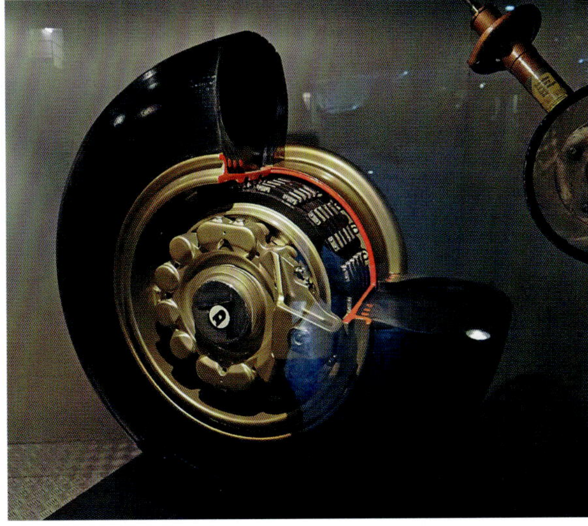

This wheel cutaway amply shows the size of the main tyres. (Jon West/G-BSST from Science Museum Group collection)

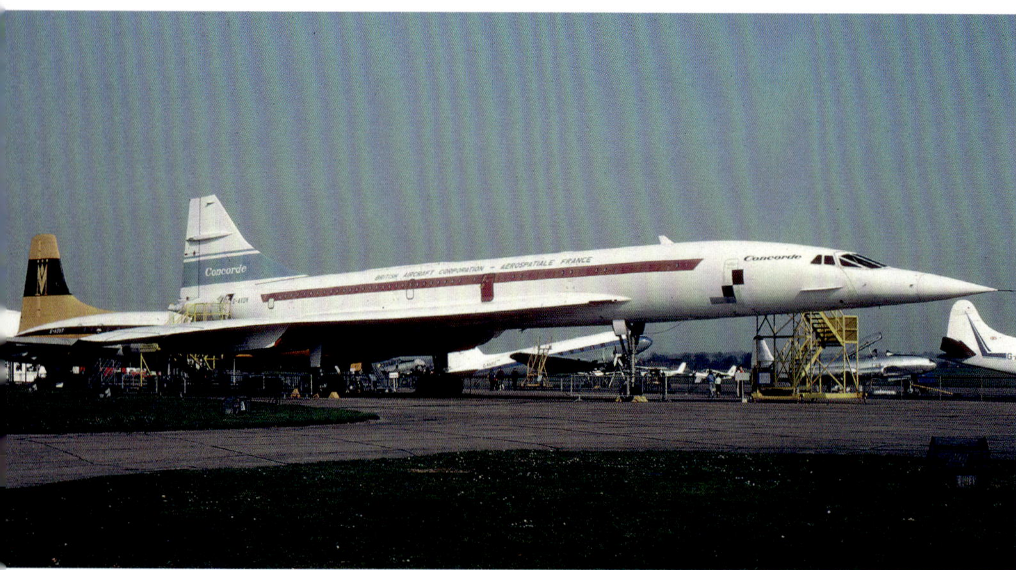

British development aircraft G-AXDN at Duxford. (Paul Seymour)

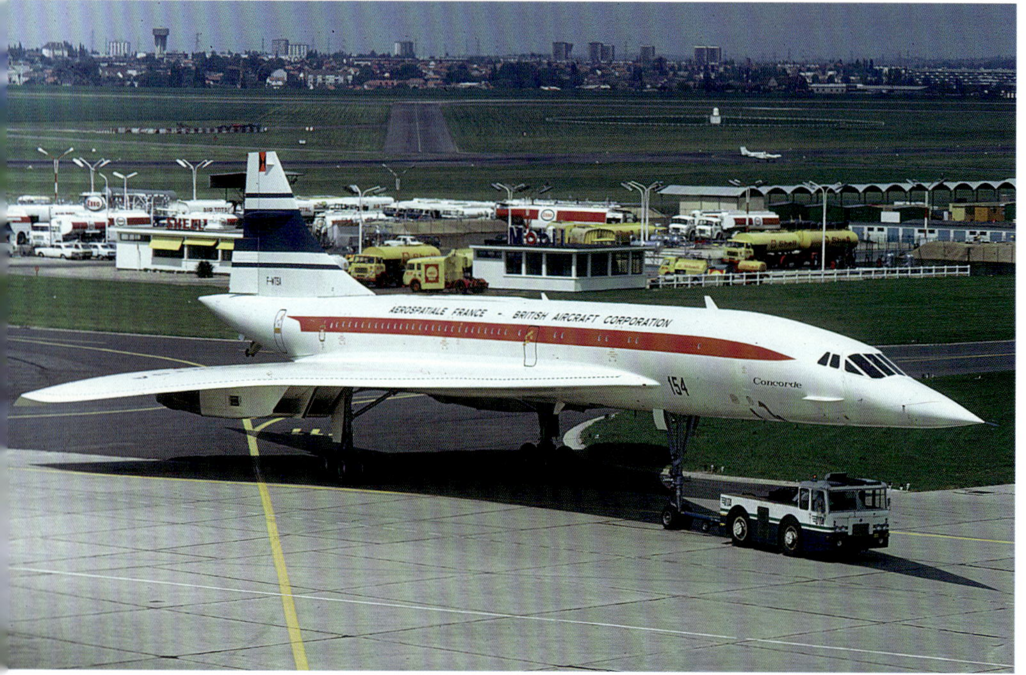

Pre-production aircraft F-WTSA in Air France colours at Le Bourget in June 1973 with Paris show number 154. (Tom Singfield collection – D. Howell)

of the reason why it took so long. Ultimately the outcome was that the introduction of safety measures that were particularly aimed at reducing the chance of fire in the fuel system. These included fitting more than 100 moulded Kevlar linings inside the fuel tanks to minimise any leaks. Also, there were new tyres that if damaged would break into small parts rather than into large chunks.

This work was carried out by engineers at both airlines, and took about eight weeks per aircraft at a cost of over £1 million per airframe. Once the engineers became more accustomed to the work involved, the time frame per aircraft was reduced. Talking to BA engineers, the size of the fuel tanks meant that only those of smaller stature could carry out this important task in the space available. While the aircraft were grounded, British Airways carried out a planned cabin upgrade with new seats, lighting and upholstery. By installing new lightweight seats, British Airways had hoped to make good savings on fuel costs; however, much of this was negated due to the cost of work on the Kevlar linings in the fuel tanks. Meanwhile, the two Concorde operators were facing one significant question – after the terrorist attack in New York on 11 September 2001, would there be sufficient people who wanted to fly in the aircraft? Since the attacks, passenger numbers, particularly in the US, had fallen while fuel costs were rising substantially.

After the safety requirements were completed to the satisfaction of the aviation authorities in France, the UK and the US, Concorde services were given the go-ahead to resume. On 7 November 2001 both Air France and British Airways re-introduced the New York JFK service. There is no doubt this was a momentous day for the staff of both airlines, as well as the many airport workers who had missed the sight and sound of this wonderful aircraft. British Airways did well on the route, with many previous customers such as celebrities and film and sports stars returning to their favourite aircraft. The figures for Air France, however, were not so good, and there was an impression that the French carrier had lost faith in the aircraft. Some reports claim that British Airways load factors on the New York route were about 50 per cent, while those of Air France were reportedly down to 20 per cent.

Engineers stated that the Concorde fleet was handling its age extremely well, and British Airways had intended to operate the Concorde fleet until about 2015. It therefore came as a shock to many when Airbus, by now the parent company, suddenly announced in April 2003 that it would no longer support Concorde after 31 October that year. That meant, without a certificate of airworthiness, it would no longer be able to fly commercial services. Meanwhile, Air France announced that they were going to suspend Concorde services at the end of May.

Was this just a coincidence? Many, myself included, do not think so. Had Air France Concorde services been as successful of those of British Airways, I do not think for a minute Airbus would have made such a decision. Many, including Lord Marshall, the head of British Airways at the time, alleged that the airline wanted to continue Concorde operations, but the decision by Airbus was forced upon them, with claims that the French wanted to kill off the aircraft. The official statement from British Airways, however, stated that that the decision to curtail Concorde operations was made jointly with both airlines and Airbus.

Ironically, in the final six months of service, British Airways load factors on Concorde services was about 90 per cent or more, and even Air France was showing 70 per cent in the final months. Many took a final opportunity to fly in it before it was retired, including me.

Would the aircraft have been more successful in sales orders if there had been a 'stretched' version carrying, say, 150 passengers? Sadly, we shall never know. Nevertheless, Concorde is an aircraft whose many achievements are still unparalleled. It is quite amazing that nearly fifty years after entering service it is still unchallenged when it comes to speed for an airliner. With Concorde services gone, and no sign of a supersonic successor, for the first time in aviation history we have taken a step backwards!

There are many superlatives that can be used for Concorde, such as 'it flew on the edge of space', and that it was 'a dream in the sky', 'a national icon' and 'an icon of the twentieth century'.

British development aircraft G-BBDG spent its whole life at Filton. At the end of its flying career, it was stored in a hangar there and apparently sometimes used by BA as a spares source. In 2004 it was moved by road to the Brooklands museum, where it is now displayed in BA colours.

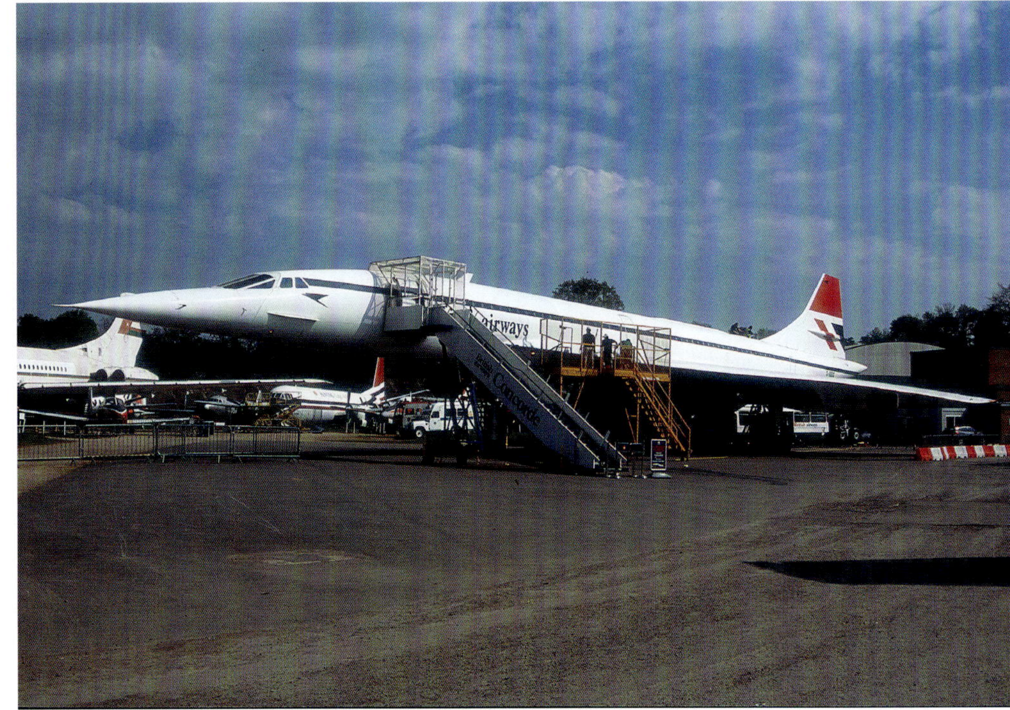

French development aircraft F-WTSB in Air France livery at Paris Orly in June 1975. (Tom Singfield collection)

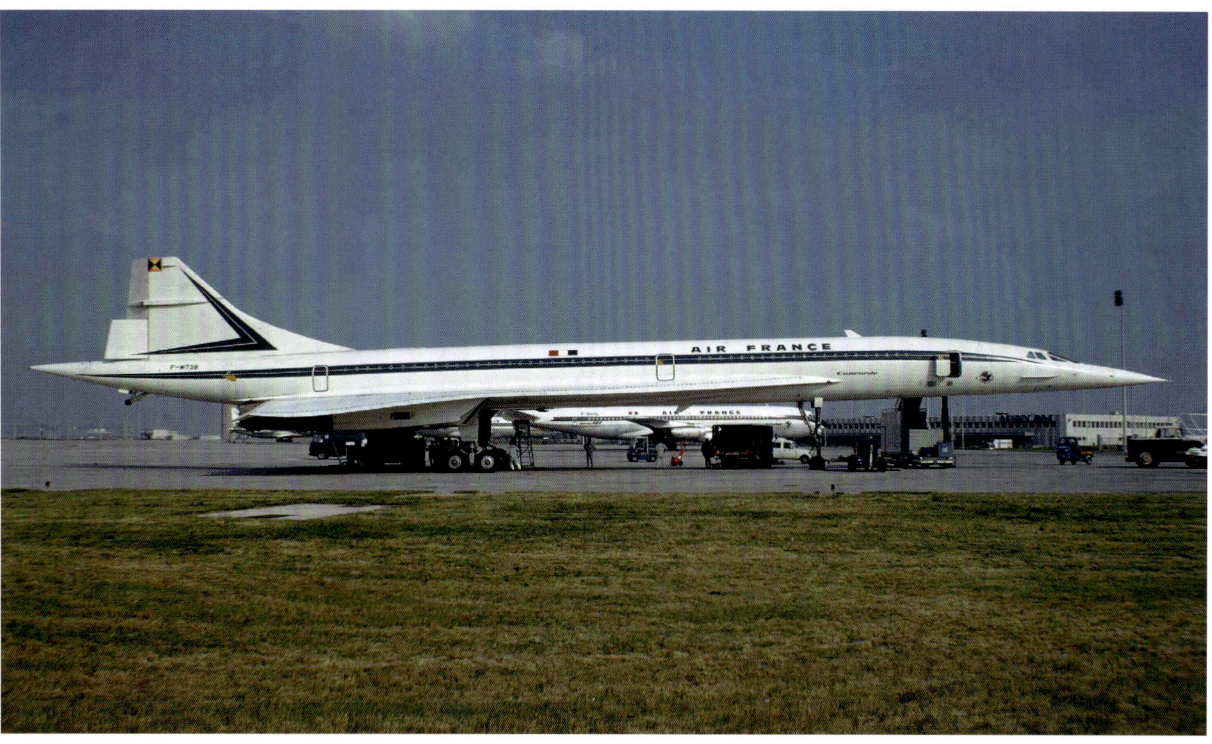

A nice shot of F-WTSA at Prestwick in July 1974 in Air France livery of the period. This French pre-production aircraft makes a good subject in excellent light conditions. (Tom Singfield collection – Gordon Bain)

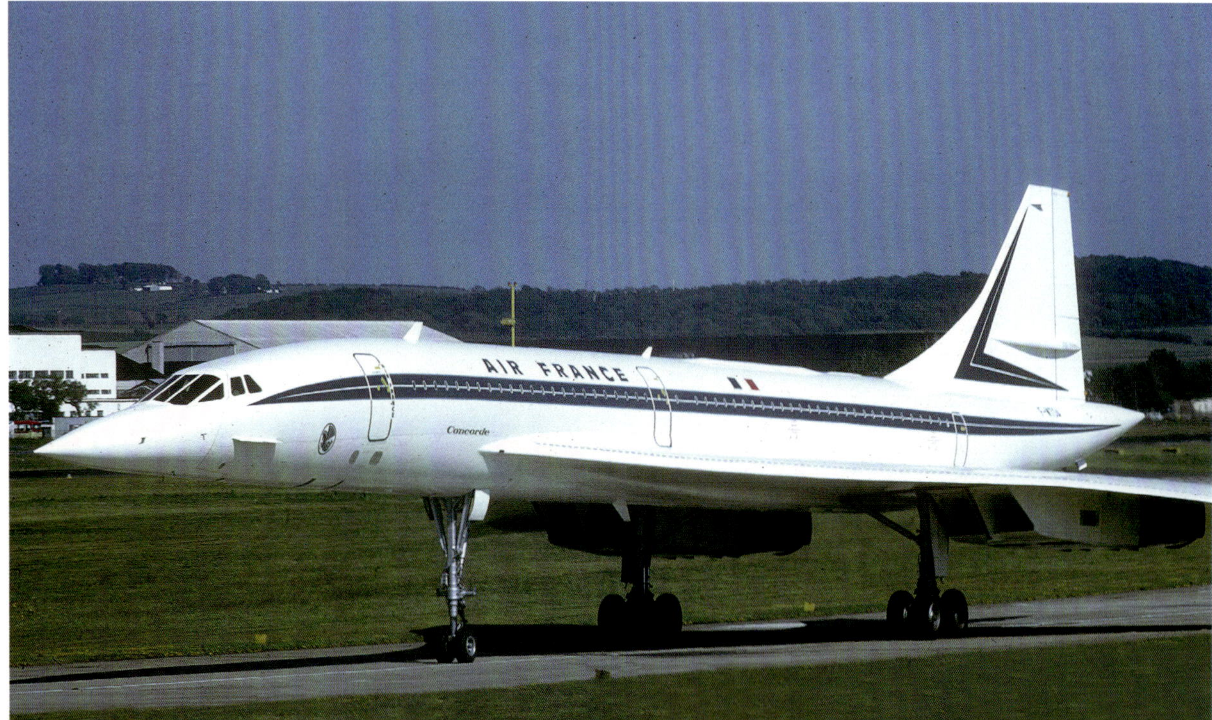

FACTS AND FIGURES

Length: 203ft 9in (62.1m)
Wingspan: 83ft 8in (26.5m)
Height: 37ft 1in (11.3m)
Fuselage width: 9ft 6in (2.9m)
Range: 4,143 miles (6,667km)
Powerplant: Four Rolls-Royce/SNECMA Olympus 593 engines, with reheat
Landing gear: Eight main wheels on two bogies, two nosewheels
Crew: Two pilots, flight engineer, six cabin crew
Capacity: 100 passengers, 2.5 tonnes of cargo
Cruising speed: 1,350mph (2,160kph), Mach 2
Ceiling: 60,000ft (18,288m)
Take-off speed: 250mph (400kph)
Landing speed: 187mph (300kph)
Maximum take-off weight (MTOW): 408,000lb (185 tonnes)
Fuel capacity: 26,286 imperial gallons (119,500 litres)
Fuel consumption: 5,638 imperial gallons (25,629 litres) per hour
First commercial flight: 21 January 1976, Paris Charles de Gaulle–Dakar–Rio de Janeiro and London Heathrow–Bahrain
Last commercial flight: 24 October 2003, New York JFK–London Heathrow

PROTOTYPES

C/N	Series	Customer	Reg.	Delivered	Currently
001	Prototype	Sud Aviation	F-WTSS	2 March 1969	Musée de l'Air et de l'Espace, Paris, France
002	Prototype	British Aircraft Corporation	G-BSST	9 April 1969	Fleet Air Arm Museum, Yeovilton, UK
101	Pre-Prod.	British Aircraft Corporation	G-AXDN	17 December 1971	Imperial War Museum, Duxford, UK
102	Pre-Prod.	Sud Aviation	F-WTSA	10 January 1973	Musée Delta, Athis-Mons, near Paris Orly, France
201	Development	Sud Aviation	F-WTSB	6 January 1973	Aeroscopia, Toulouse, France
202	Development	British Aircraft Corporation	G-BBDG	13 December 1974	Brooklands Museum, Surrey, UK

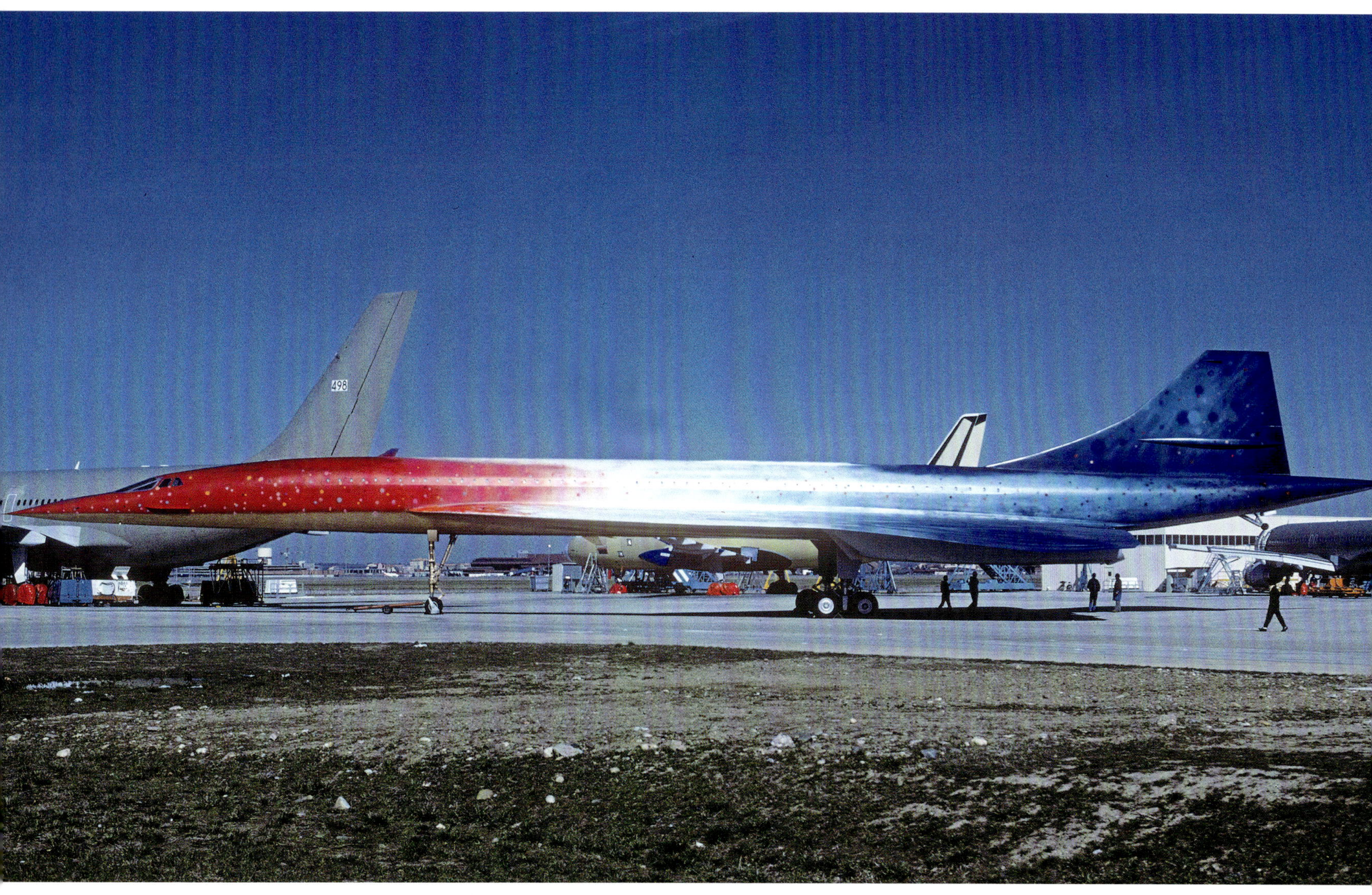

F-WTSB in stylish livery at Toulouse in March 1989 to celebrate Concorde's twentieth anniversary. In the 1980s this development aircraft spent three years in storage at Châteauroux. Its final flight on 19 April 1985 was from Châteauroux to Toulouse, where it joined the Aeroscopia museum. (Tom Singfield collection – Jean M. Magendie)

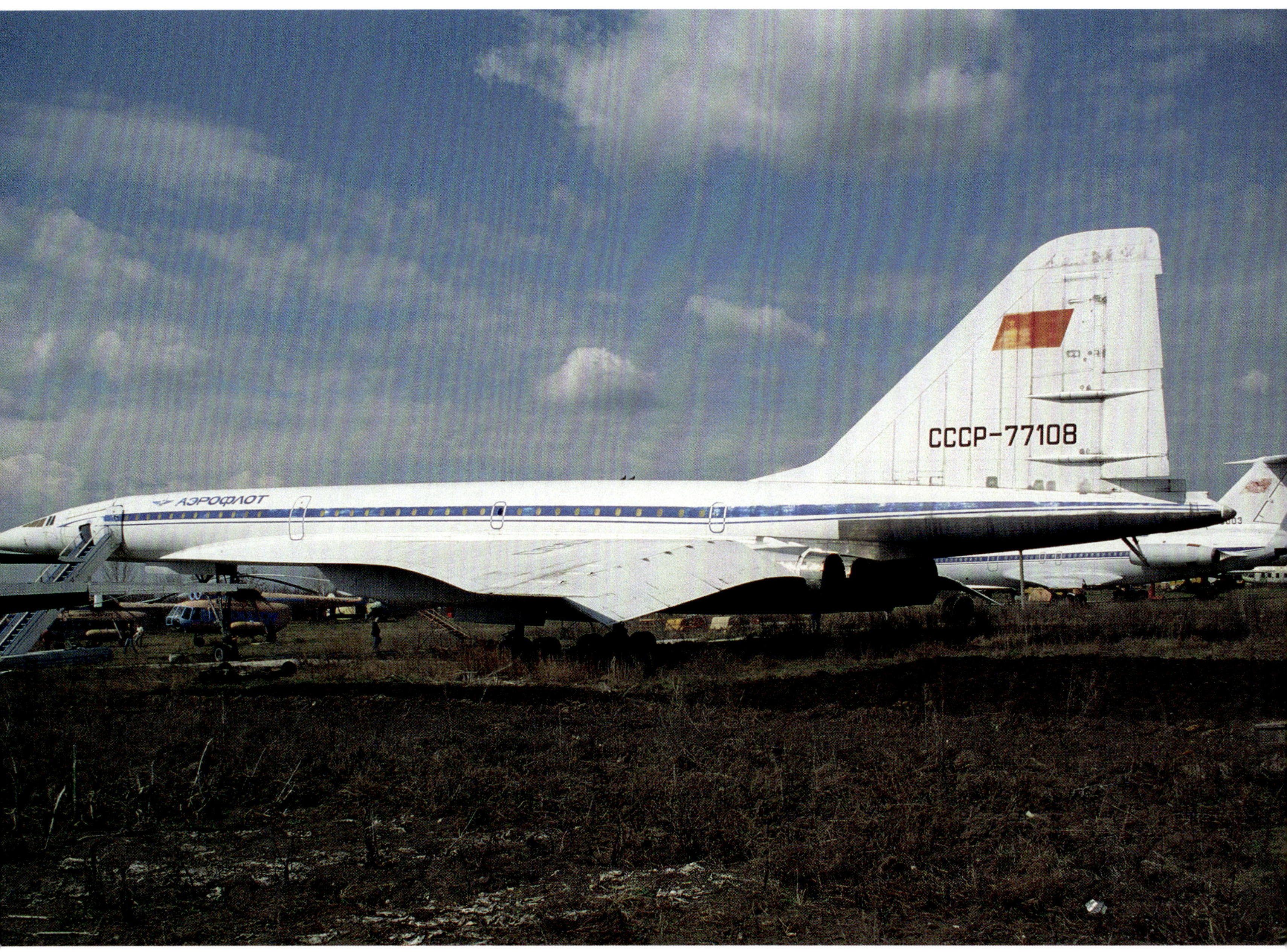

Tupolev Tu-144 'Concordski' CCCP-77108 at the Samara State University on 26 April 1993. (Paul Seymour)

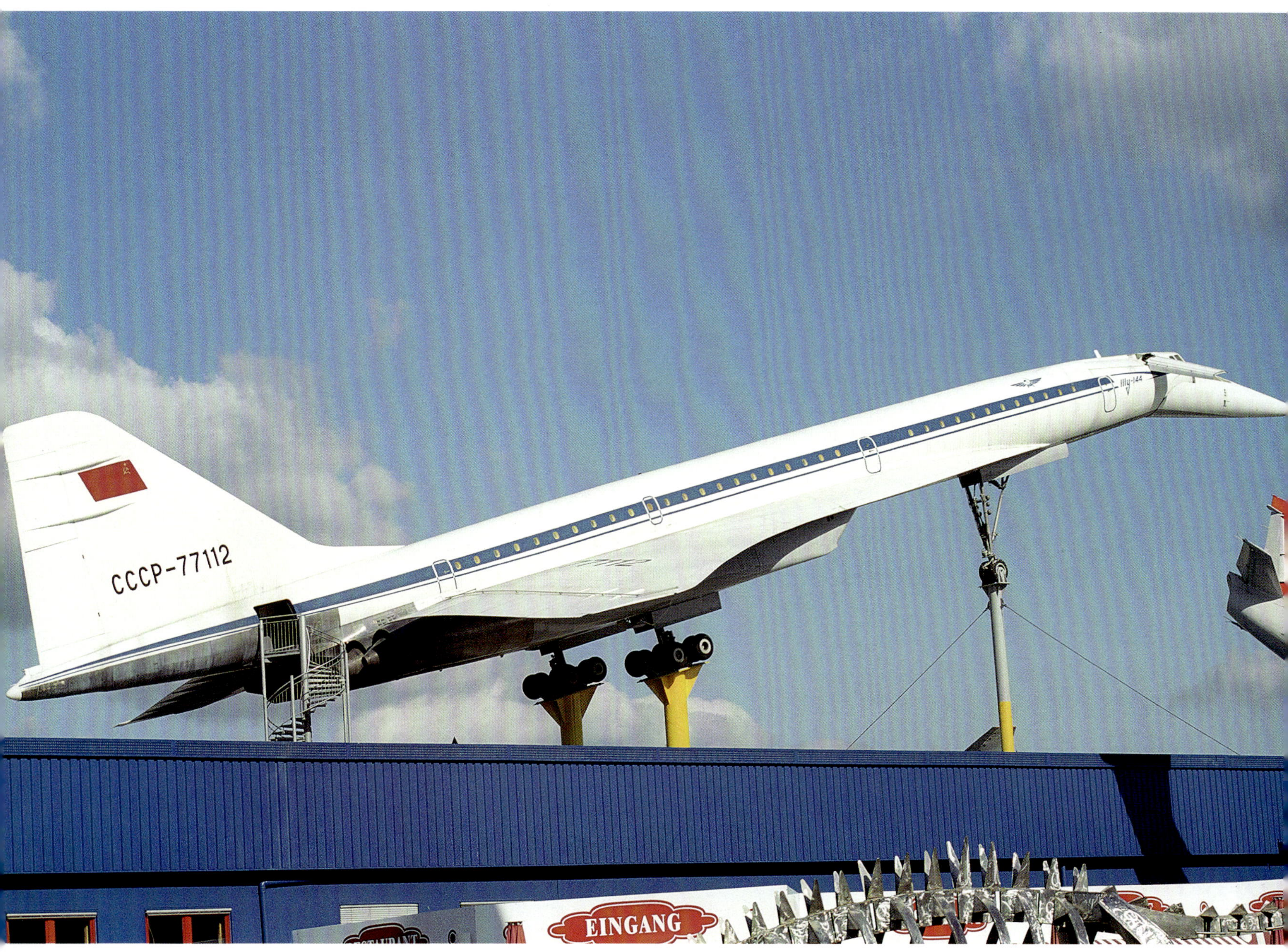

Tu-144 CCCP-77112 at the fabulous Technik Museum Sinsheim in Germany. This amazing museum has both a Concorde and Tupolev Tu-144. (Paul Seymour)

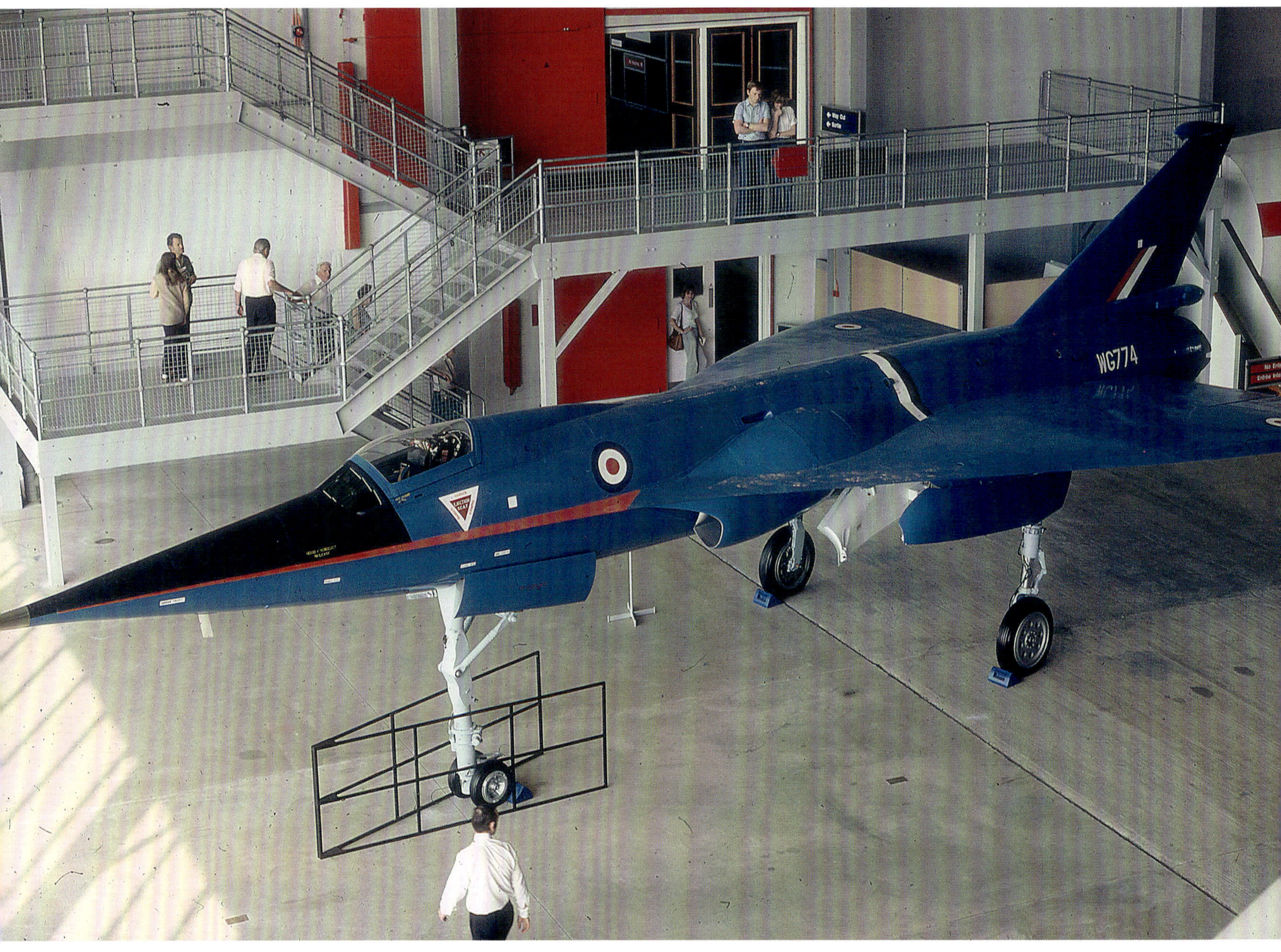

Research aircraft BAC 221, formerly known as the FD2, at Yeovilton's Fleet Air Arm Museum. It carries the military registration WG774 from its time with the Royal Aircraft Establishment (RAE). (BAC221 from Science Museum Group collection)

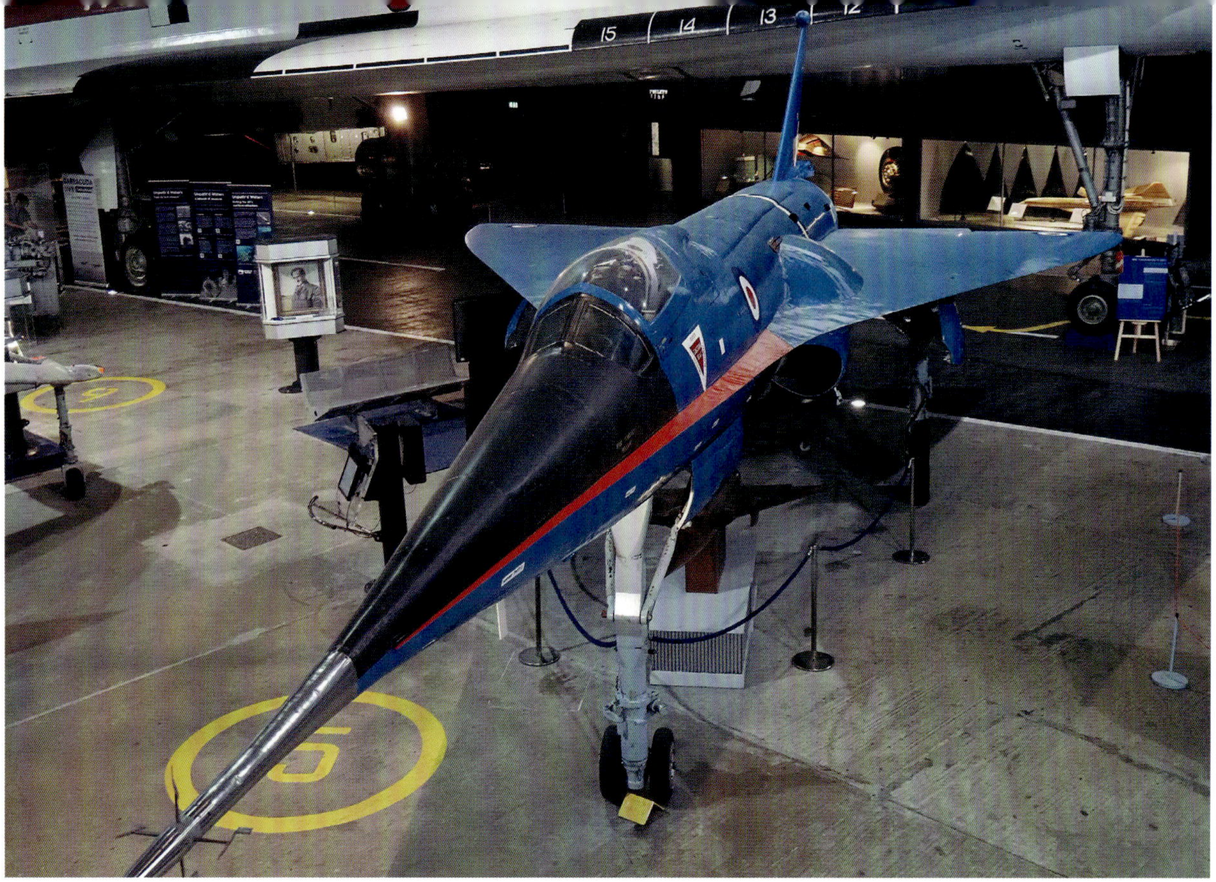

BAC 221 WG774, formerly known as the Fairey Delta 2, of which two were built. It was used by the RAE for research into flight and control at transonic and supersonic speeds. (Jon West/BAC221 from Science Museum Group collection)

Handley Page HP.115 XP841 was used by RAE Bedford for research in the Concorde programme. It is now preserved at the Fleet Air Arm Museum. It was used for test into low-speed handling of the slender delta wing design. The blue-coloured BAC 221 is also visible. (HP.115 XP841 from Science Museum Group collection)

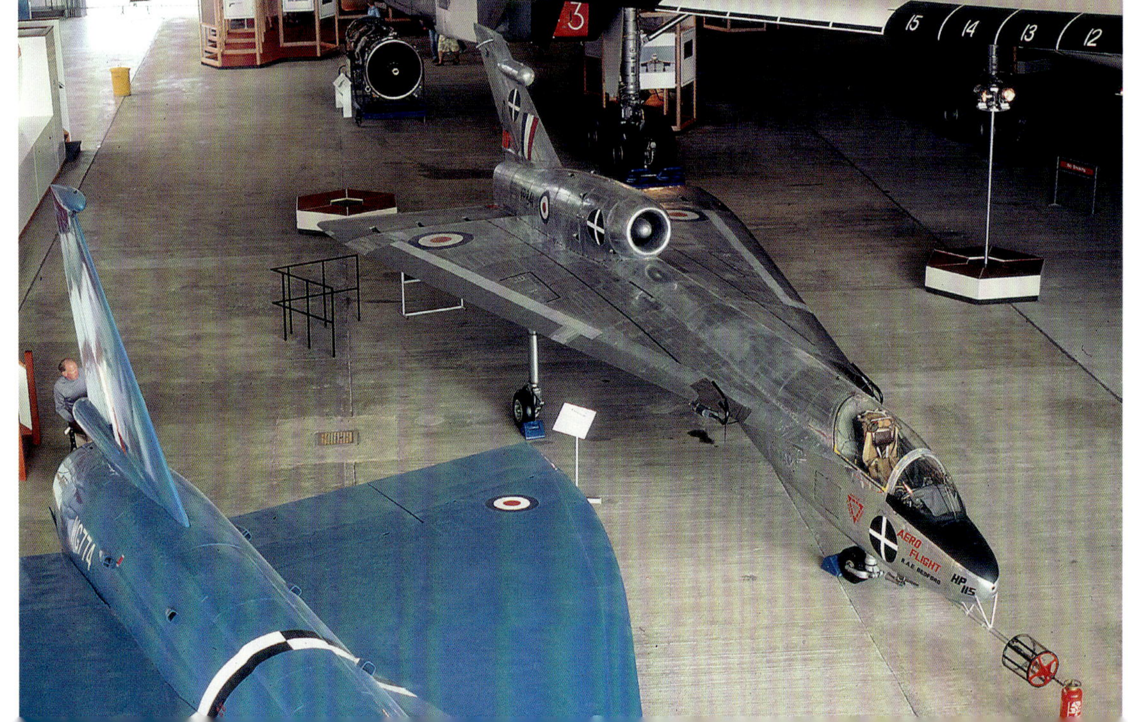

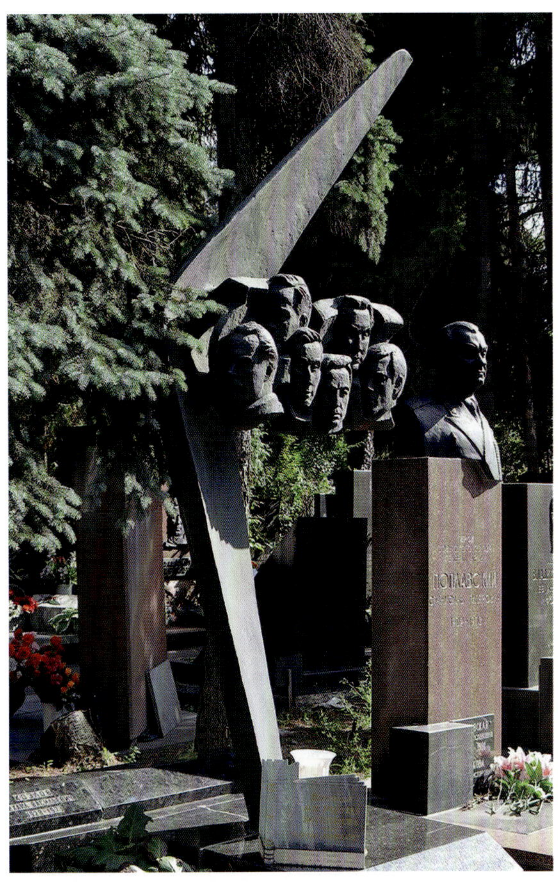

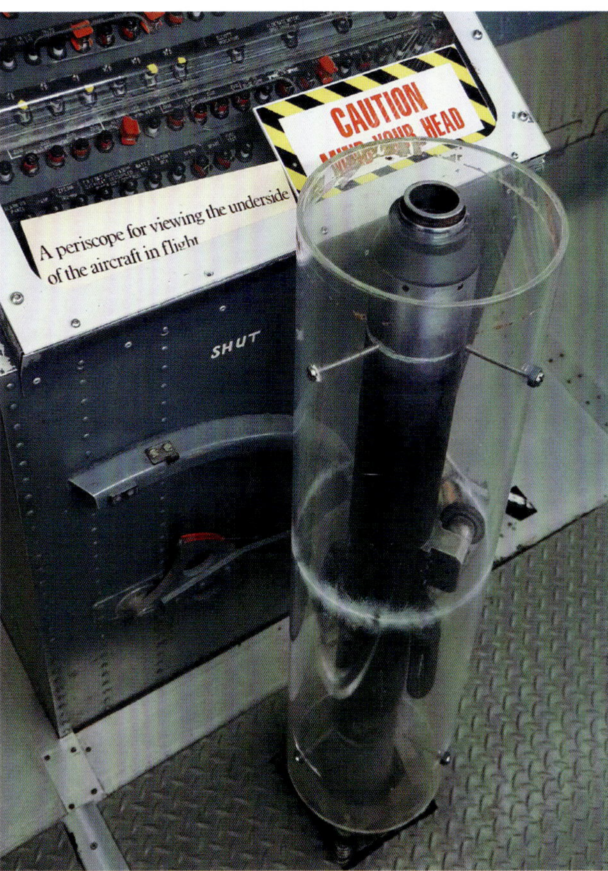

Left: Memorial to the flight crew of the Tupolev Tu-144 that crashed at the Paris Air Show at the Novodevichy cemetery in Moscow in 2014.

Right: On the British prototype G-BSST, a periscope was fitted to enable the crew to inspect the undersides of the aircraft. (Jon West/G-BSST from Science Museum Group collection)

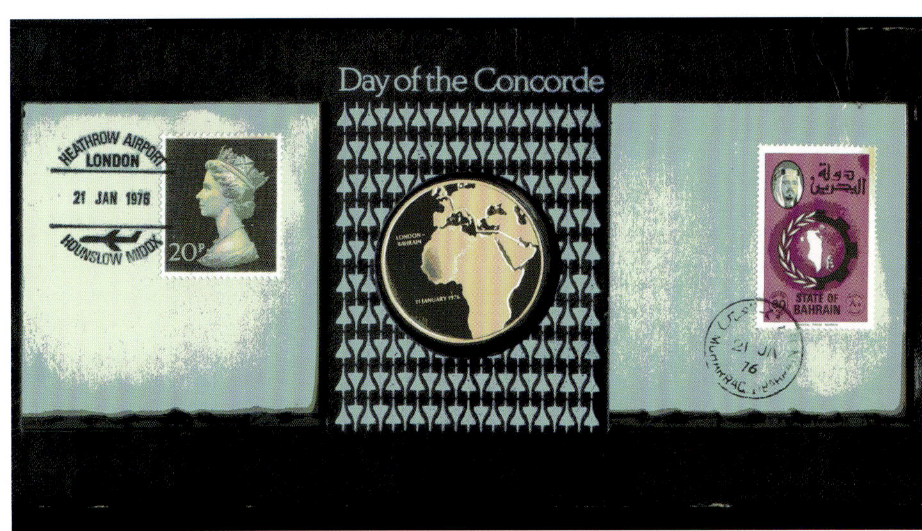

First day cover for stamp collectors of the inaugural British Airways Concorde London–Bahrain flight on 21 January 1976.

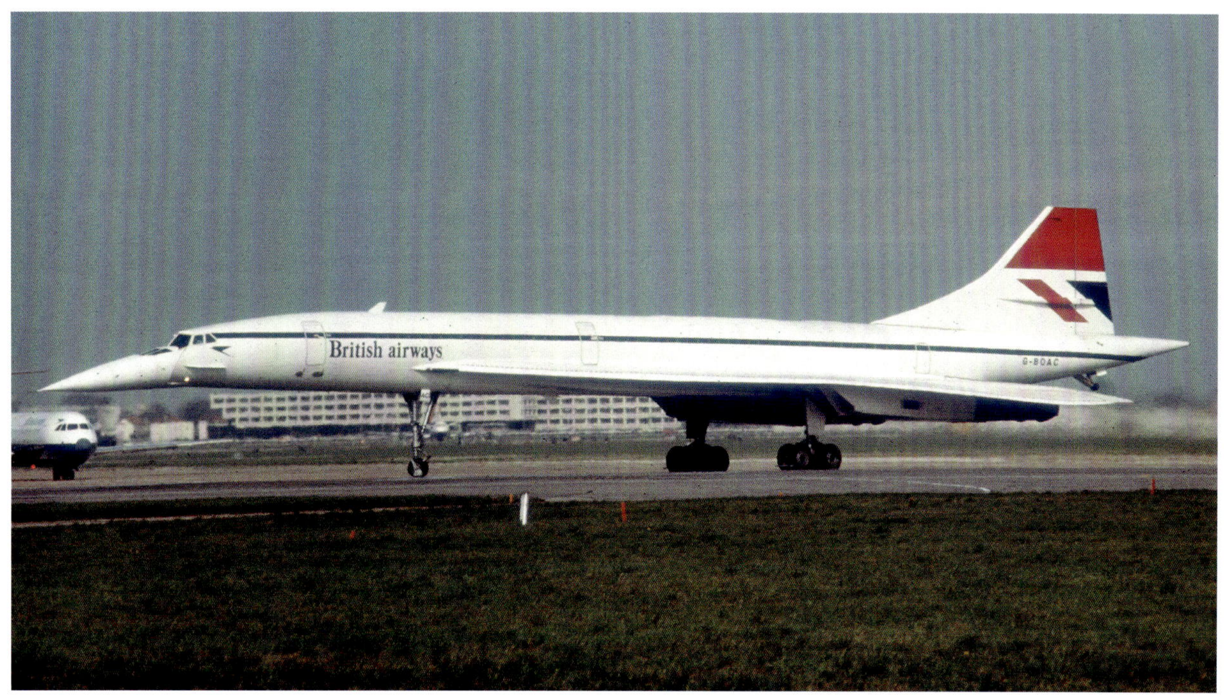

G-BOAC of British Airways in Negus & Negus livery gets ready to depart runway 27L at Heathrow. (Paul Seymour)

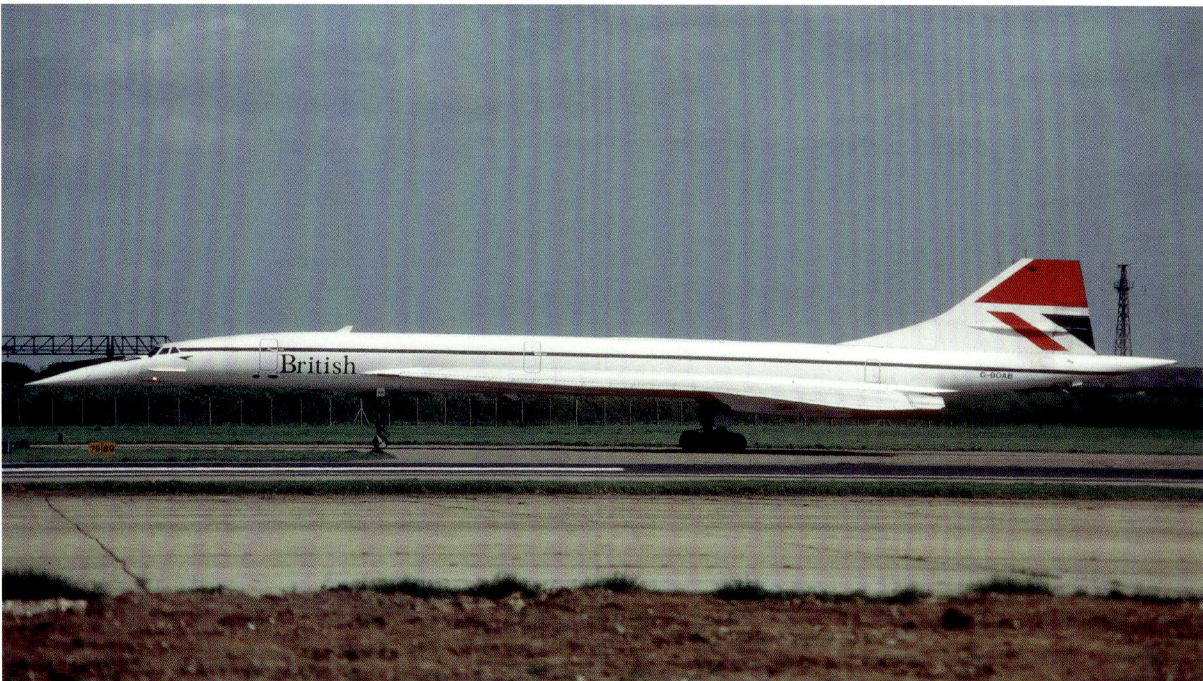

G-BOAB in its Negus & Negus livery at Heathrow. (Paul Seymour)

BRITISH AIRWAYS – CONCORDE 102

The seven-strong British Airways Concorde fleet were registered G-BOAA to G-BOAG.

C/N	Series	Customer	Reg.	Delivered	Currently
204	102	British Airways	G-BOAC	13 February 1976	Manchester Airport viewing park UK
206	102	British Airways	G-BOAA	14 January 1976	National Museum of Flight, East Fortune, Scotland
208	102	British Airways	G-BOAB	30 September 1976	British Airways training, Heathrow maintenance base, UK
210	102	British Airways	G-BOAD	6 December 1976	USS Intrepid Museum, New York, USA
212	102	British Airways	G-BOAE	20 July 1977	Bridgetown Airport, Barbados
214	102	British Airways	G-BOAG[*]	6 February 1980	The Museum of Flight, Seattle, USA
216	102	British Airways	G-BOAF[**]	6 September 1980	Bristol Aerospace Museum, Filton, UK

[*] G-BFKW was delivered to BA as such in 1980, becoming G-BOAG for service entry in 1981. However, this aircraft spent several years at British Airways' Heathrow maintenance base being used as a 'Christmas tree' – in other words it was used as a spares source with parts removed to help keep the rest of the fleet flying. During this time, it was painted all white, and did make the occasional flight as a back-up aircraft. One of these was a Goodwood Travel flight to Greenland, when BA had two aircraft on the ground at Kangerlussuaq in Greenland at the same time. After work to bring it back to operational status, it re-joined the Concorde fleet in April 1985. As it was the final Concorde to be delivered, and because of its time being used as a spares source, this aircraft flew fewer hours than any others in the fleet.

[**] G-BFKX first flew as such and was delivered to BA in June 1980 with US registration N94AF before taking up G-BOAF.

On 21 January 1976 Concorde finally entered commercial service from London Heathrow to Bahrain. As much of the routing took the flight over Europe, where supersonic travel was not permitted, it was not an ideal way to show off the Concorde's attributes, as the aircraft could only fly supersonic over the Mediterranean Sea. It did, however, still knock more than two hours off the subsonic flight time.

On 4 February 1976 the US authorities relented and permitted Concorde to fly to Washington DC. Both airlines started their service simultaneously on 24 May 1976. This first transatlantic service from Heathrow was ideal for Concorde and just what British Airways wanted. British Airways operated this route between the capital cities for eighteen years, until it was suspended in November 1994. A flight to Singapore was also started in December 1977, though after only three services it was suspended as the Malaysian Government objected to the aircraft passing through its airspace for noise reasons. After re-routing, the service was restarted in January 1979. However, the route was not a commercial success and discontinued in November 1980.

The service that both airlines wanted, but BA in particular, was to New York. JFK airport was operated by the Port of New York Authority and, despite the prestige of a Concorde service, it was strongly against it, as were many of the residents around the airport, who claimed it was too noisy and a pollutant. The US judicial authorities, however, sided with Concorde and, after much legal wrangling, it was permitted to fly into the airport.

On 22 November 1977 JFK services finally started. Operating twice daily, this would be the jewel in the crown of British Airways services, which was evident in the allocation of the flight number BA001, with BA002 operating the return. The later flight was BA003/004. British Airways also operated a once-, sometimes twice-weekly London–Barbados schedule for up to four months in the winter season. These flights proved very popular with the wealthy escaping for some winter sunshine. There were also occasional flights to Toronto's Lester B. Pearson International Airport. The schedules meant that, with three aircraft generally under maintenance at any one time, two and sometimes three aircraft were earmarked for scheduled services, and up to two aircraft for the ever-expanding charter market, which accounted for 20 per cent of the aircraft's utilisation.

A January 1979 lease agreement saw Braniff International Airlines operate both British Airways and Air France Concordes on a thrice-weekly Washington–Dallas service. As the route was overland it had to be flown subsonic. However,

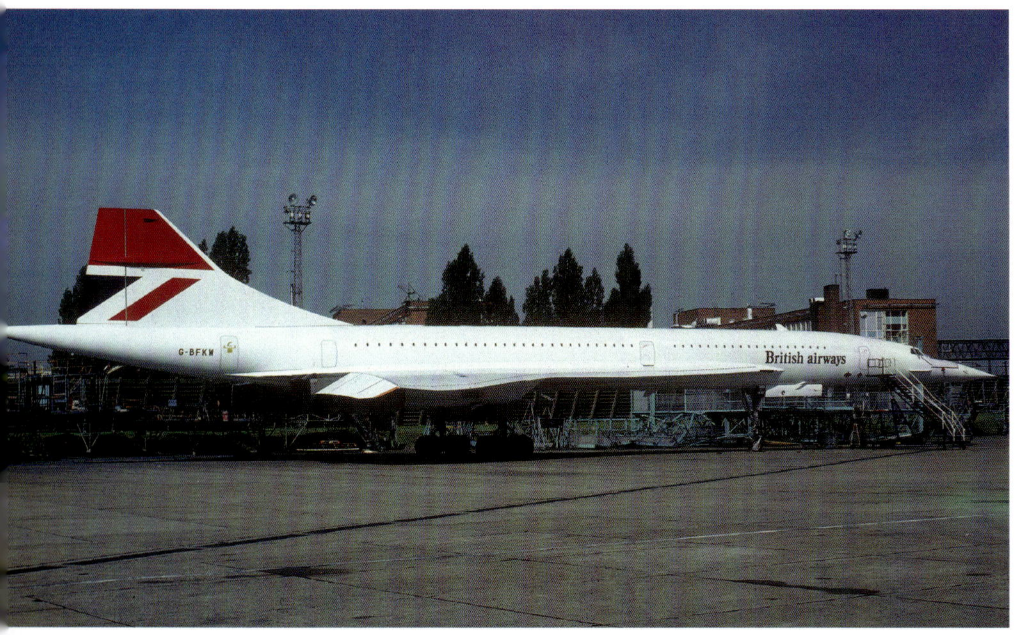

The newly delivered G-BFKW at Heathrow in August 1980. This aircraft was manufactured at Filton but had no buyer, hence the strange registration. It was then loaned to British Airways for a six-month period, and was eventually purchased by the airline, being re-registered as G-BOAG on 9 February 1981. (Tom Singfield collection)

this service only lasted for eighteen months, with services ceasing in June 1980. In March 1984 British Airways Concorde services were extended from Washington to Miami thrice weekly but this service was not a great success and was eventually dropped in 1991.

In 1984 Concorde's future was secured through an agreement whereby BA took over responsibility for all support costs. BA actually acquired an eighth Concorde as the first development aircraft at Filton (G-BBDG) was retained as a spares source. It was around this time that the airline started to make a profit from its supersonic aircraft. It increased the price of a flight to almost double that of a first-class ticket on a subsonic aircraft. British Airways flew a Washington Dulles–Dallas Fort Worth service in its own right from June 1988 (as the airline did not have domestic passenger rights for this route it was only available to those flying the international leg). Like the Braniff service, it was a commercial failure and folded after just four months.

After the Air France crash on 25 July 2000, all Concorde aircraft were immediately grounded. A British Airways service bound for New York was taxiing for departure at Heathrow when the news was received and it was instructed to return to the gate straight away. After the safety modifications had been completed, British Airways restarted the JFK service on 7 November 2001, nearly seventeen months after they were halted by the grounding.

Throughout its British Airways history, the Concorde fleet wore three different liveries. The first, worn from 1976 to 1984, is known as the Negus & Negus scheme, so named after the designers. Then came the Landor scheme of 1985–97, again named after the designers. These were the colours worn for the longest time and

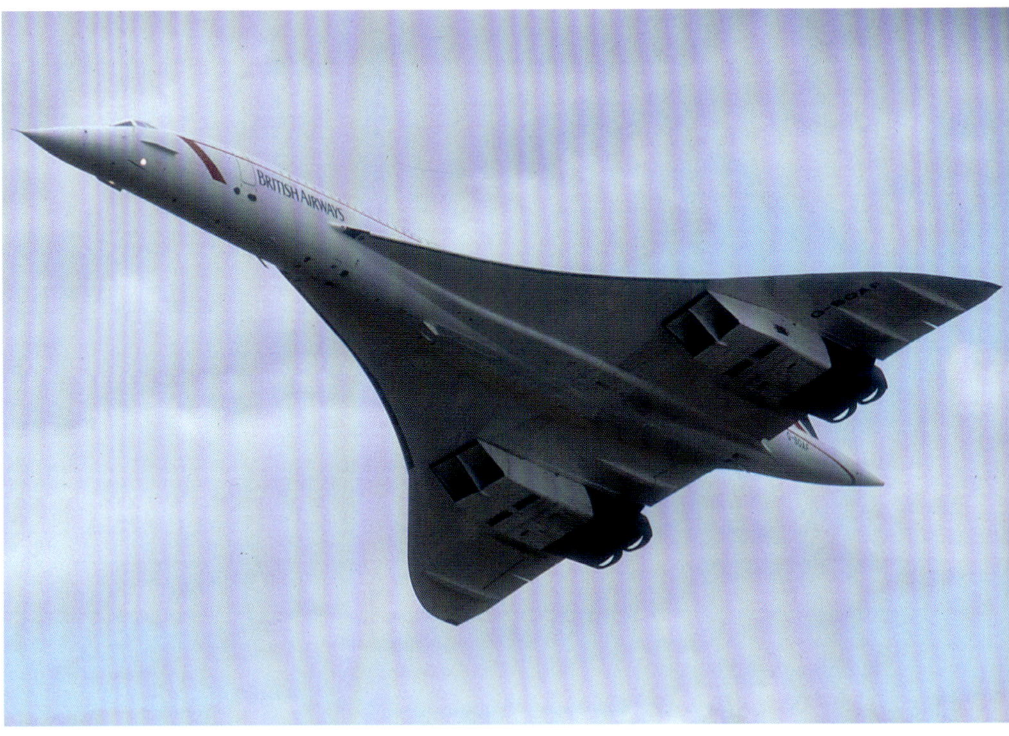

G-BOAF performing a flypast at the Duxford Air Show on 15 September 1985.

hence photographs of the aircraft in this scheme predominate in this book. The last was the 1998–2003 Union Flag scheme, which came about under Project Utopia, where the airline's fleet bore an inventive livery of schemes from artists around the world. Former Prime Minister Margaret Thatcher was one who publicly disliked the idea, but it was liked by many, especially enthusiasts.

After the retirement decision was made, British Airways' Concorde G-BOAG carried out a North American farewell tour in October 2003, taking in Toronto and New York JFK. Other aircraft in the fleet visited locations such as Boston and Washington Dulles. With 23,397 hours on the clock, G-BOAD had the highest number of flying hours of any Concorde built, and significantly more than any Air France example.

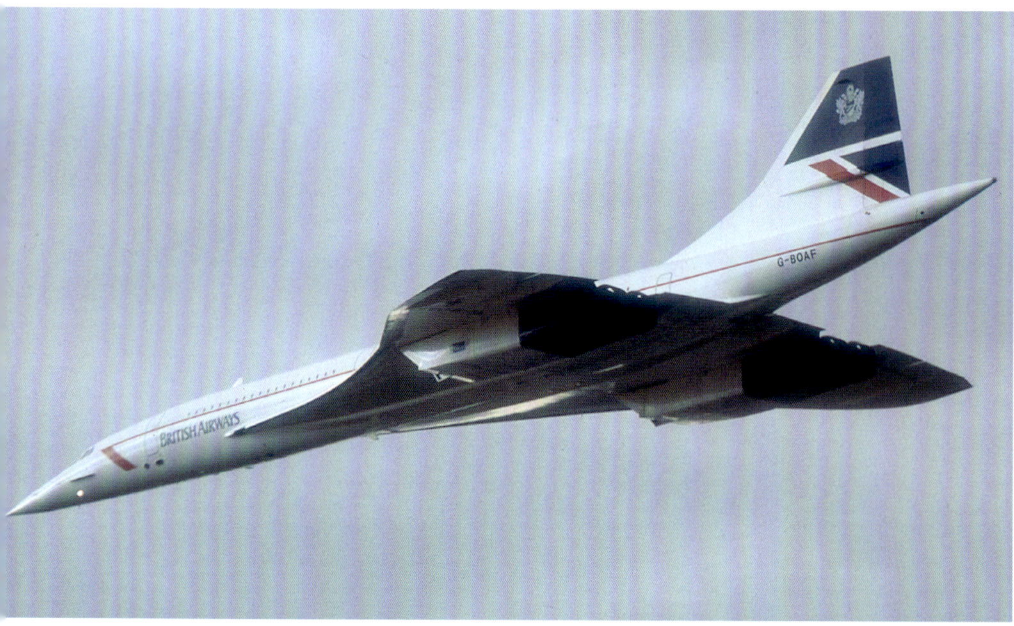

G-BOAF showing the spectacular Concorde design at Duxford.

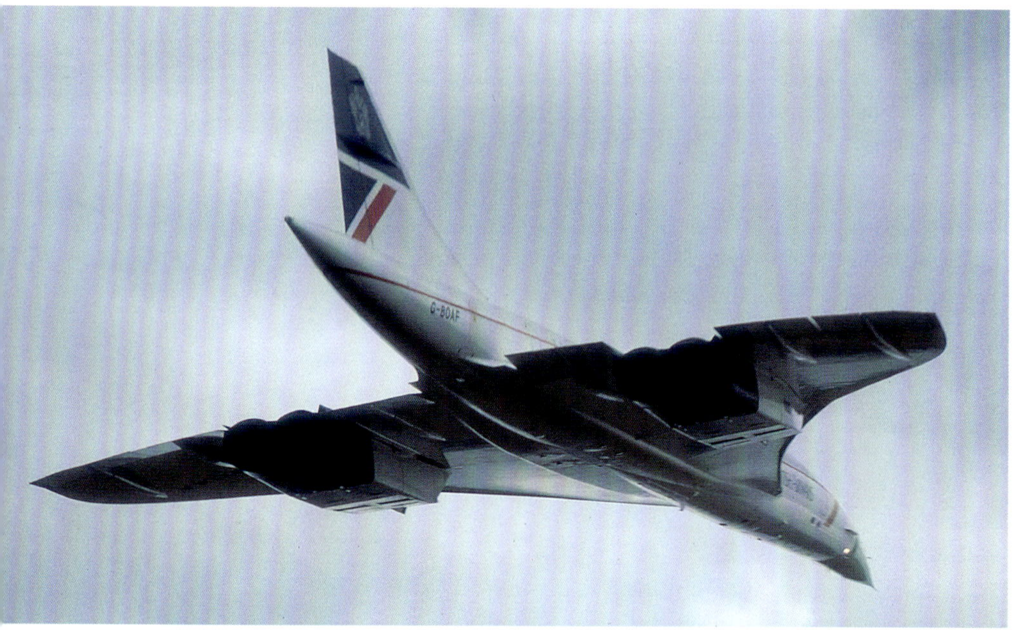

The classic lines of Concorde are on display as G-BOAF powers away from Duxford at the end of its performance.

CHARTERS

While Concorde proved a success with the passengers, it was the use of the aircraft on many charter flights that brought it home to the general public, as then it meant that it was not only the rich and famous who could fly in it. Although these trips were not cheap, they were available to all. Until then, both Air France and British Airways had struggled to make their Concorde operations viable.

In addition to regular New York and Washington scheduled flights, the airline often operated a winter schedule to Barbados, which for many of the affluent meant a relaxing time in the Caribbean sun. Another was to Rovaniemi in Finnish Lapland – the home of Santa Claus. These winter charters were good for British Airways' prestige. For the affluent, many destinations around the world became accessible, often with a supersonic leg, and many world speed records were broken. In fact, Concorde was seen in many places round the world, ranging from Greenland to New Zealand.

The first British Airways Concorde charter was on 19 September 1978 after a conversation between BA pilot Brian Calvert and the landlord at his local watering hole, the Bell Inn at Aldworth in Berkshire. It was the landlord's suggestion that they should fly in 'the old girl'. Brian put the proposal to BA and the outcome was a two-and-a-half-hour supersonic flight over the Bay of Biscay. The seed was sewn. Another early flight was when Concorde stewardess Jeannette Hartley had an idea to hire Concorde for herself and some friends. This was suggested to BA, which was not averse to the idea, though it would cost £20,000 – or £200 a head. Initially Jeannette only took eleven bookings, but after she was interviewed by a women's magazine and the national press, the flight was fully booked within three weeks. She ended up organising two flights, and did the seating plan and passenger check-in herself. Another charter was organised by Concorde pilot Christopher Orlebar to mark the fiftieth anniversary of a cousin's participation in the 1931 Schneider Trophy air race in a Supermarine S.6B seaplane.

Perhaps the most well-known series of charters was Goodwood Travel's 'Flight of Fantasy' programme. To quote some words from the Flight of Fantasy brochure, 'British Airways' Concorde is the supreme expression of aeronautical excellence. Its unique style, its marriage of aesthetics and sophisticated engineering, its reputation for comfort and unfaltering efficiency have assured it of landmark status in the annals of civil aviation.'*

Goodwood Travel was formed in 1981 by Jan Knott, Colin Mitchell and George Stevens, and undertook its first BA Concorde flight in 1982. The company soon became renowned as specialists in Concorde flights. Indeed, I was one of their customers when, to mark a forthcoming twenty-fifth anniversary, I bought my wife a trip to the Monaco Grand Prix in 1997, as she was into F1 at the time. I could not go as I was on shift at Gatwick! On the day of her flight, three Concordes took passengers to Nice for the event, one from Air France and two from British Airways.

By then Goodwood Travel had become synonymous with Concorde charters. It operated regular supersonic daytrips that included lunch, but it was the amazing variety of flights on offer that I think made the company number one. It flew regular trips too, and by late 1997 had taken Concorde to

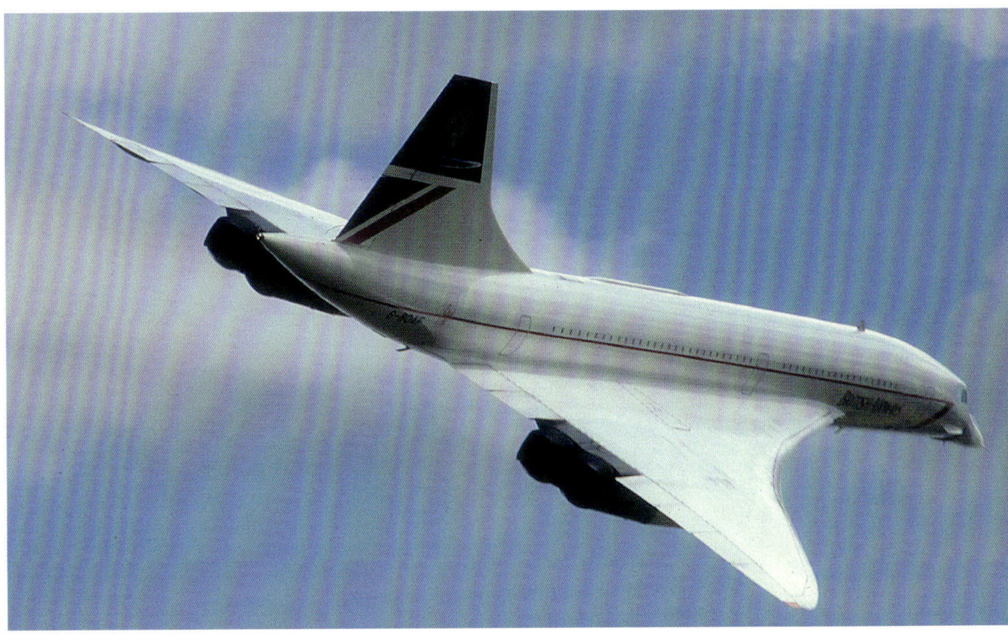

G-BOAF departing Duxford during the air show.

forty-seven destinations around the world, including Aqaba (Jordan), Barbados, Kangerlussuaq (Greenland), Moscow and New York, to name just a few. Goodwood would arrange trips supersonic one way and subsonic the other. In the case of locations like Barbados and New York, it could be supersonic one way and ocean-going liner like the *QE2* the other. These trips could be one-day or week-long events and could range from a return flight to Cairo with a week on the Nile by boat to safari trips in South Africa. Among the trips I would like to have gone on were two magical places I have been to but not by Concorde. The first was to Aqaba on the Red Sea, then to the Red Rose City of Petra, surely one of the wonders of the world. Another was via Kangerlussuaq in Greenland to Ilulissat. After landing at Kangerlussuaq, customers were then flown by commuter aircraft to Ilulissat. The magical giant icebergs in Disko Bay really are something, and it

---

* Goodwood Travel 'Flights of Fantasy' Brochure, 1997.

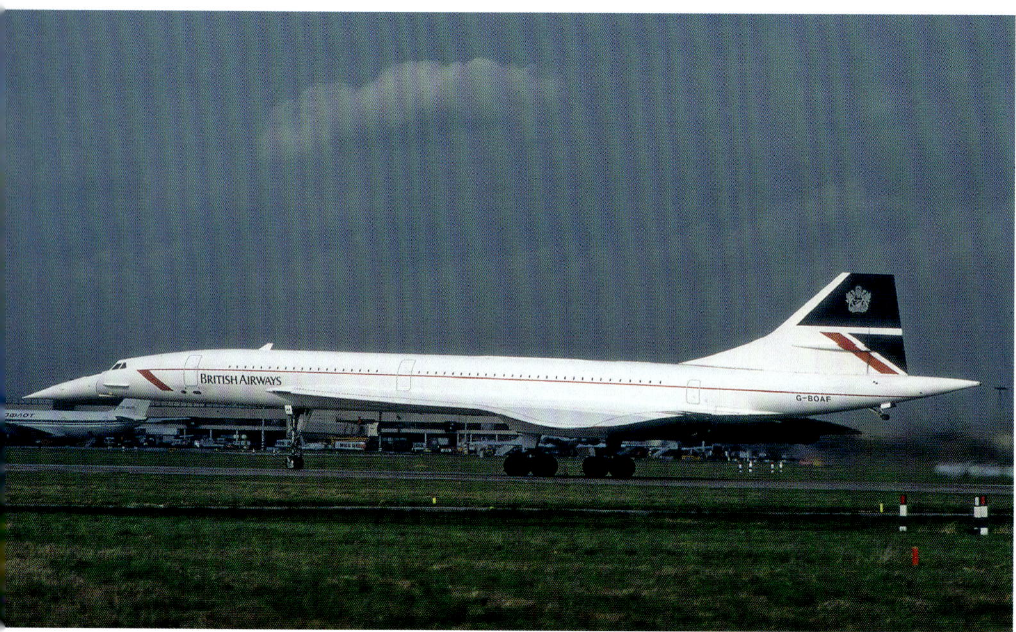

G-BOAF awaiting departure from Heathrow's runway 27L on 5 March 1989.

on the aircraft. The company even organised Concorde simulator trips at Bristol Filton.

However, Goodwood Travel was one of several travel companies that would charter a whole aircraft, or even part of the load. For years Bournemouth-based Bath Travel was heavily involved in travel from the Bournemouth area, and at one time even had its own aircraft, a BAe 146. When the runway at Bournemouth's Hurn airport was extended, Bath Travel could realise a dream, operating Concorde from the airport. It did this several times, even filling seats on Concorde's subsonic positioning flight from Heathrow.

American Express and Kuoni were regular customers. One of the more popular (and cheaper) charters was around the Bay of Biscay, where the aircraft could fly supersonic. Another company was David Gladwin Concorde Ltd. Gladwin was a former British Airways pilot who set up subsonic flights from regional airports such as Belfast, Birmingham, East Midlands, Exeter and Manchester to Heathrow; being subsonic flights, they were much cheaper. The company also booked supersonic charters to New York, Paris and Rovaniemi (Finland). A popular one was a day or weekend trip to Cairo to see the Pyramids, with a supersonic dash down the Mediterranean. BA flew winter Concorde charters to the north to enable passengers to view the Aurora Borealis simply because, unlike most other airliners, Concorde could fly above any cloud cover.

is said to be one of the most productive glaciers in the world, with the ice moving about 35m a day. It is thought that the iceberg that sank *Titanic* came from there. A flight to Ilulissat on Concorde was never possible as the runway is only 800m long and used by short take-off and landing (STOL) aircraft on regional services.

Goodwood Travel held several Concorde records. One was that they chartered *three* British Airways Concordes on one day to go to Nice for the Monaco Grand Prix. Another was that three Concordes were chartered in one day to three different destinations. Then there was the March 1987 'Concorde World Air Cruise' that went around the world in eighteen days, the grand route taking in cities including London, Moscow, Cairo, Delhi, Hong Kong, Beijing, Guam, Honolulu, Mexico City, Barbados and New York – what a journey. By the time Concorde retired, Goodwood could claim to have flown more than 100,000 passengers

Concorde Spirit Tours (USA) first chartered Concorde in November 1985 for a Miami–Aruba trip, which was so successful that the company later ran round-the-world tours, one of these being a New York–Toulouse–Dubai–Bangkok–Guam–Honolulu–Acapulco extravaganza, with the over-water legs being supersonic. This was completed in a flying time of thirty-one hours, twenty-seven minutes and forty-nine seconds.

During the late 1990s British Airways was operating in the region of 300 charter flights a year, which really is quite astounding and a testimony to the attraction and popularity of Concorde.

Apart from Antarctica, Concorde visited every continent on Earth. Amazingly, it visited more than 250 destinations, including 76 in the United States alone. Some of these prestigious flights were the trips of a lifetime for many, and were often enjoyed by those whose taxes had paid for the aircraft.

BRANIFF INTERNATIONAL AIRLINES

Although a number of US airlines, such as American, Continental, Eastern, Pan American, Trans World and United, had options on Concorde, it was Braniff that became the sole American operator of the type, despite not having any Concordes of its own. It began a Washington Dulles to Dallas Fort Worth service using aircraft leased from both Air France and British Airways, and was an extension of the European carrier's services to Washington from London and Paris. It certainly was an unusual agreement, with the aircraft retaining their owner's livery, but using Braniff cockpit and cabin crew. Of course, as the sector was over land the aircraft had to fly subsonic. To comply with US regulations, the aircraft had to wear American registrations. These were taped over the European registrations for the domestic sector, then removed again at Washington prior to the transatlantic return flight. However, the service was not a commercial success for Braniff, and it only operated from January 1979 to May 1980.

It has been reported that load factors on these sectors averaged only 20 per cent, and when you add the cost of Braniff crews training on Concorde, it is not hard to see why the venture was unprofitable. Braniff had in fact hoped to operate its own Concordes on South American services, but a financial recession put paid to that.

As a requirement of its insurers, British Airways was forced to fly a captain and flight engineer as cockpit observers for US segments, as in reality the aircraft were still BA-owned for insurance purposes. For Braniff, fourteen pilots (three captains, five first officers, four flight engineers, a check pilot and a check engineer) were trained in both France and the UK to operate the type, at both the subsonic speeds required for their services and also up to Mach 2 cruising speed. This added significantly to Braniff's costs. This service was flown five times a week, with the aircraft night-stopping

G-BOAA lining up on runway 27L at Heathrow awaiting take-off clearance on 5 March 1989. Note another Concorde visible behind it waiting to line up from the other side of the runway.

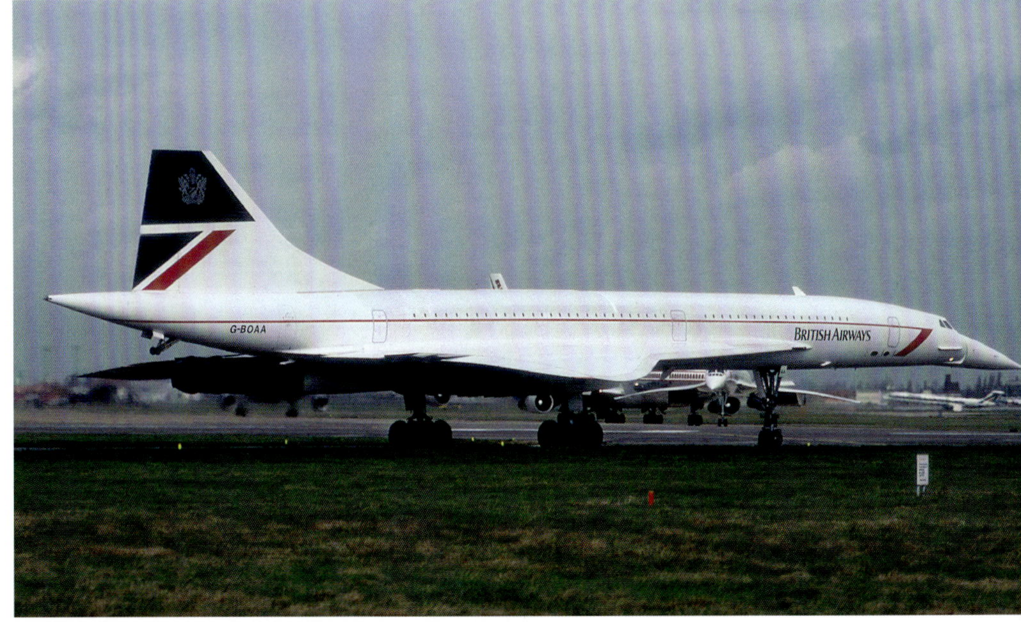

at Dallas Fort Worth, then carrying on to Dulles the following morning in time for the transatlantic leg. Braniff joint ops were suspended just after G-N94AF (G-BOAF) was delivered in June 1980.

The US registrations applied were:

F-BTSD – N94SD
F-BVFA – N94FA
F-BVFB – N94FB
F-BVFC – N94FC
F-BVFD – N94FD
G-BOAA – G-N94AA – N94AA
G-BOAB – G-N94AB – N94AB
G-BOAC – G-N81AC – N81AC
G-BOAD – G-N94AD – N94AD
G-BOAE – G-N94AE – N94AE
G-BOAF – G-N94AF – N94AF

SINGAPORE AIRLINES

For several years Concorde G-BOAD had Singapore Airlines livery on the port side and British Airways on the starboard. This was when the airlines operated a joint service from London Heathrow to Singapore Paya Lebar Airport via Bahrain. The cabin crew on board were from both airlines. The service began on 9 December 1977 but had to be stopped after just three days as the Malaysian Government complained about the noise of Concorde as it passed through its airspace. After re-routing, the service restarted on 24 January 1979, but only lasted until 1 November 1980 because of unsatisfactory passenger loads. The airline had initially hoped that this service would continue on to Australia, but this never materialised.

G-BOAE coming out of Terminal 4 and heading for runway 27L at Heathrow on 25 April 1990.

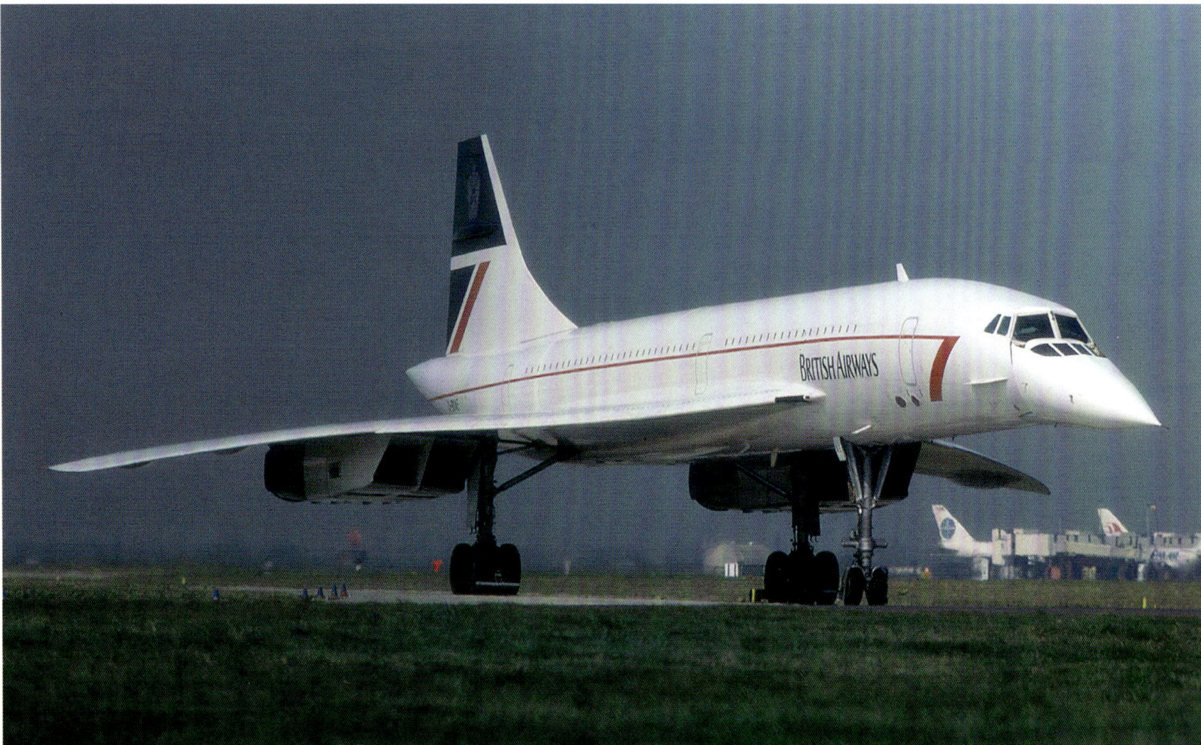

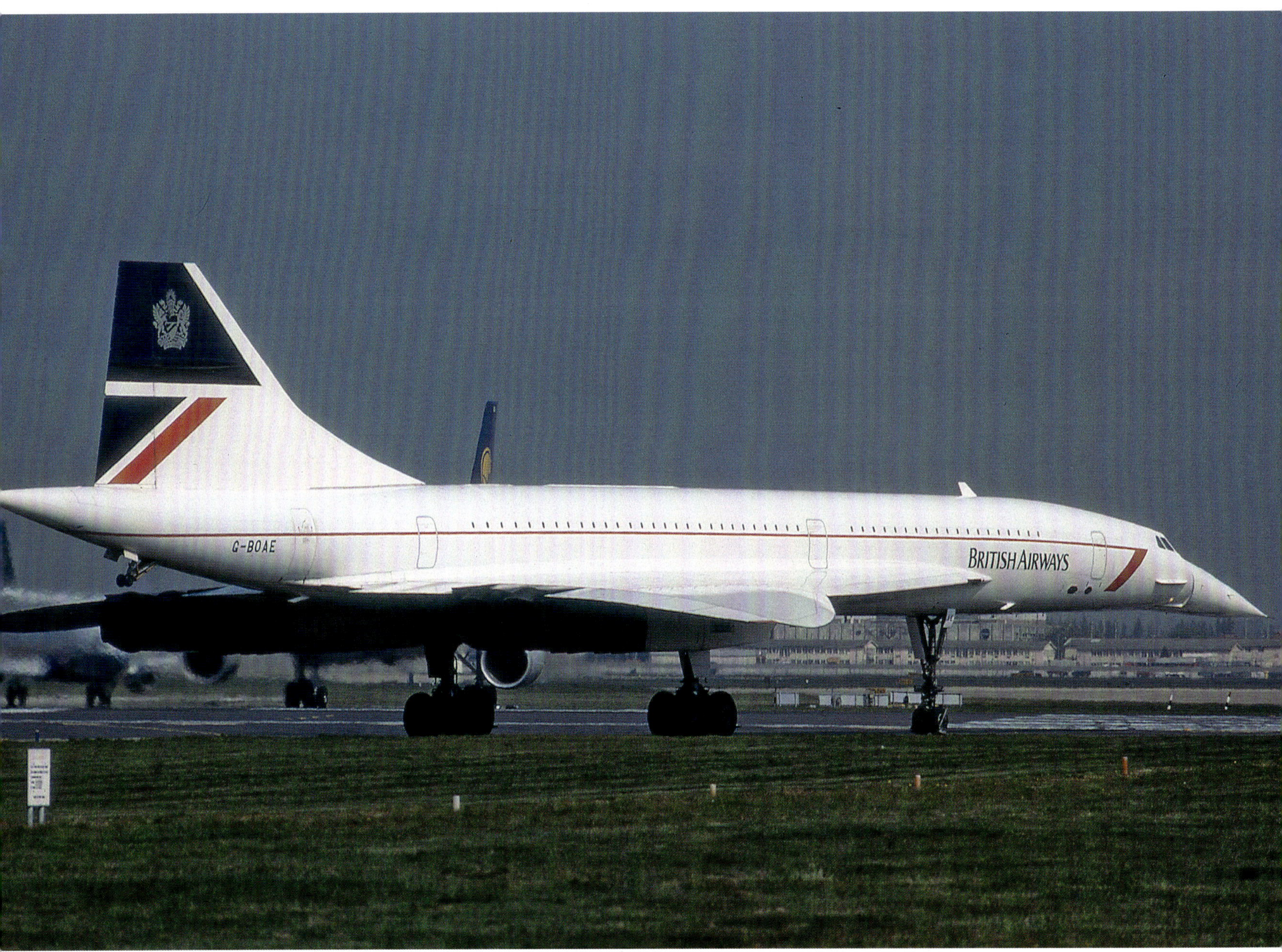

G-BOAE awaiting line-up clearance at the holding point of 27L at Heathrow on 25 April 1990.

The small window on Concorde. The clouds high above show that this photo was taken during the descent.

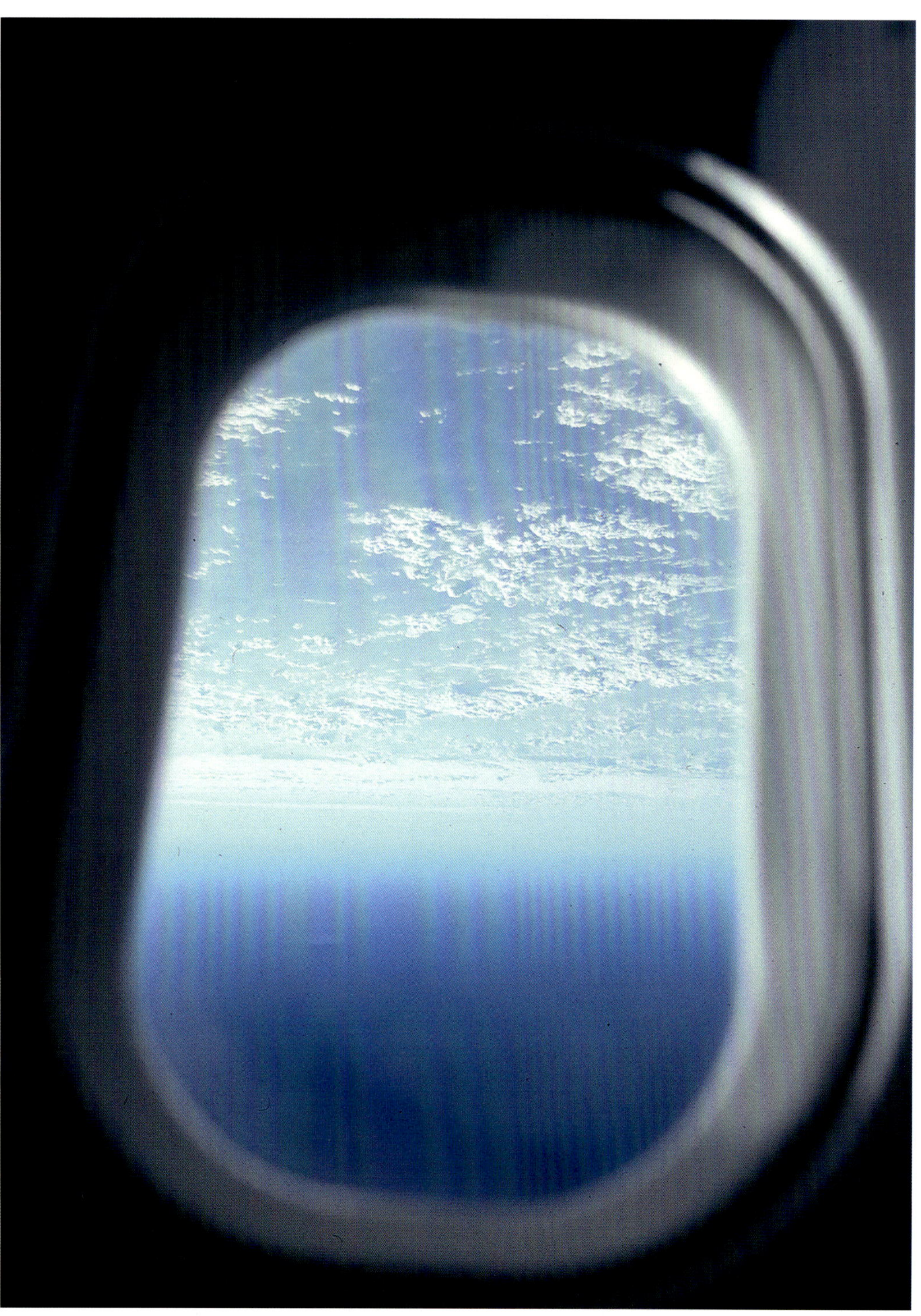

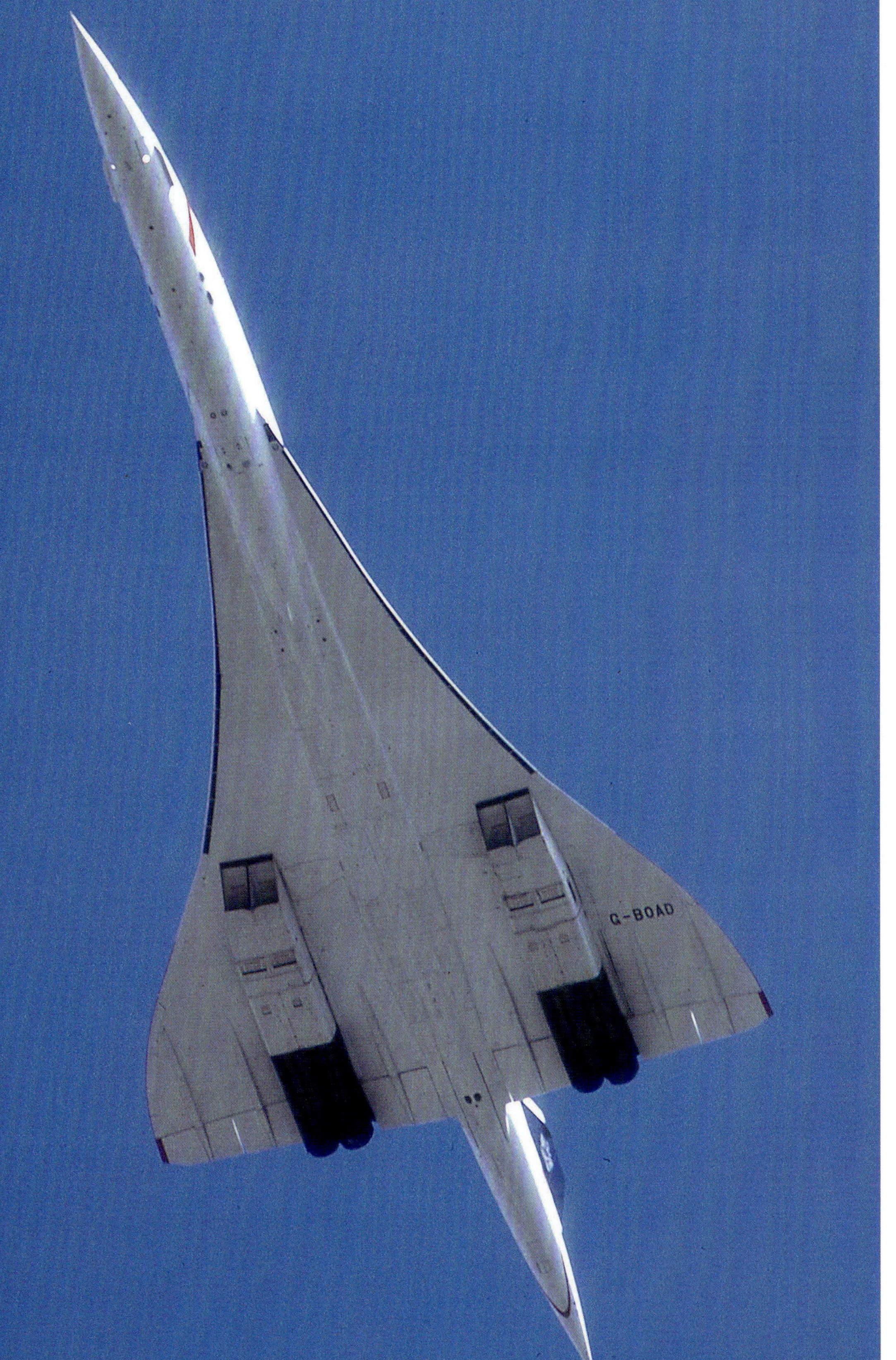

The sleek lines of Concorde
G-BOAD during a flypast at
the Farnborough Air Show
on 7 September 1990.

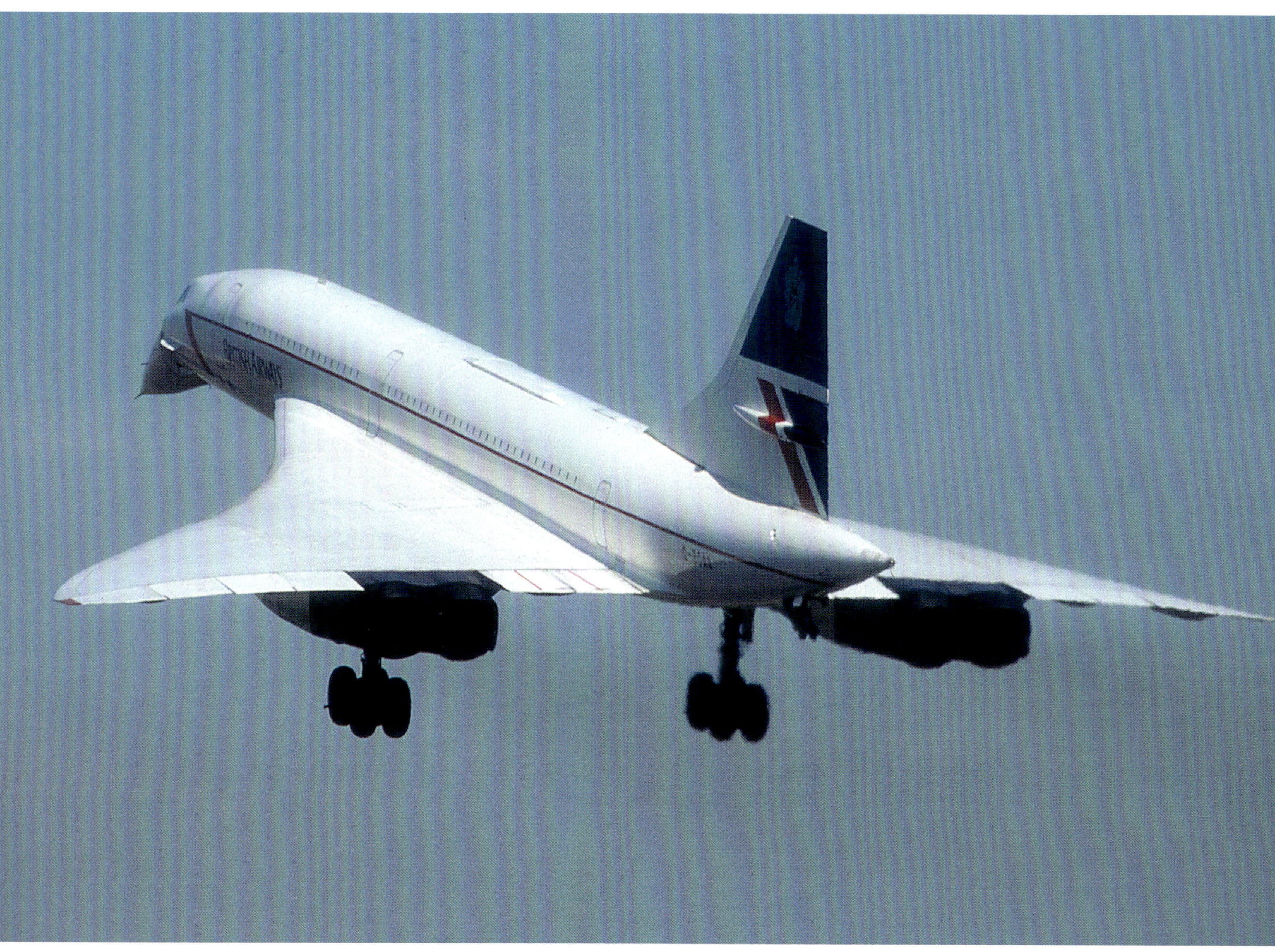

A dramatic three-quarters rear shot of G-BOAA about to land on 27L at Heathrow on 28 June 1993.

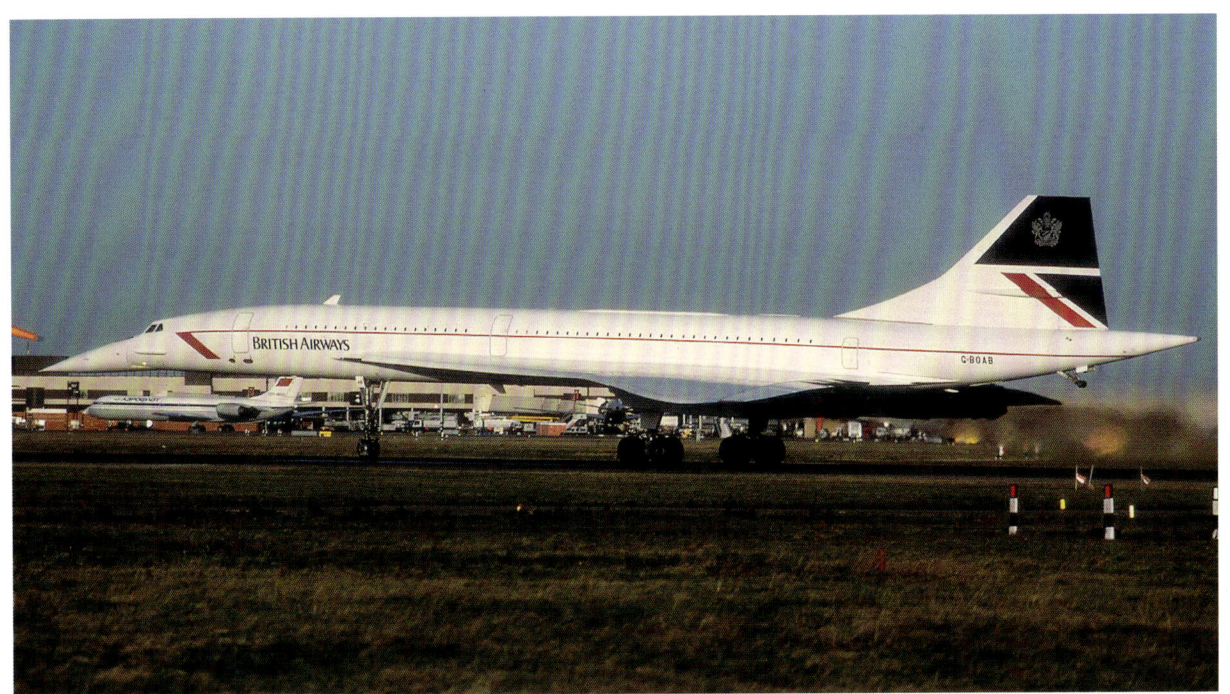

G-BOAB in the Landor livery at Heathrow ready for departure on runway 27L on 6 January 1991.

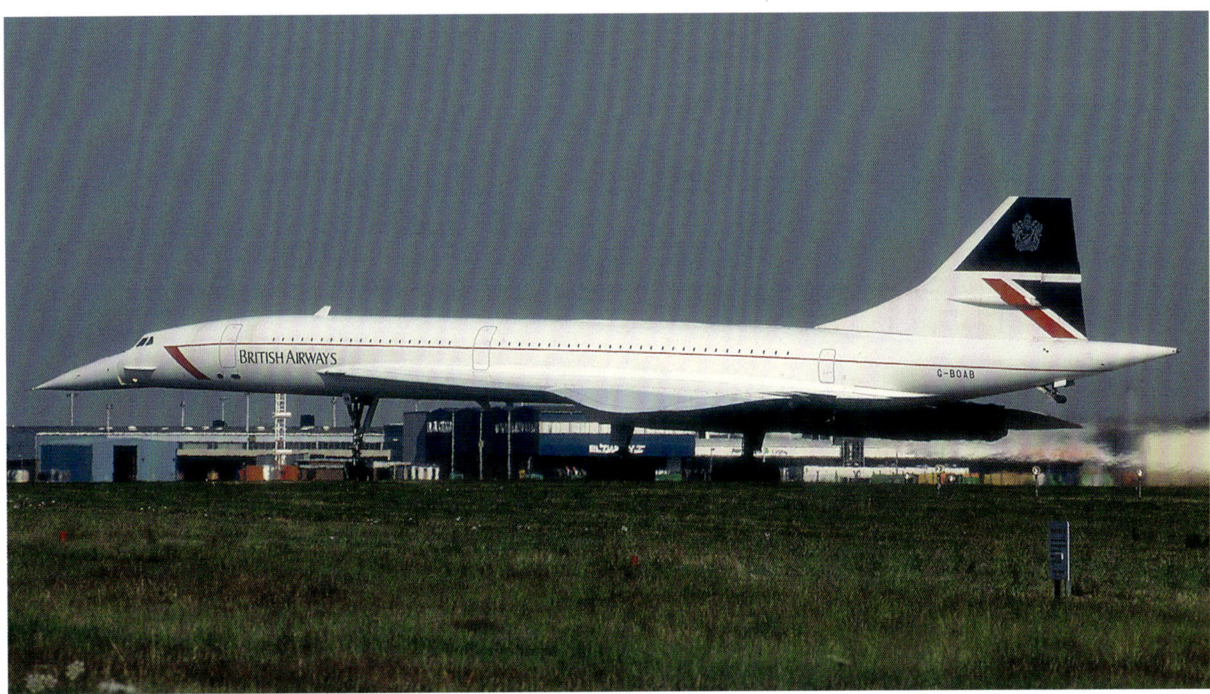

G-BOAB ready to release the brakes on runway 27L at Heathrow on 28 June 1993.

G-BOAD on its way to the 27L holding point at Heathrow from Terminal 4 on 8 February 1994.

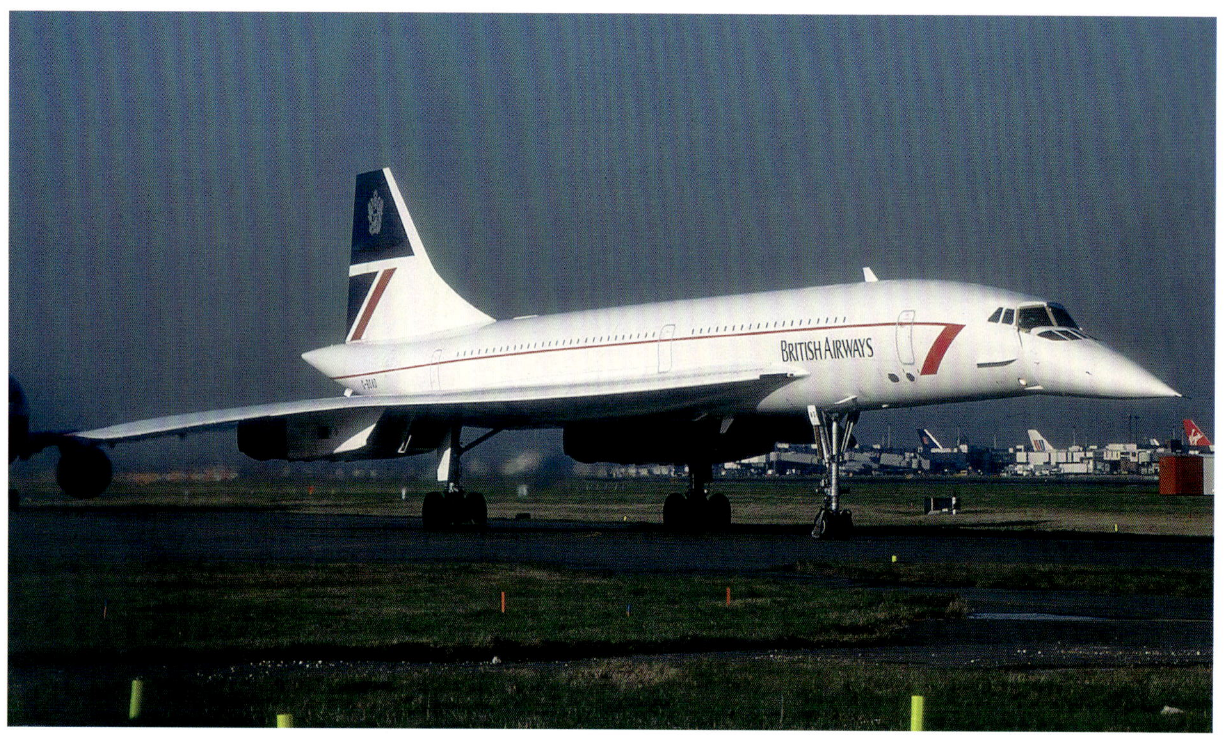

G-BOAD awaiting line-up clearance from air traffic control on runway 27L at Heathrow on 8 February 1994.

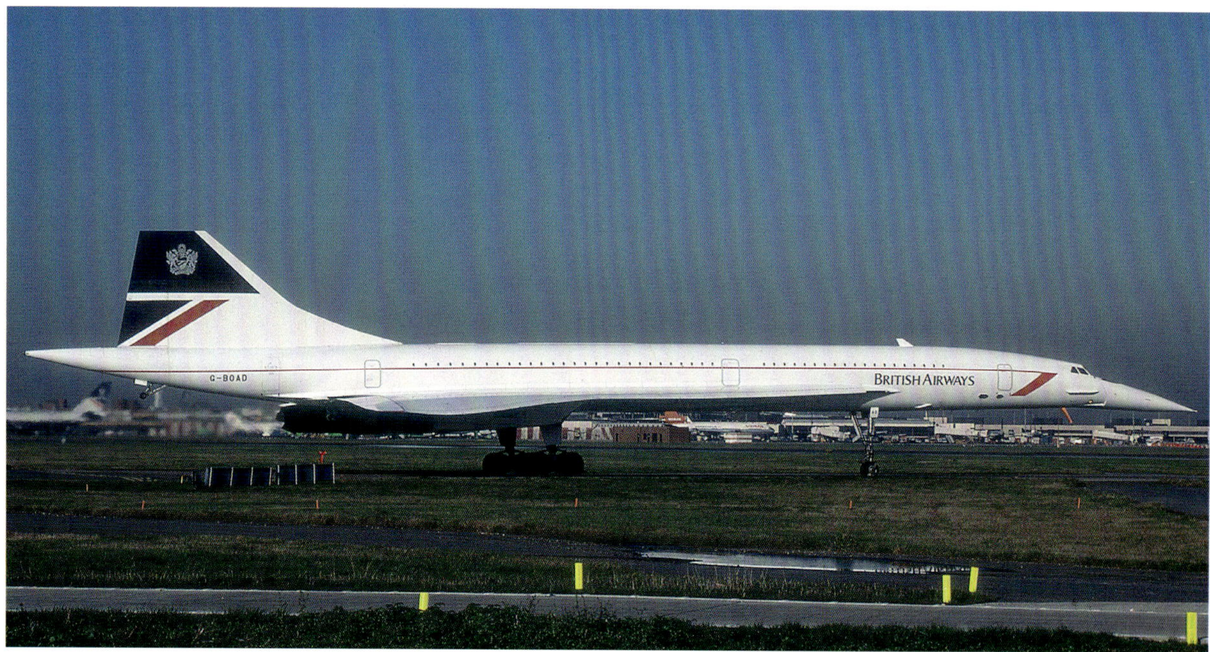

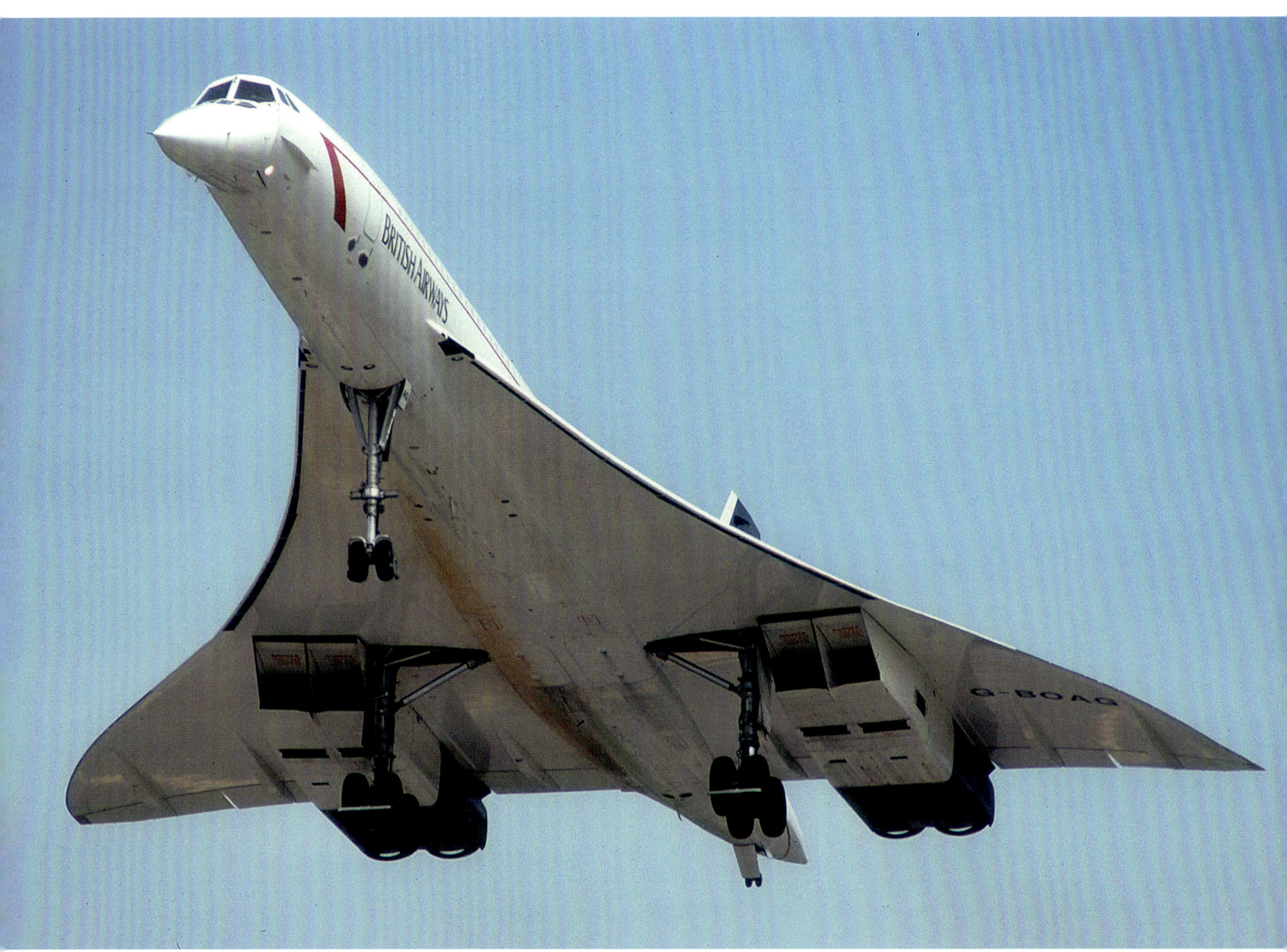

G-BOAG on very short finals for landing on 13 July 1985.

G-BOAC on approach to runway 33R at Toronto's Lester B. Pearson International Airport on 1 June 1994. The nose visor in the down position enables the pilots to view the runway properly.

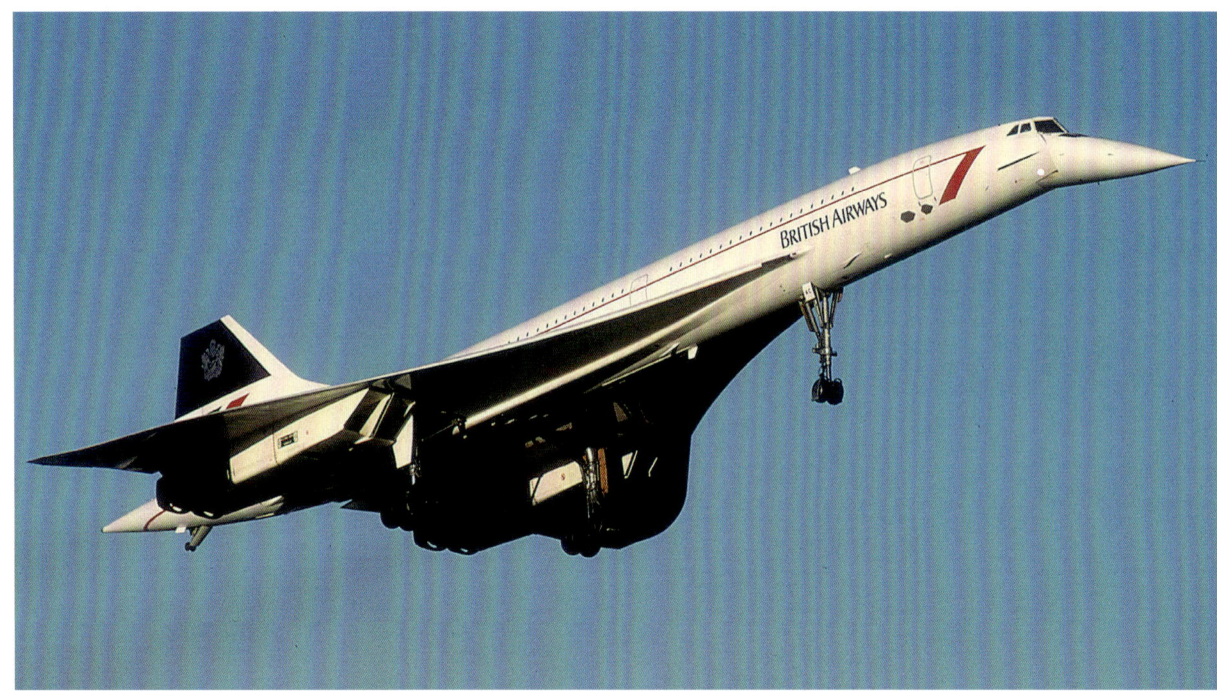

G-BOAC on approach to runway 09L at Heathrow on 10 July 1994.

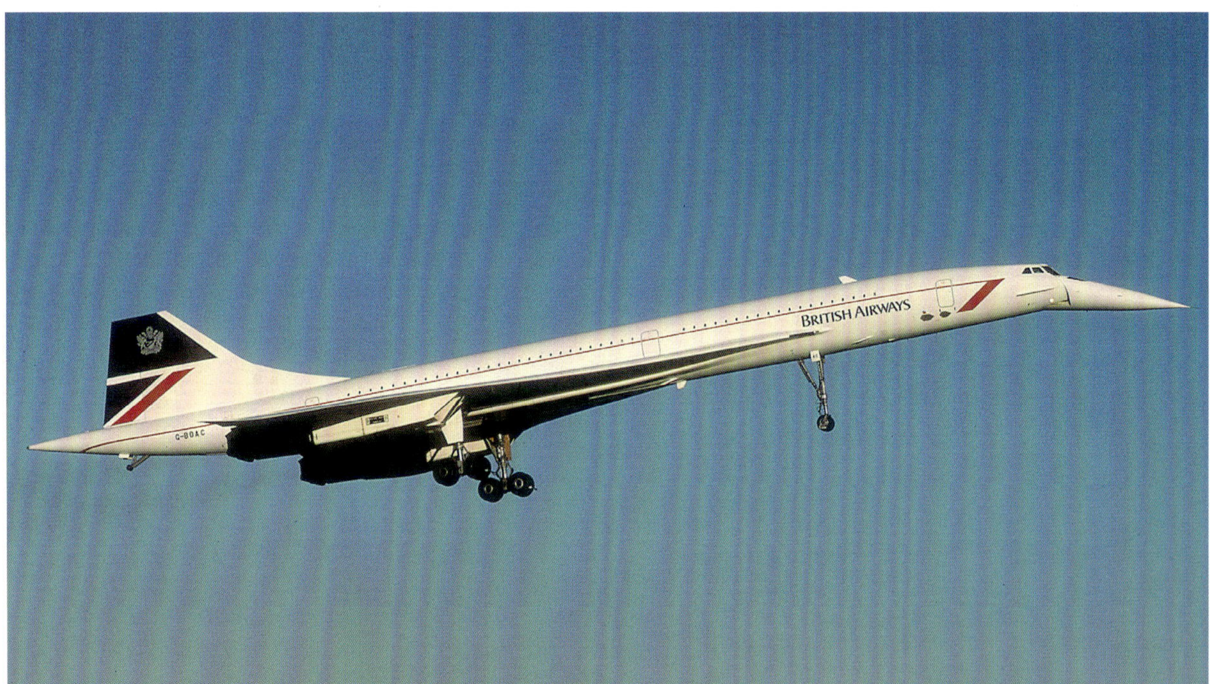

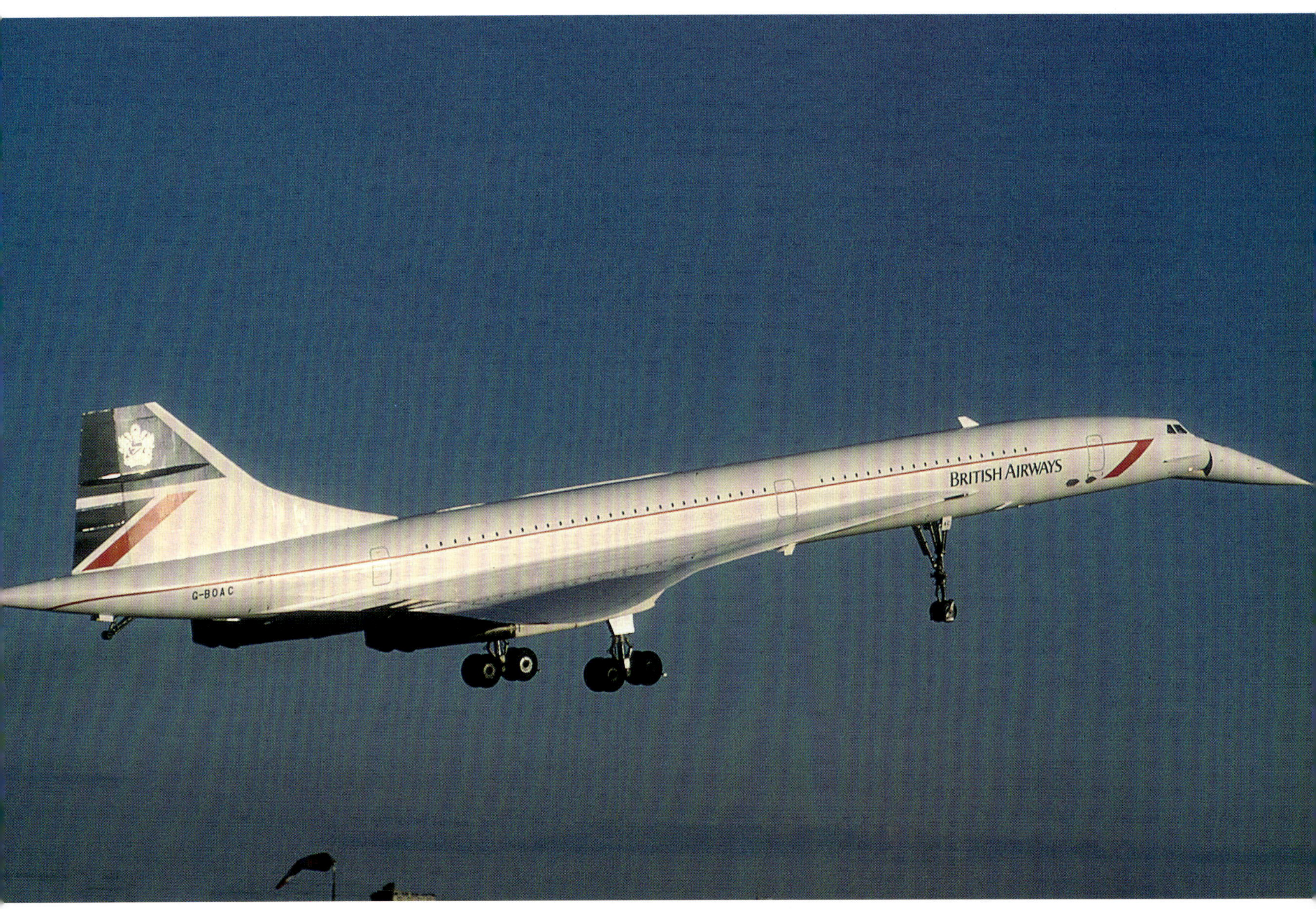

G-BOAC on very short finals to land on runway 09L at Heathrow on 10 July 1994.

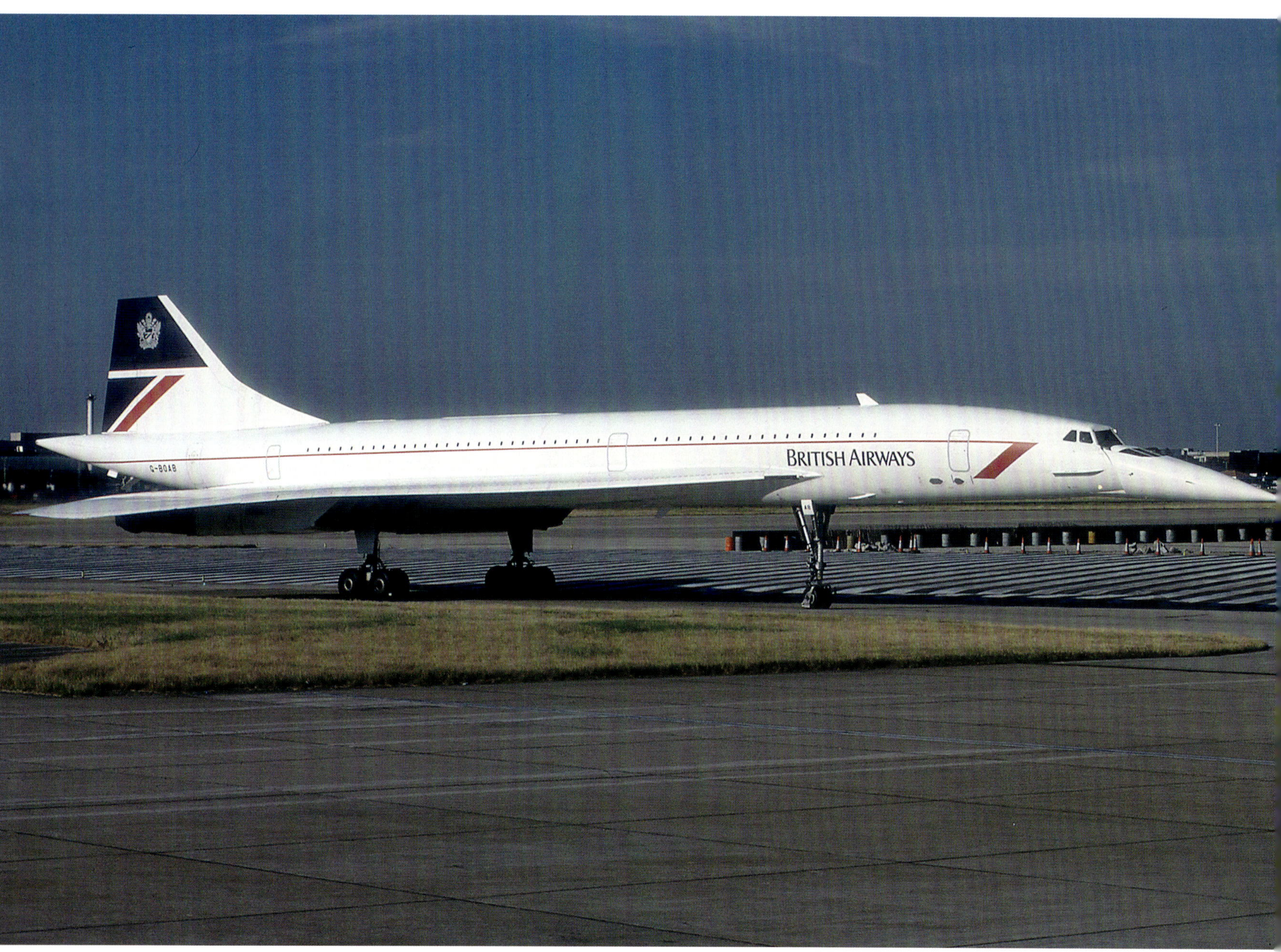

After landing on Heathrow's runway 27R, G-BOAB taxies across the airfield bound for Terminal 4 on 10 July 1994.

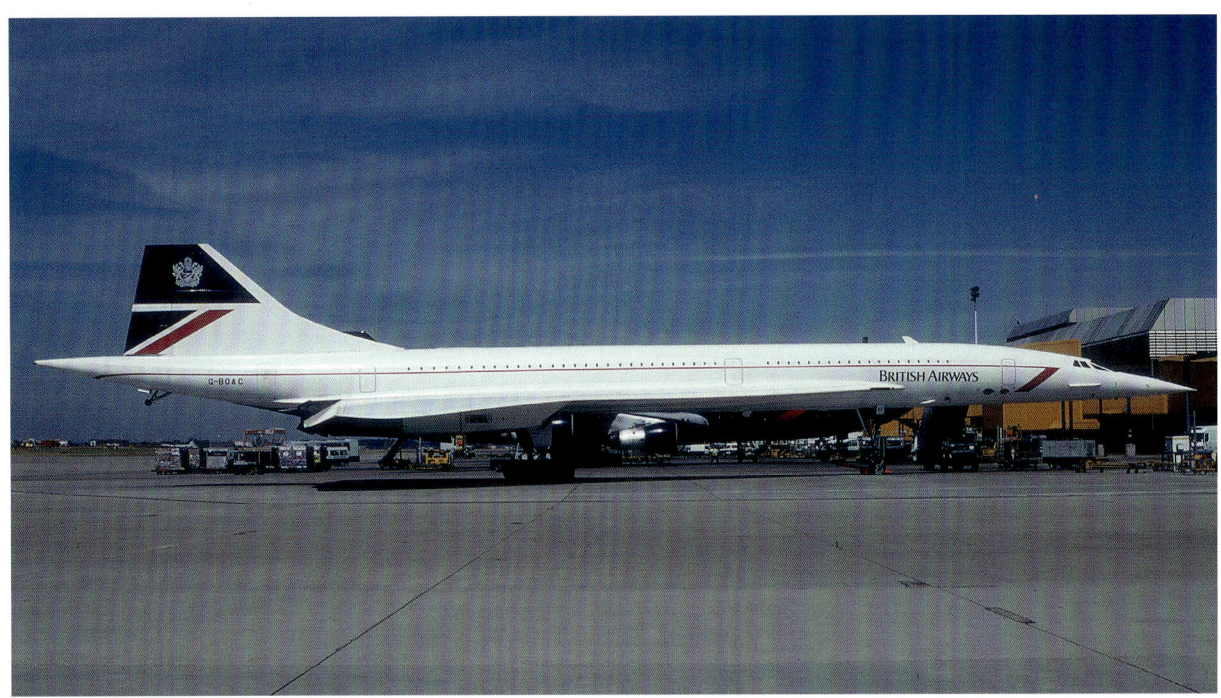

G-BOAC parked on the gate at Heathrow's Terminal 4 ready for a flight to New York.

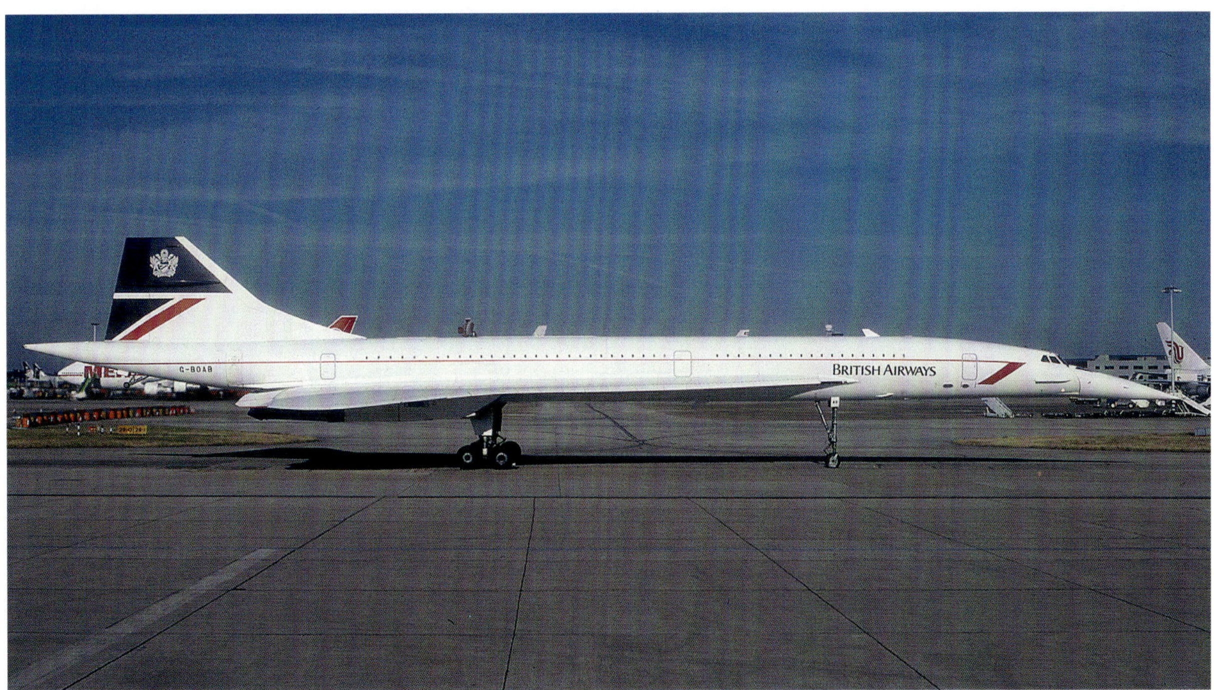

G-BOAB taxiing between the runways at Heathrow on 10 July 1995, bound for Terminal 4.

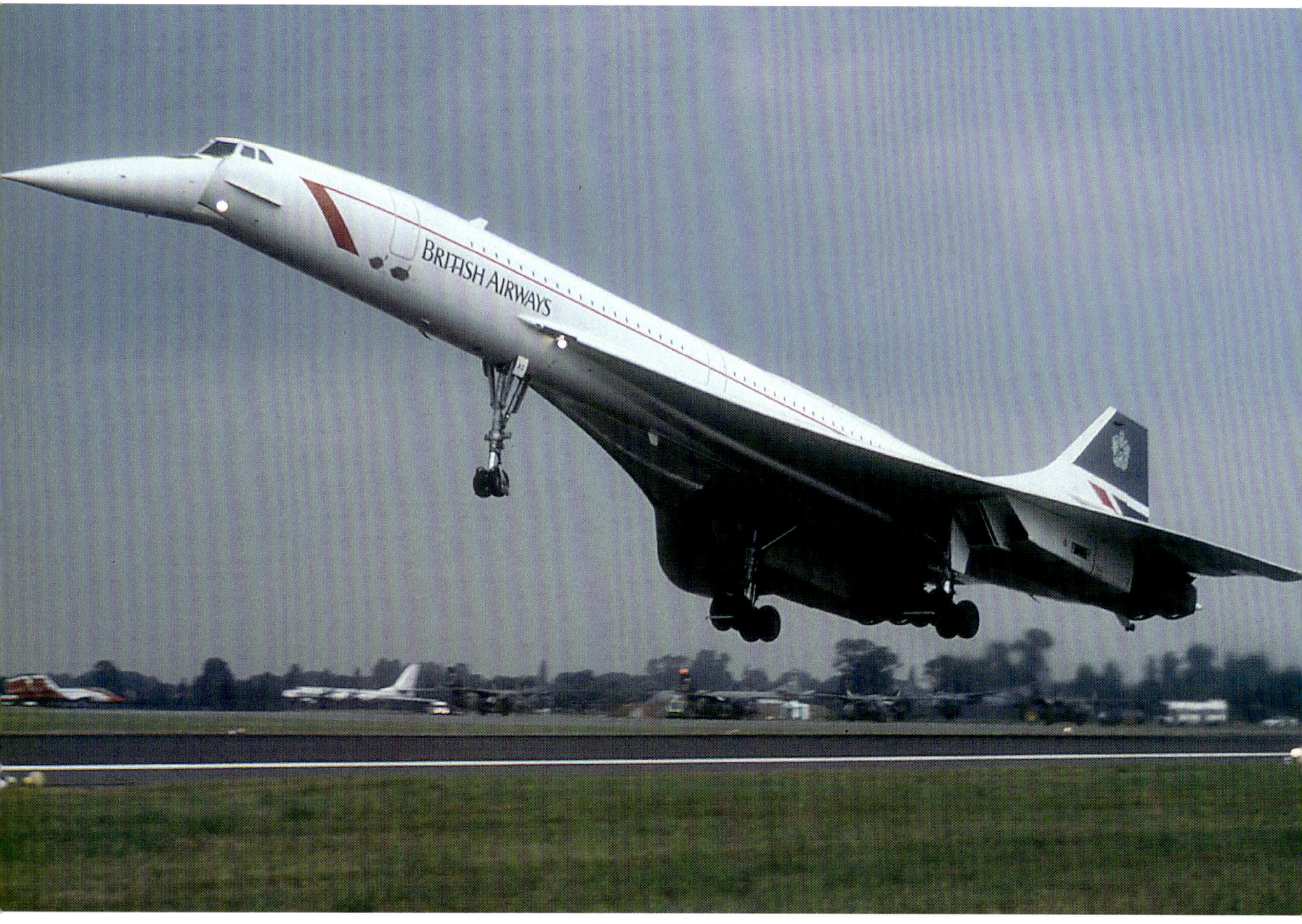

G-BOAC about to land on runway 27 at Fairford to attend the International Air Tattoo on 31 July 1994. This was probably a Goodwood charter flight from Heathrow.

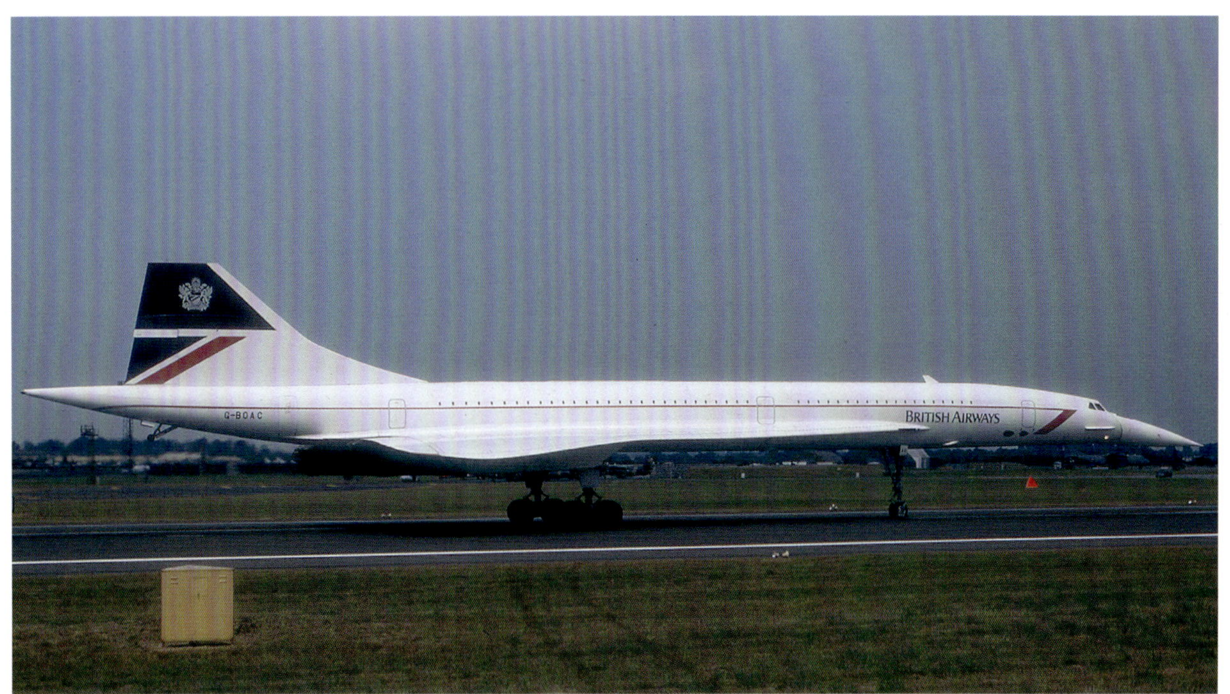

G-BOAC backtracking the runway at Fairford on 30 July 1994. The International Air Tattoo was a two-day event, and Concorde often visited on both days on Goodwood Travel charters from Heathrow.

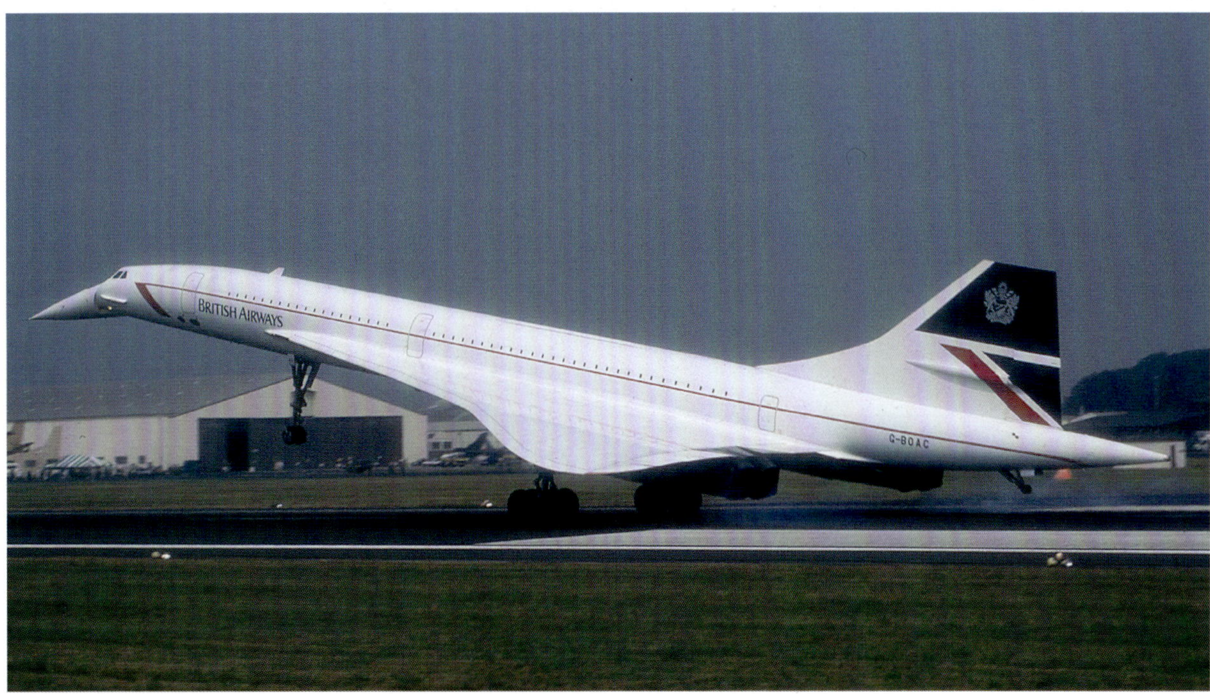

G-BOAC touching down on runway 27 at Fairford on 30 July 1994 to attend the International Air Tattoo. It had a full load of passengers on a Goodwood Travel trip from Heathrow.

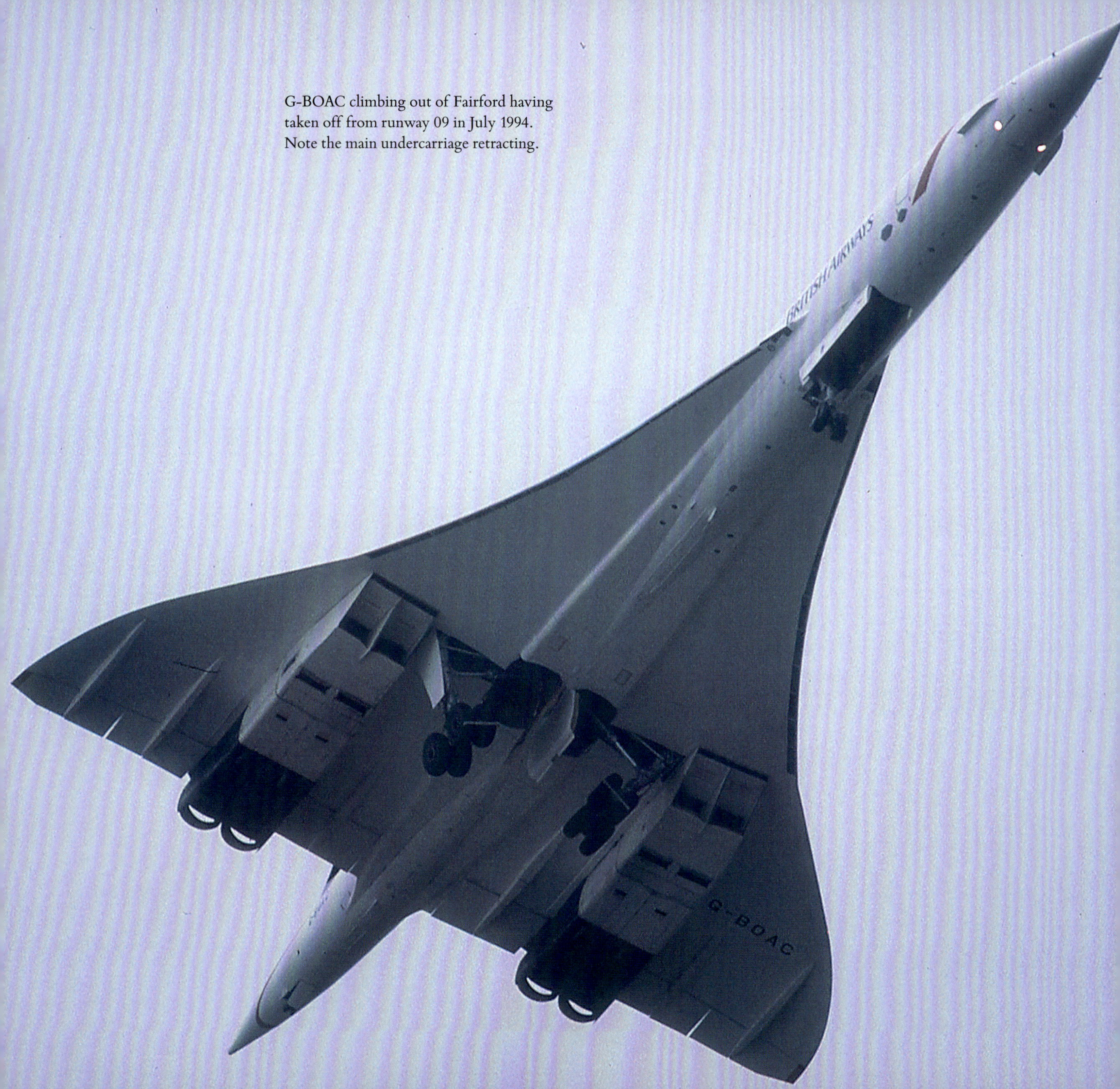

G-BOAC climbing out of Fairford having
taken off from runway 09 in July 1994.
Note the main undercarriage retracting.

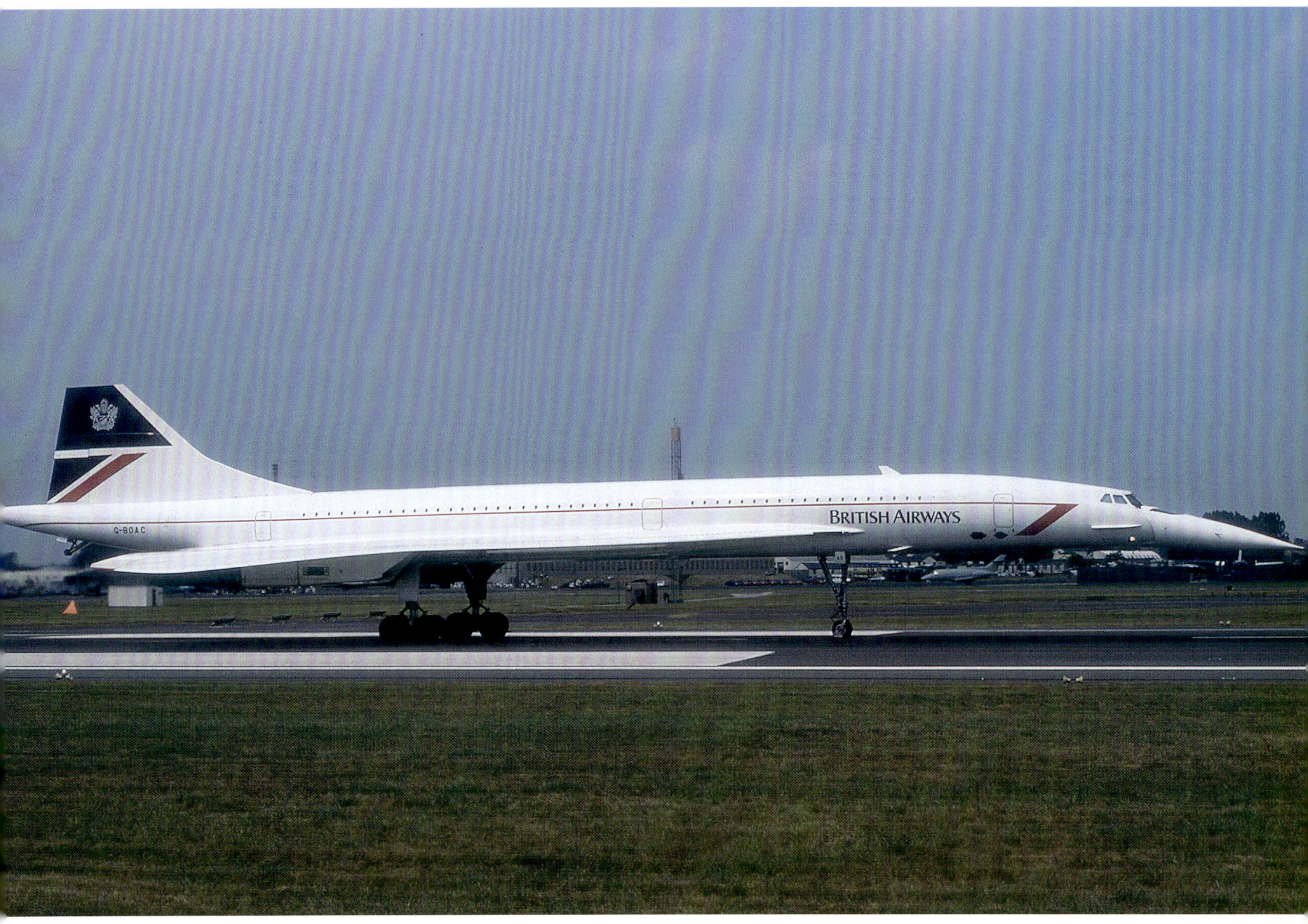

G-BOAC taxies down the runway at Fairford on 31 July 1994.

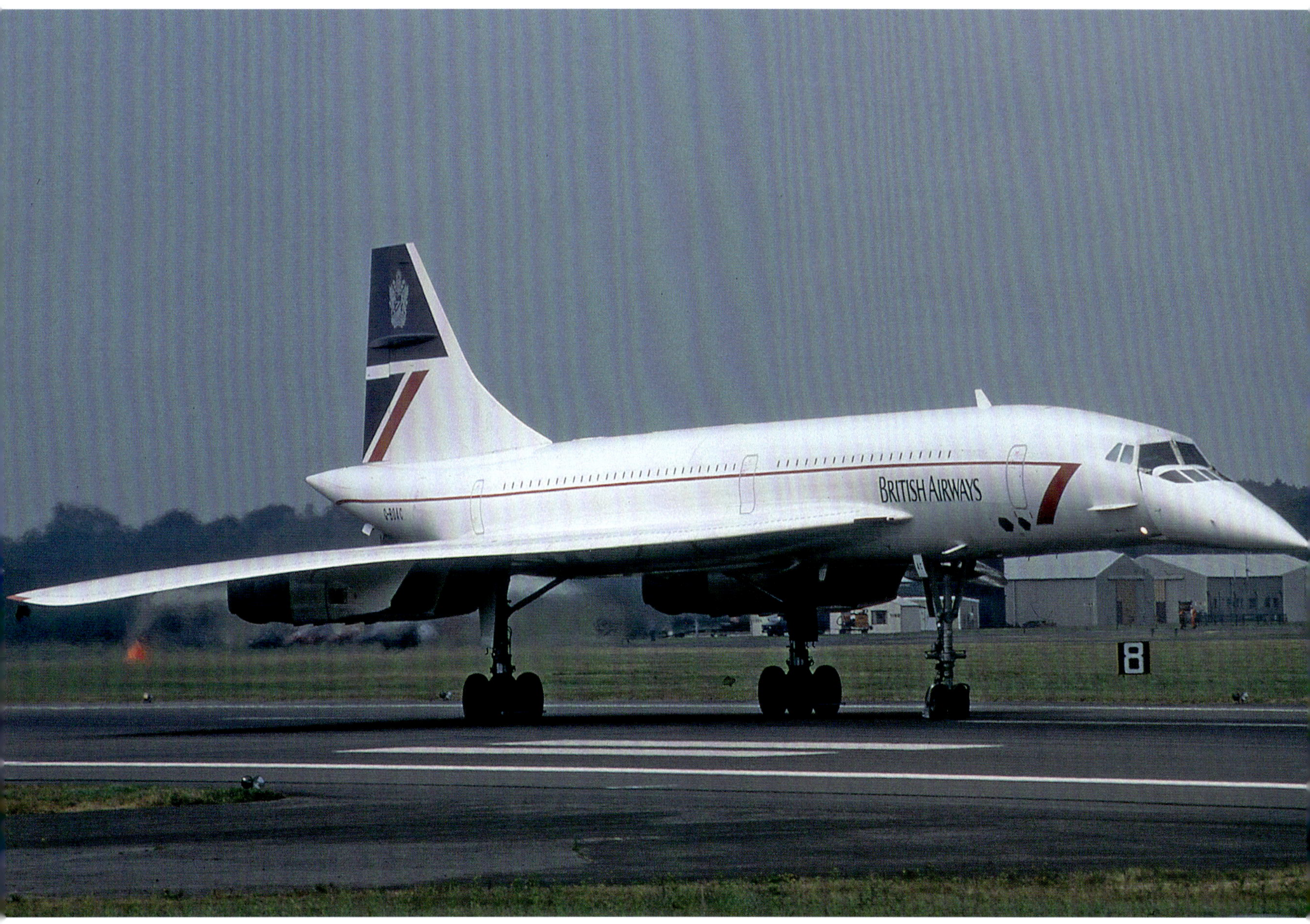

G-BOAC backtracking the runway at Fairford for a return flight to Heathrow after attending the International Air Tattoo in July 1994.

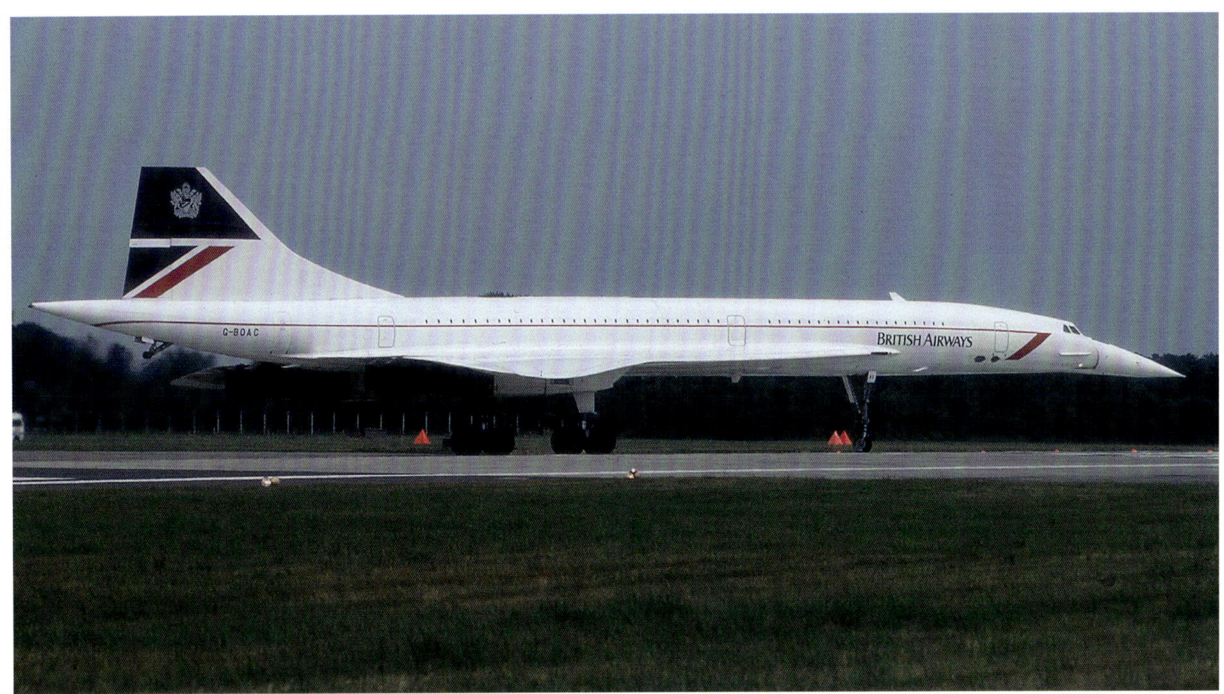

G-BOAC ready to line up for a runway 27 take-off from Fairford back to Heathrow on 30 July 1994.

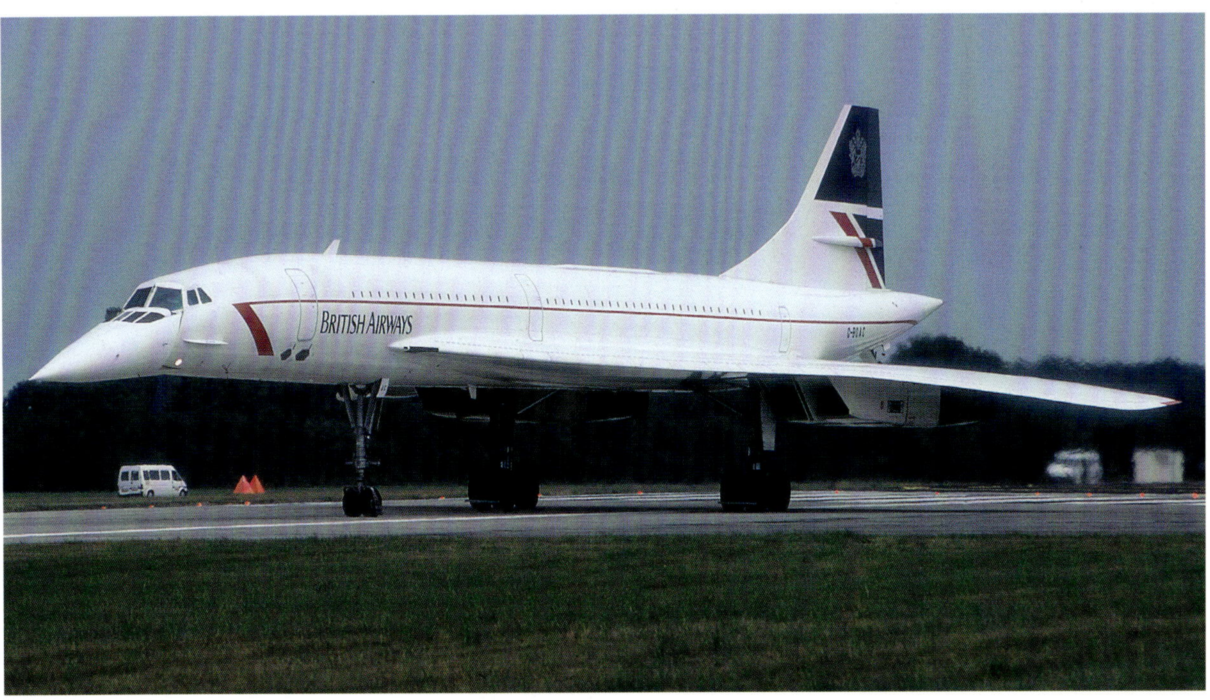

G-BOAC, seen here in Landor colour scheme, is ready for take-off at Fairford on 30 July 1994.

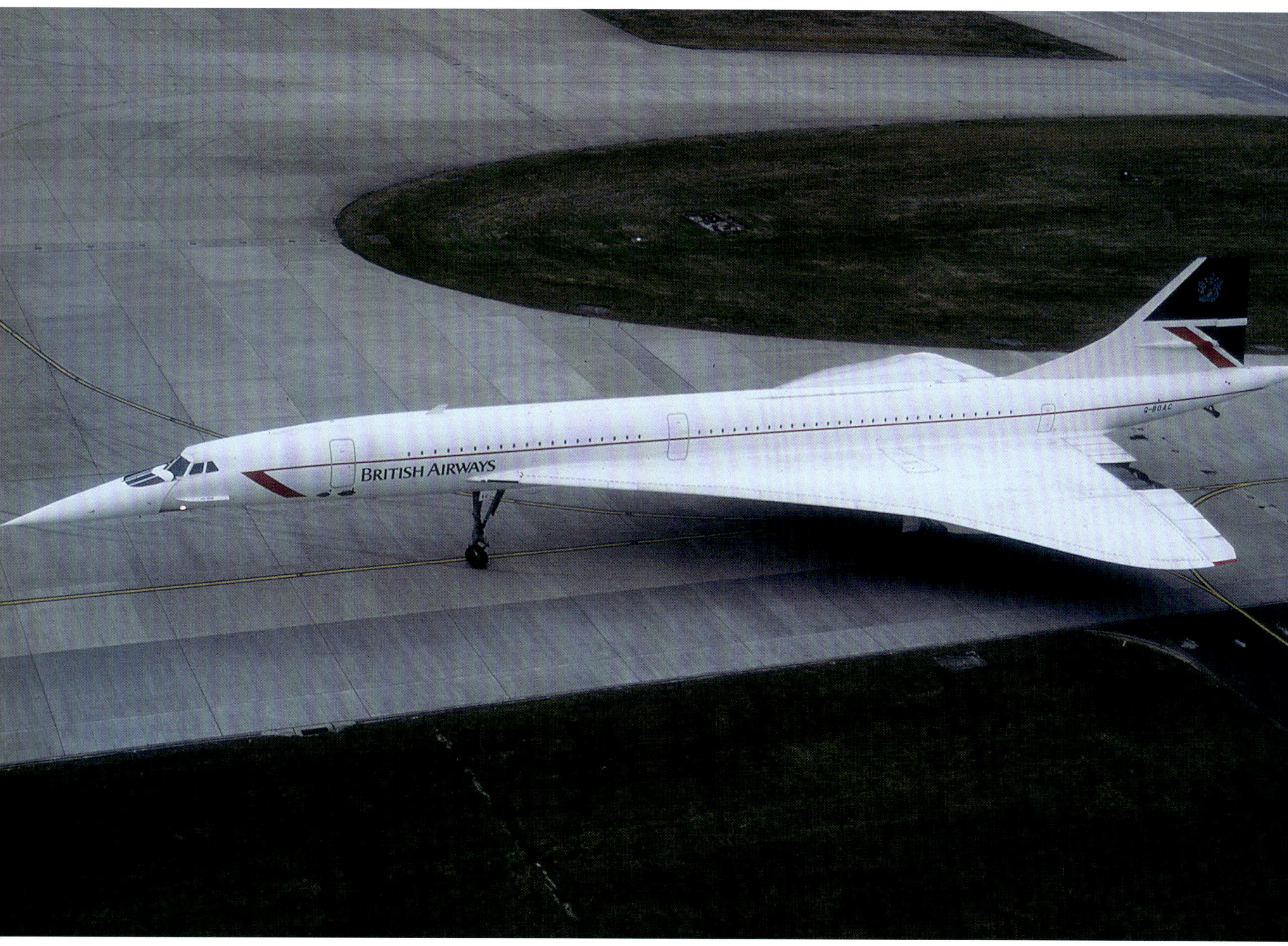

G-BOAC taxies in at Gatwick, from where it will undertake a charter flight on 26 August 1994.

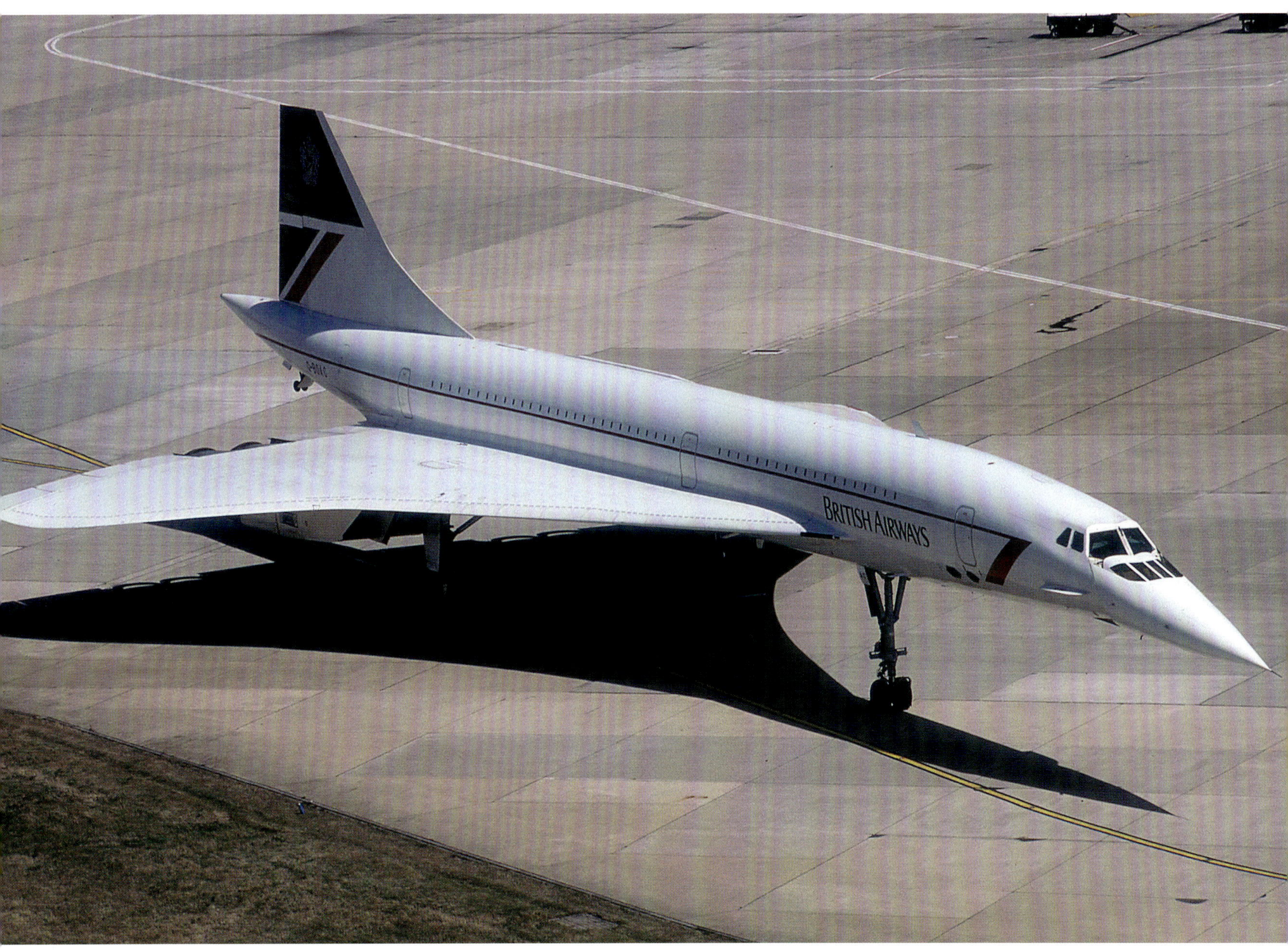

G-BOAC taxies out from Gatwick's North Terminal for a charter flight on 26 August 1994.

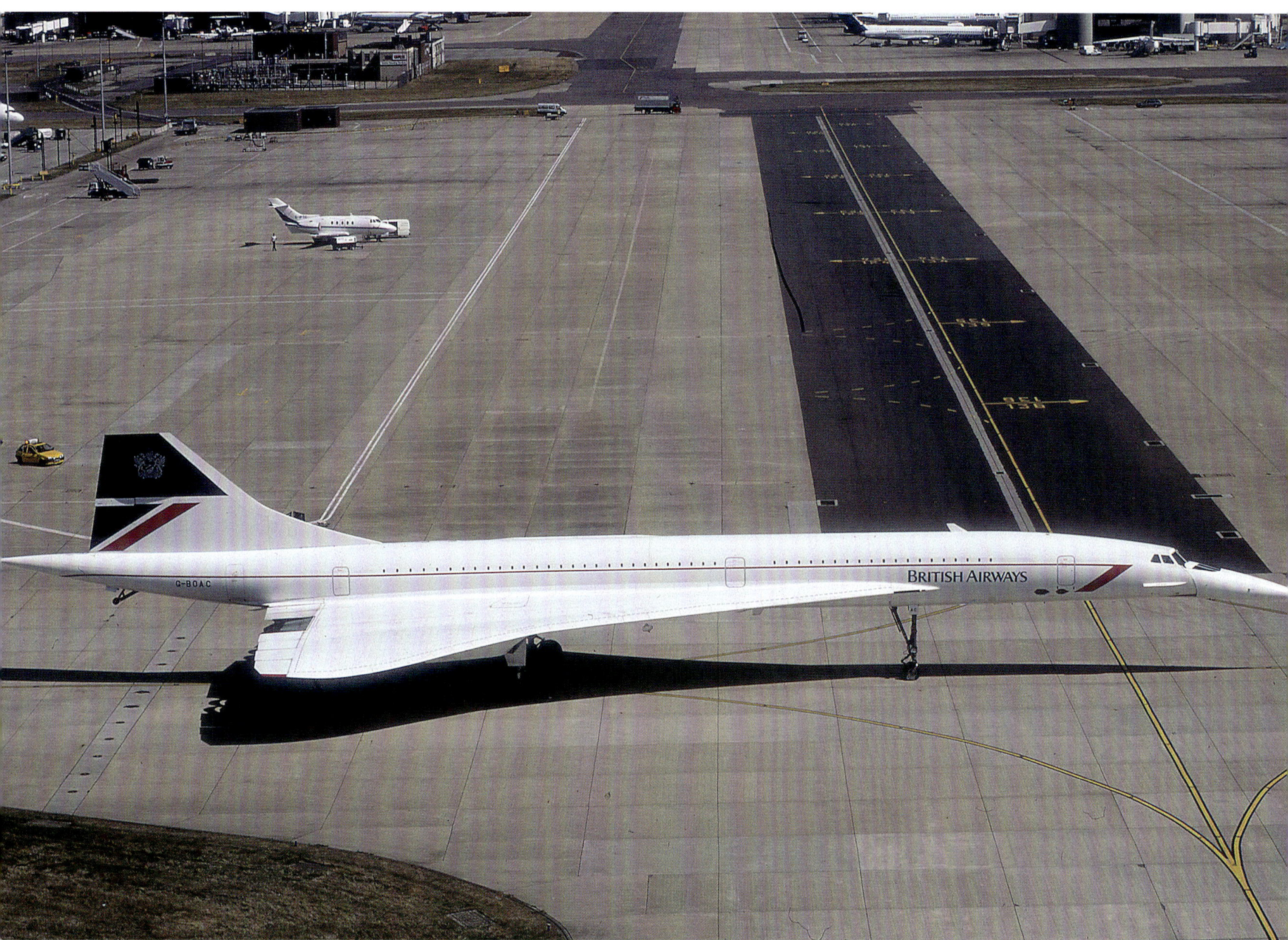

Another shot of G-BOAC at Gatwick on 26 August 1994.

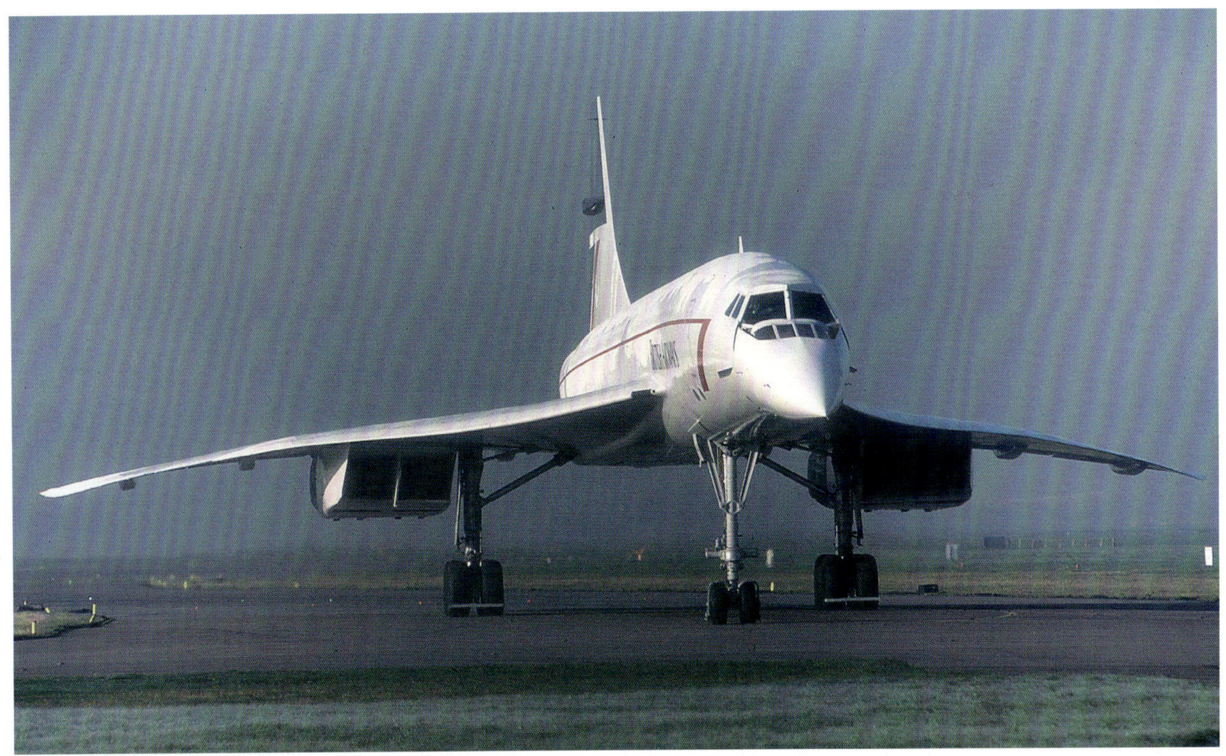

A 'classic Concorde shot' of G-BOAG as the aircraft taxies out from Terminal 4 at Heathrow, next stop New York. This angle emphasises the narrow fuselage. Note the heavy condensation on the fuselage.

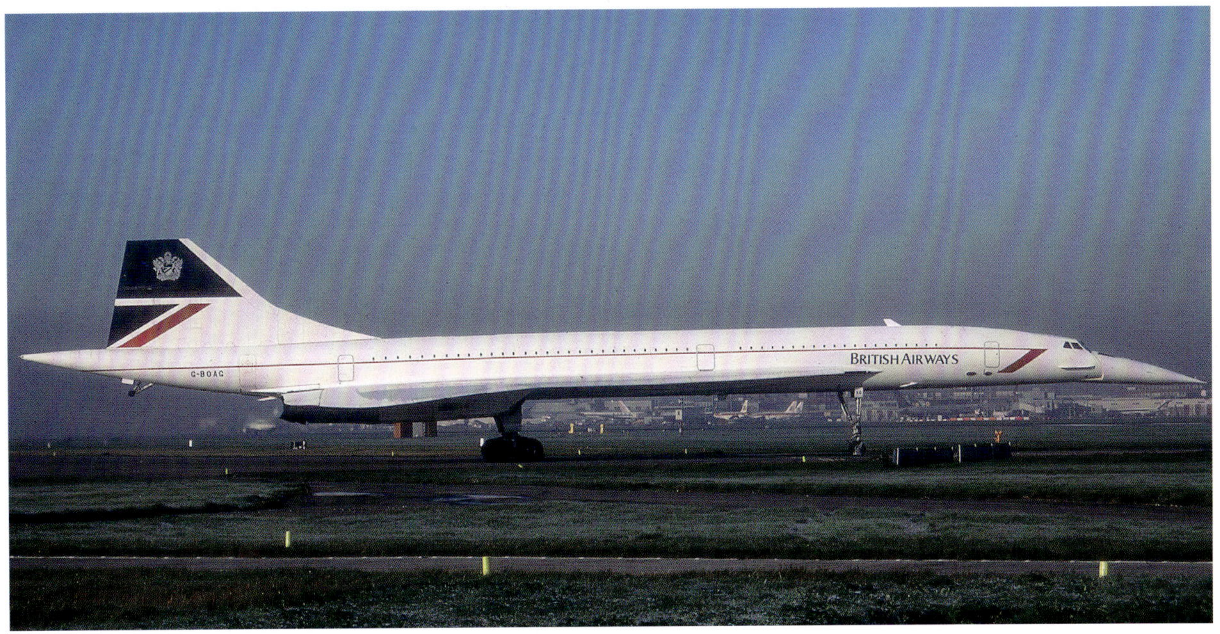

G-BOAG at the holding point for runway 27L at Heathrow.

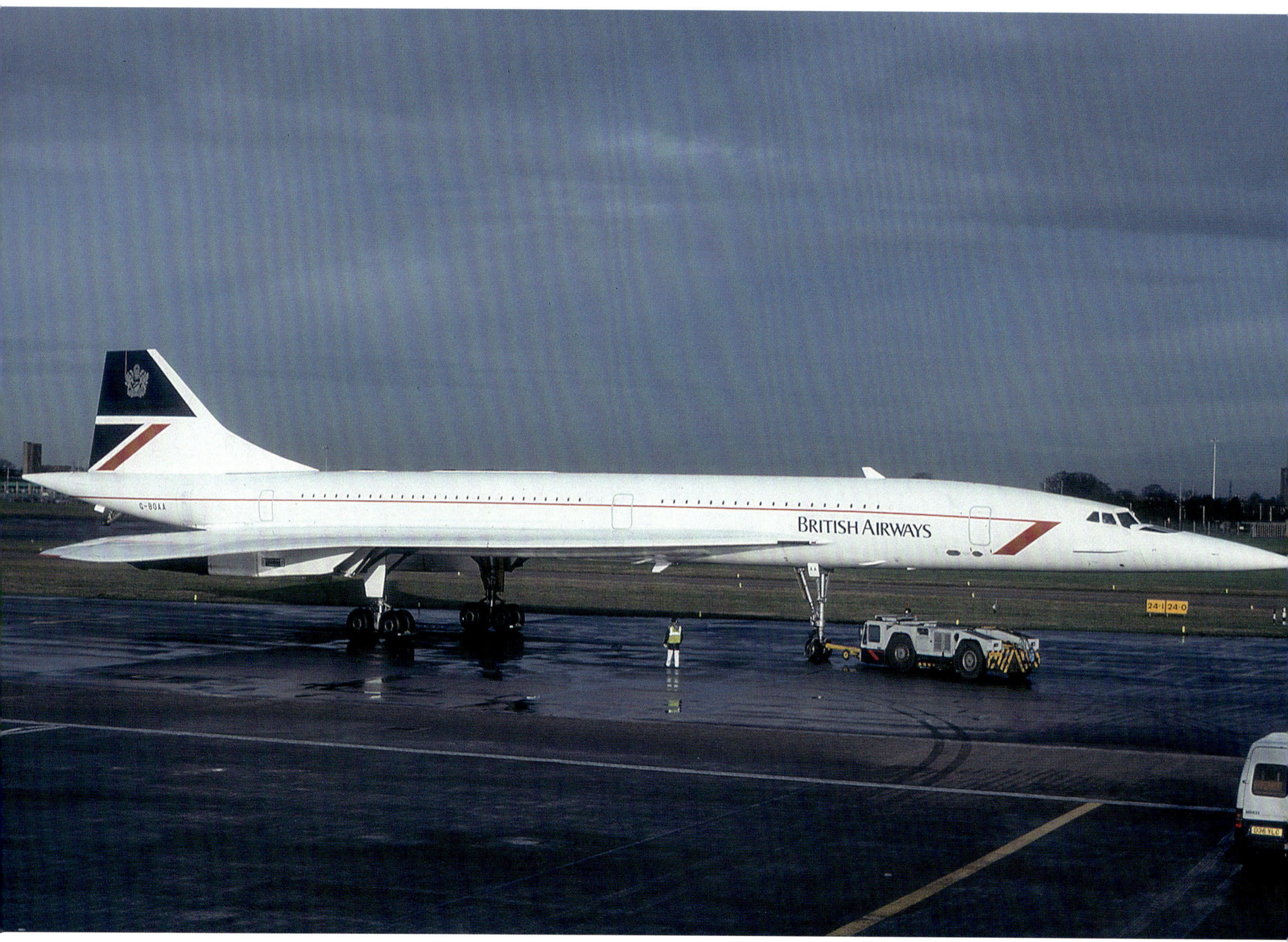

G-BOAA under tow at Heathrow. Despite the registration, this was not the first Concorde to be delivered to British Airways. (SPA Photography)

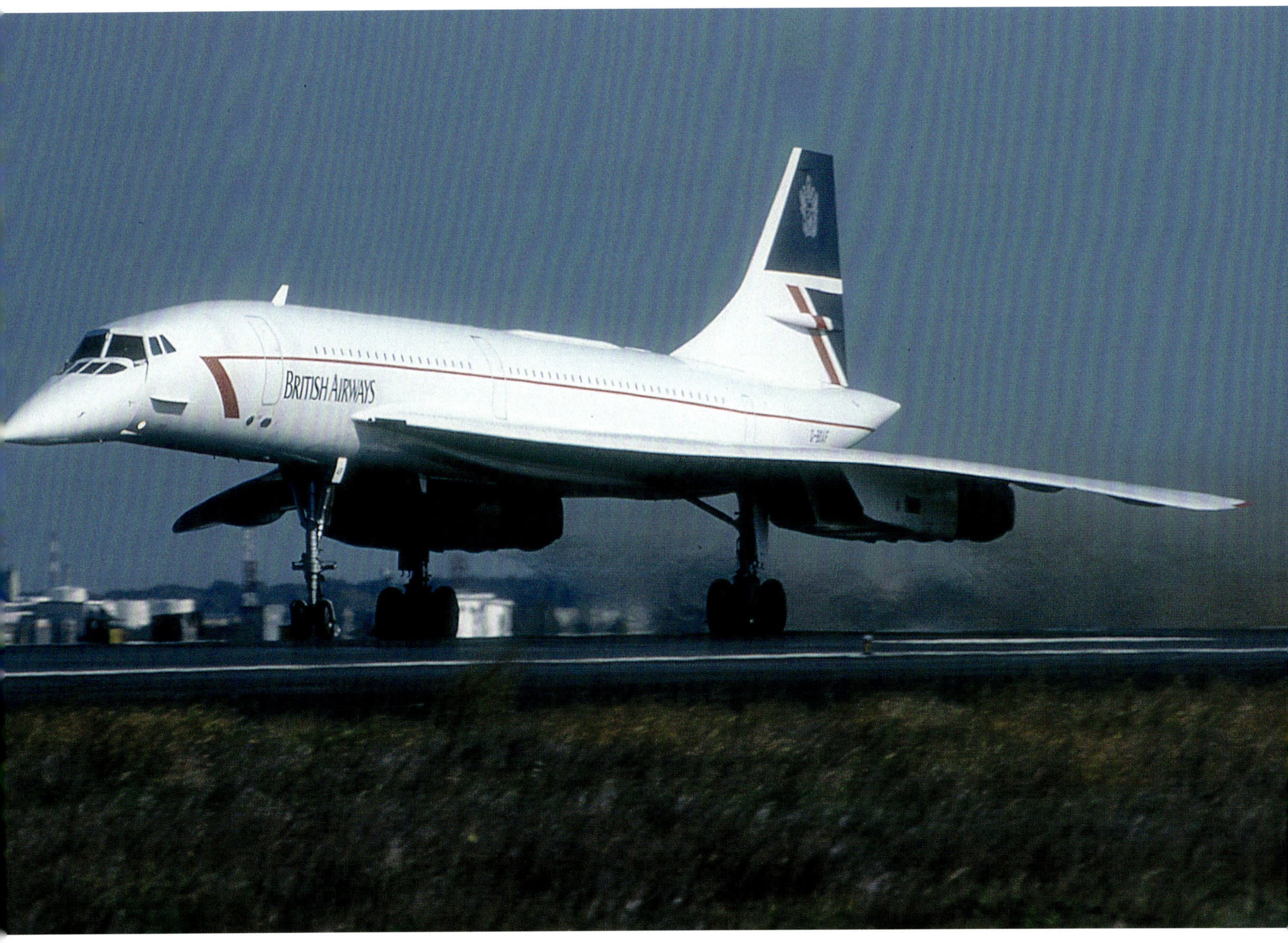

G-BOAF powering down runway 31L at JFK on 21 October 1994.

G-BOAF 'Rotate'.
Captured at the point
of rotation from JFK's
runway 31L, it is bound for
Heathrow as flight BA002
on 21 October 1994.

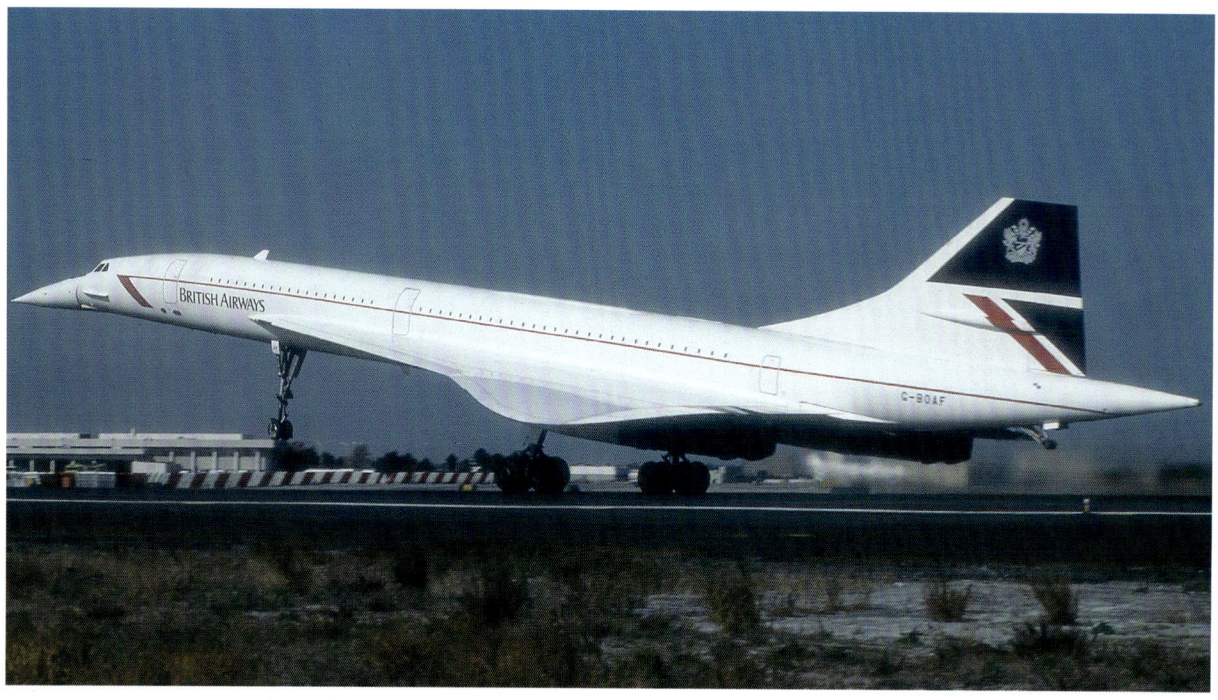

G-BOAA taxies out from
Terminal 4 at Heathrow
on 12 January 1995.

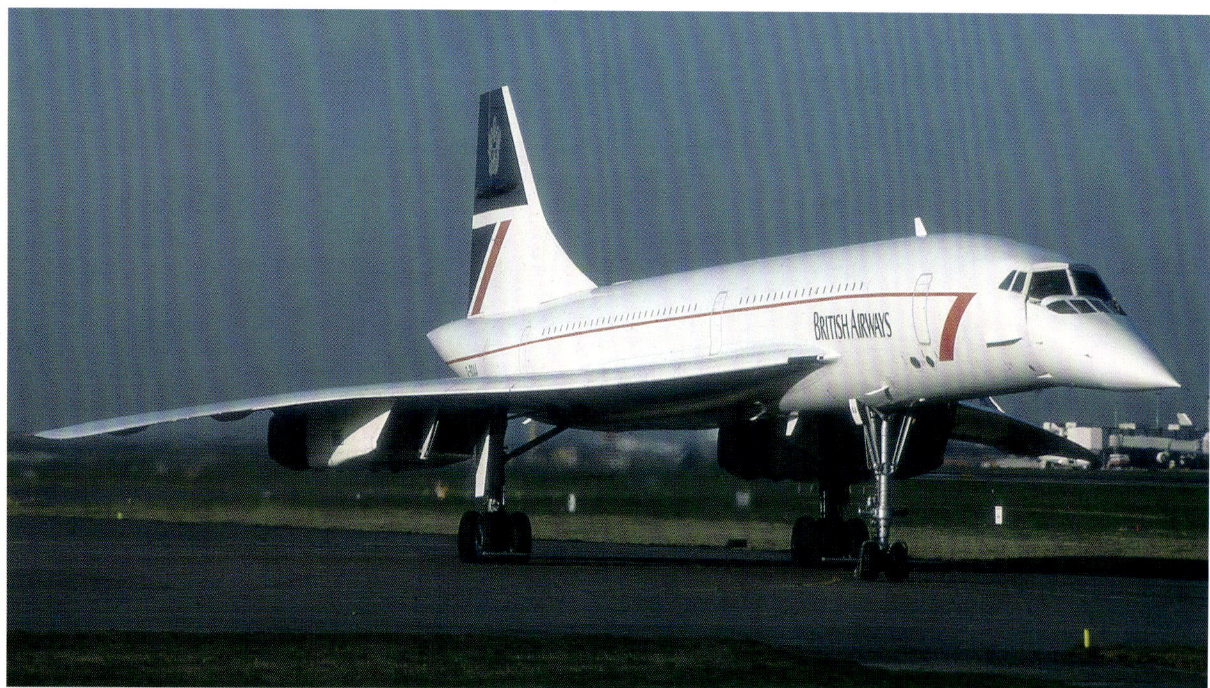

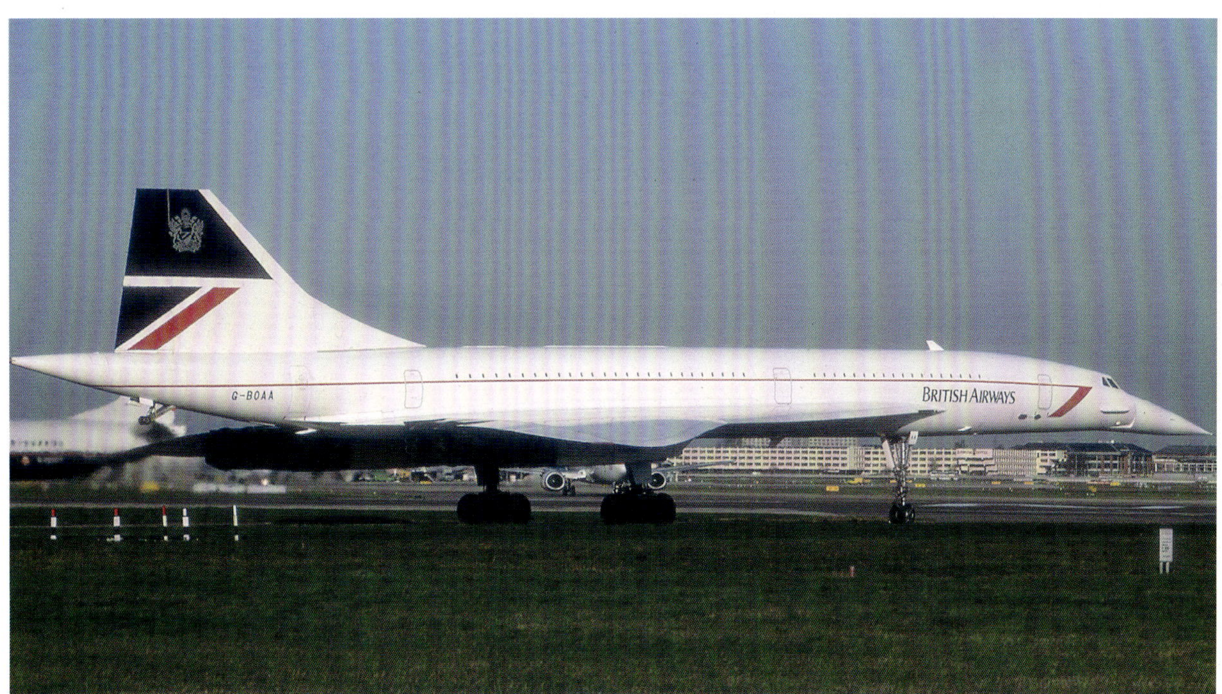

G-BOAA at the holding point for runway 27L at Heathrow on 12 January 1995.

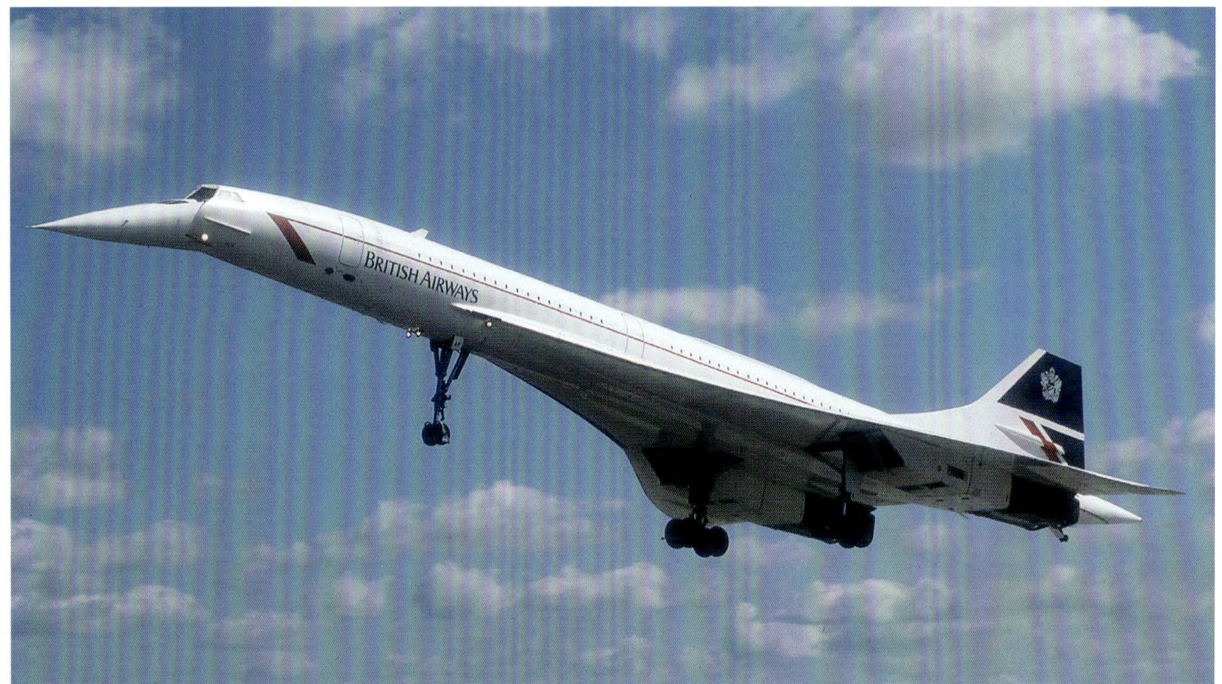

G-BOAF on final approach to Fairford on 22 July 1995.

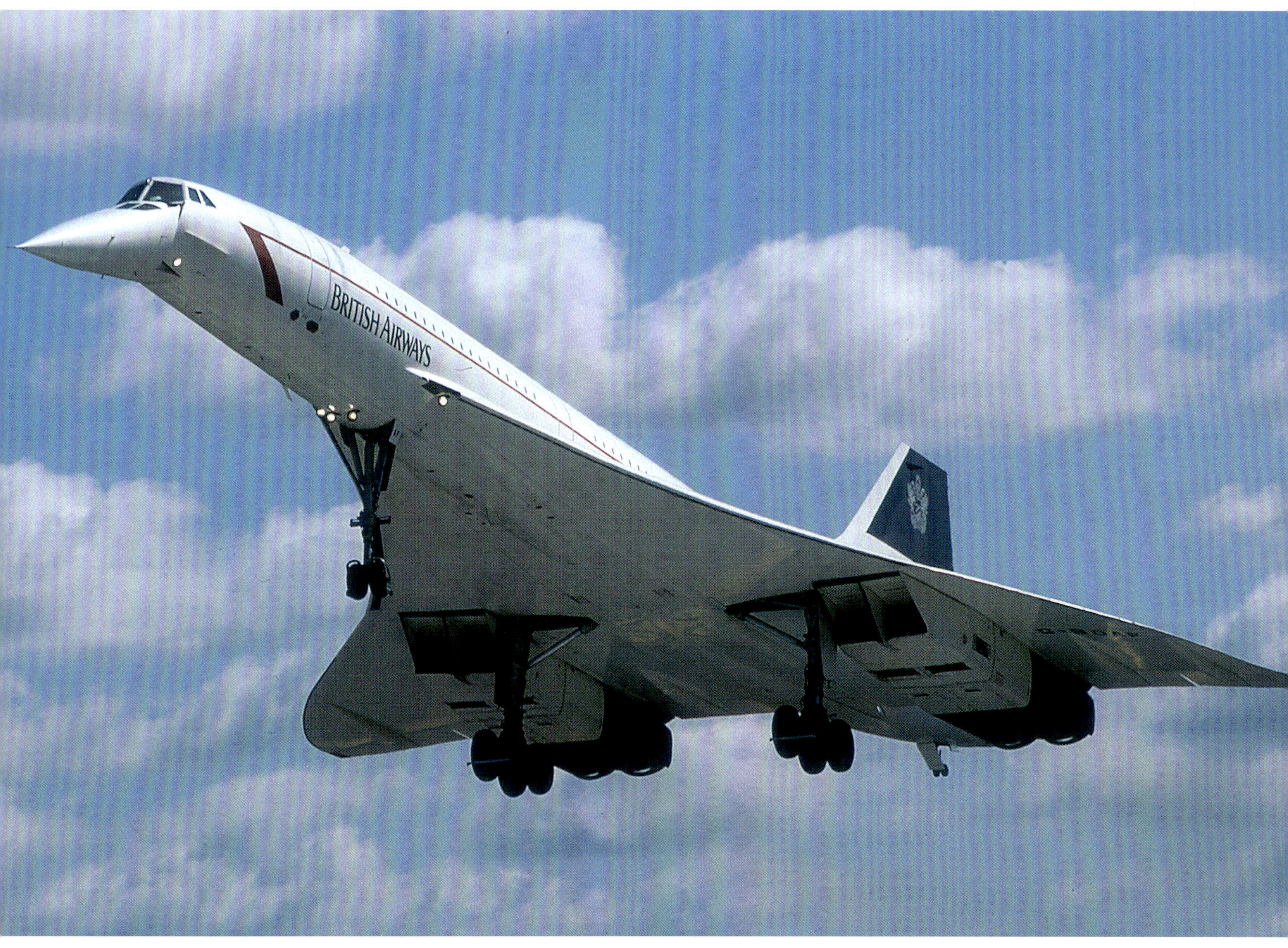

G-BOAF on final approach to land at Fairford. Fairford is officially an RAF base, but is in fact operated by the US Air Force. It was once the home to KC-135 Stratotankers but in recent years plays host to Strategic Air Command deployments, including B-52s.

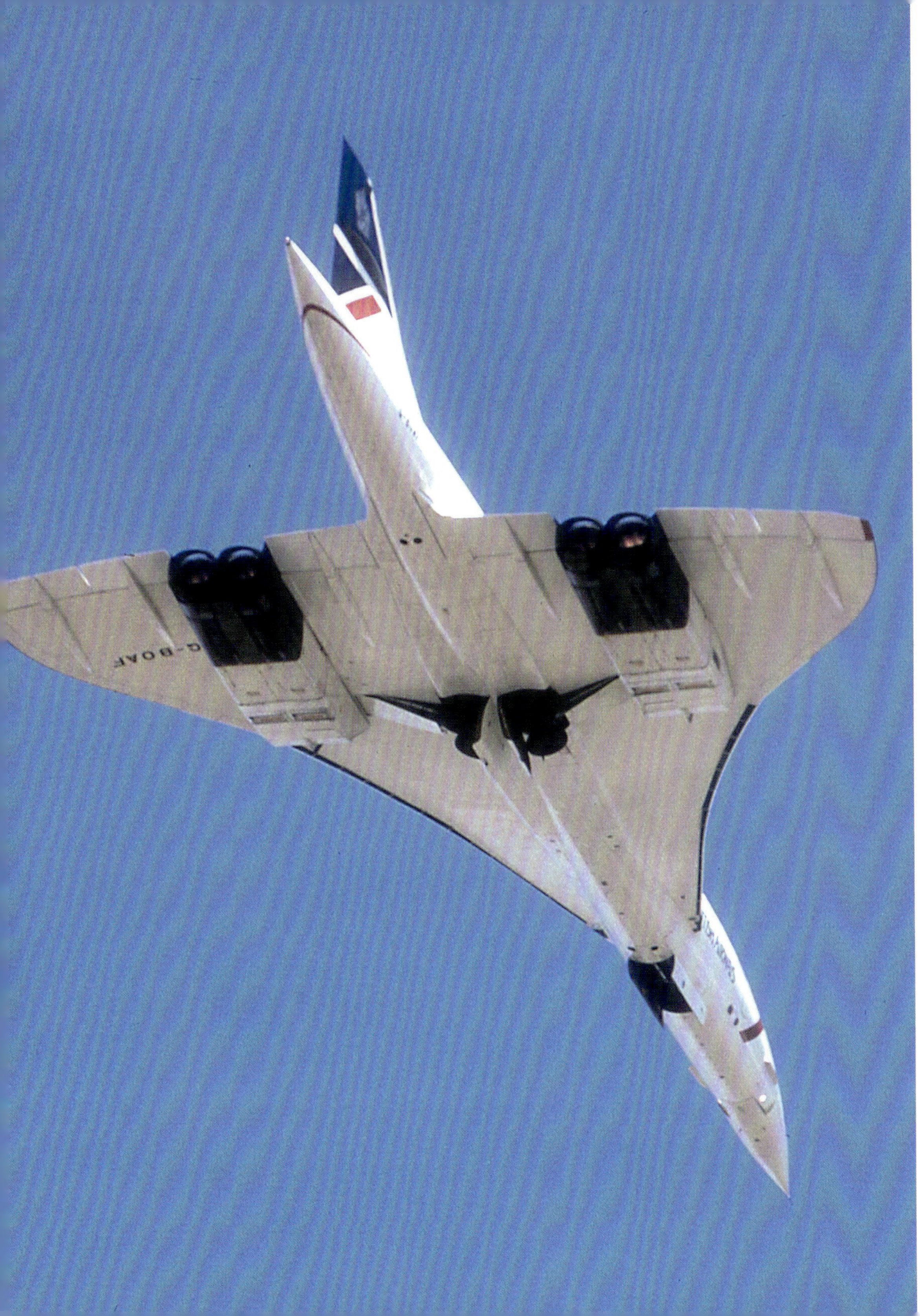

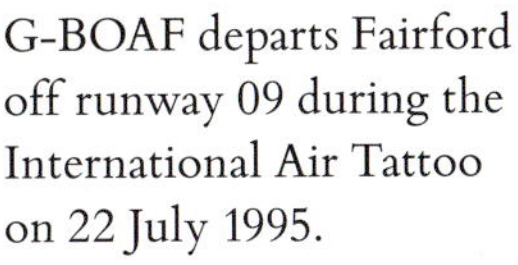

G-BOAF departs Fairford off runway 09 during the International Air Tattoo on 22 July 1995.

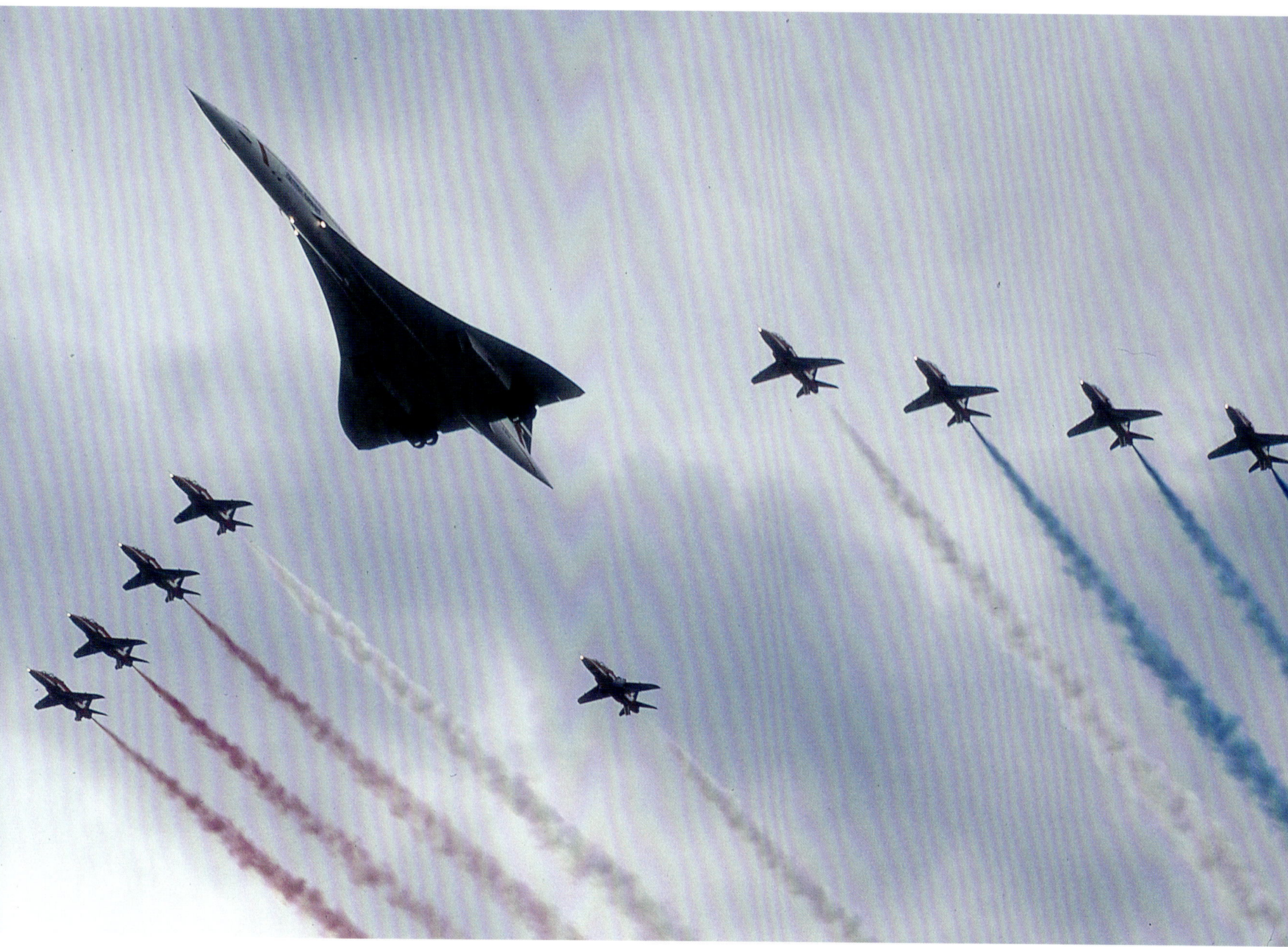

G-BOAC in formation with Hawk aircraft of the RAF Red Arrows aerobatic display team at a Heathrow flypast on 2 June 1996.

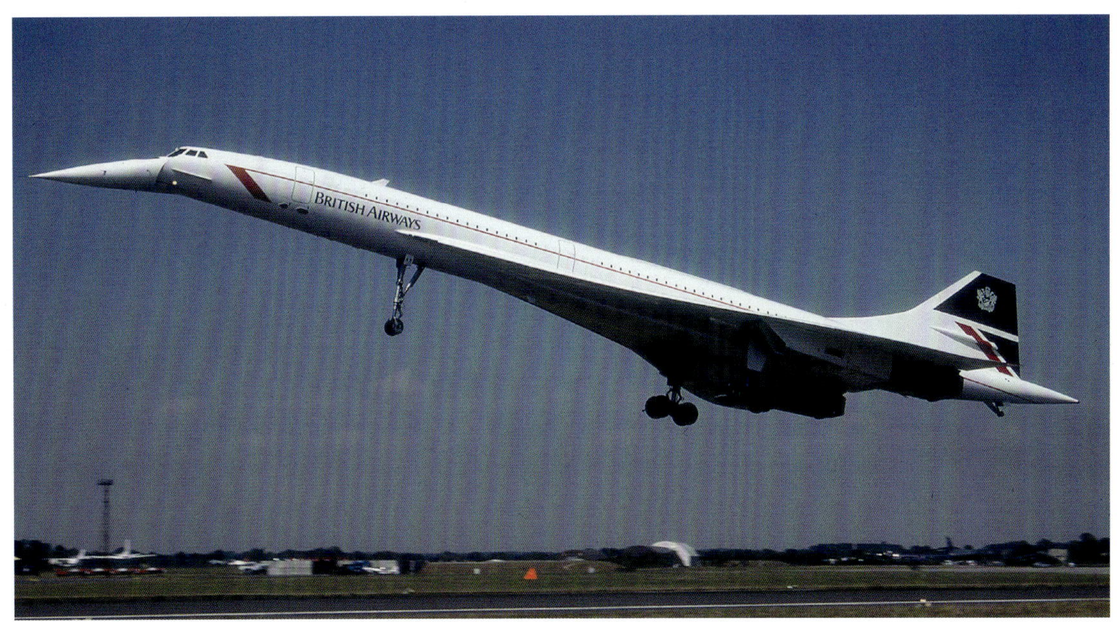

G-BOAB about to land on runway 27 at Fairford to attend the International Air Tattoo on 20 July 1996.

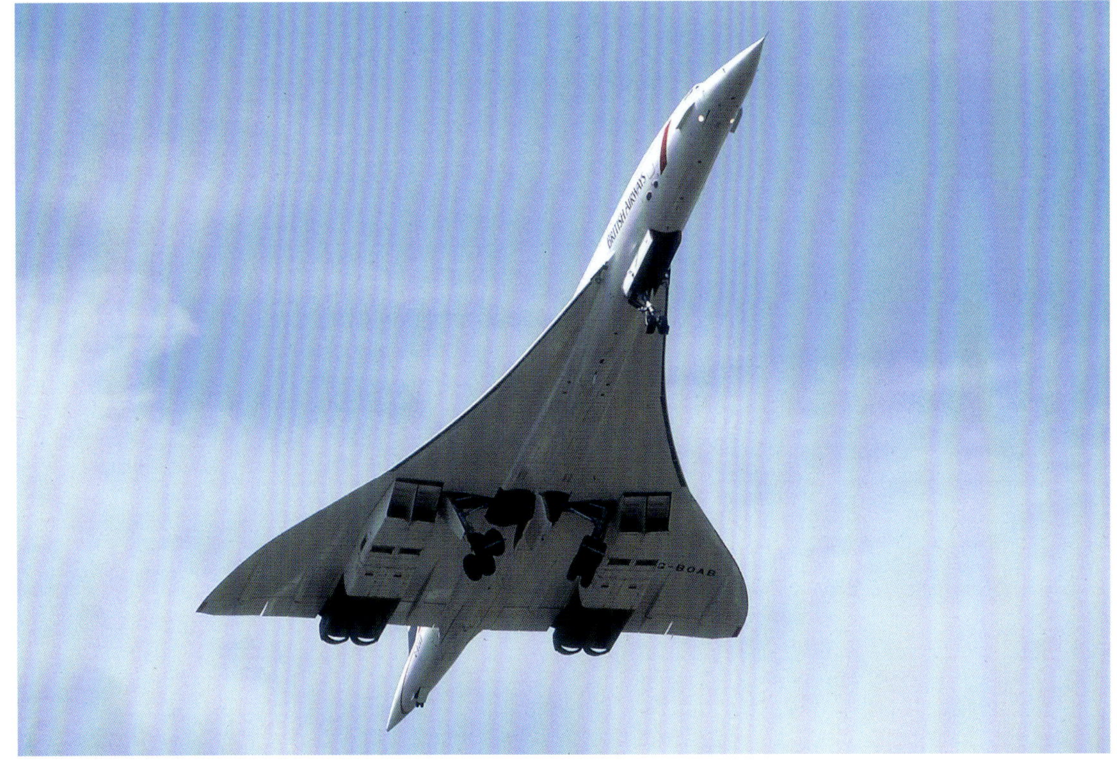

G-BOAB climbs out of Fairford after a runway 09 take-off on 20 July 1996.

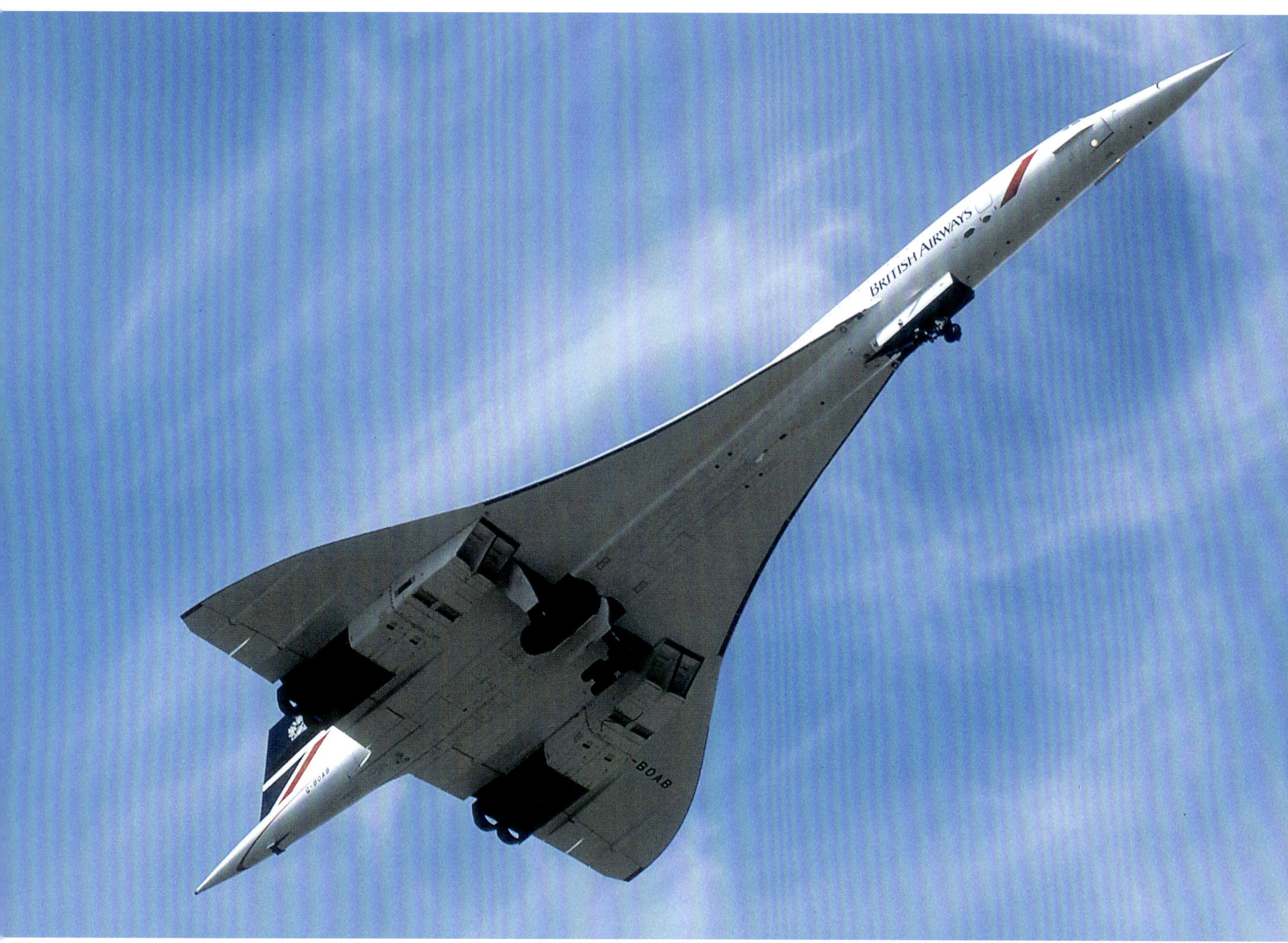

G-BOAB climbing out of Fairford on 20 July 1996.

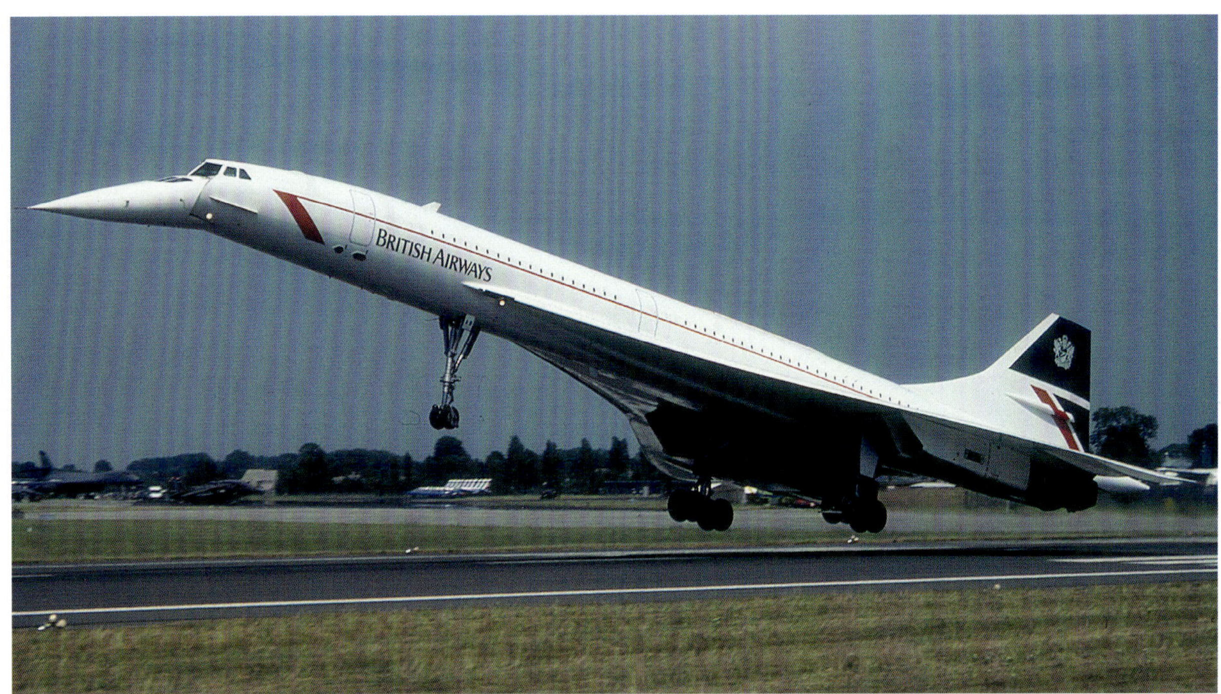

The wheels of G-BOAB about to impact the surface of runway 27 at Fairford on 21 July 1996.

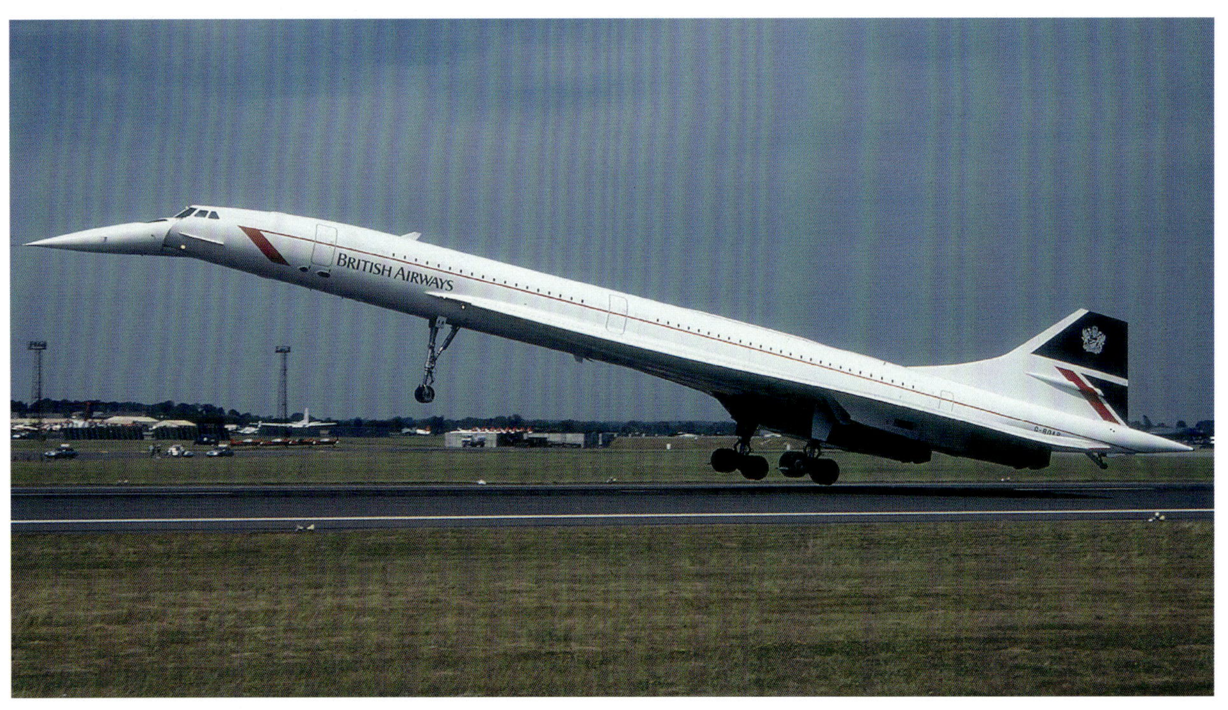

G-BOAA approaches the holding point for Heathrow's runway 27L with storm clouds gathering behind.

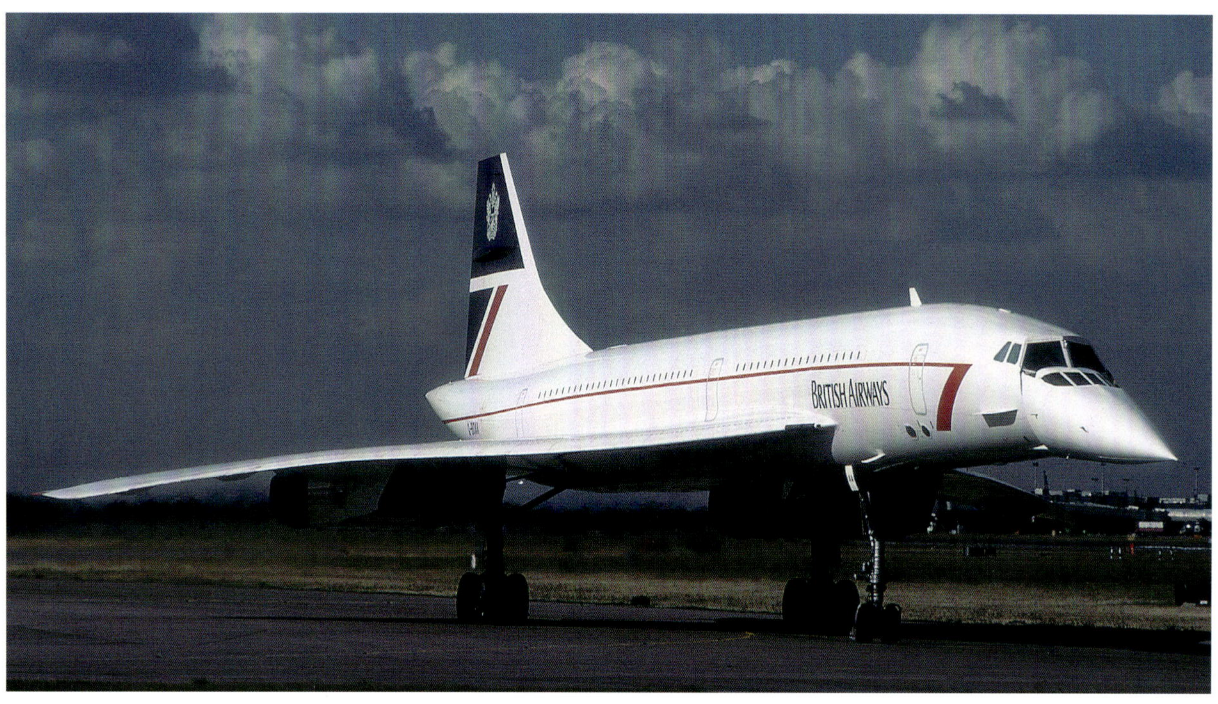

G-BOAA leads a convoy of aircraft from Heathrow's Terminal 4 to the holding point of runway 27L.

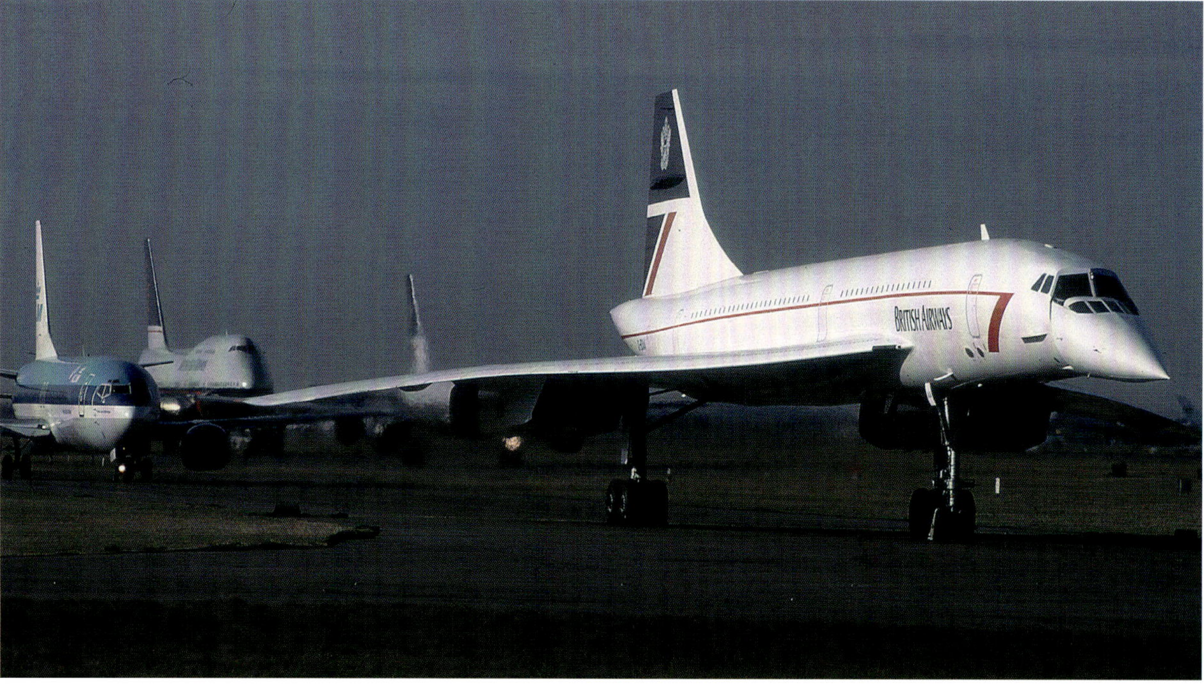

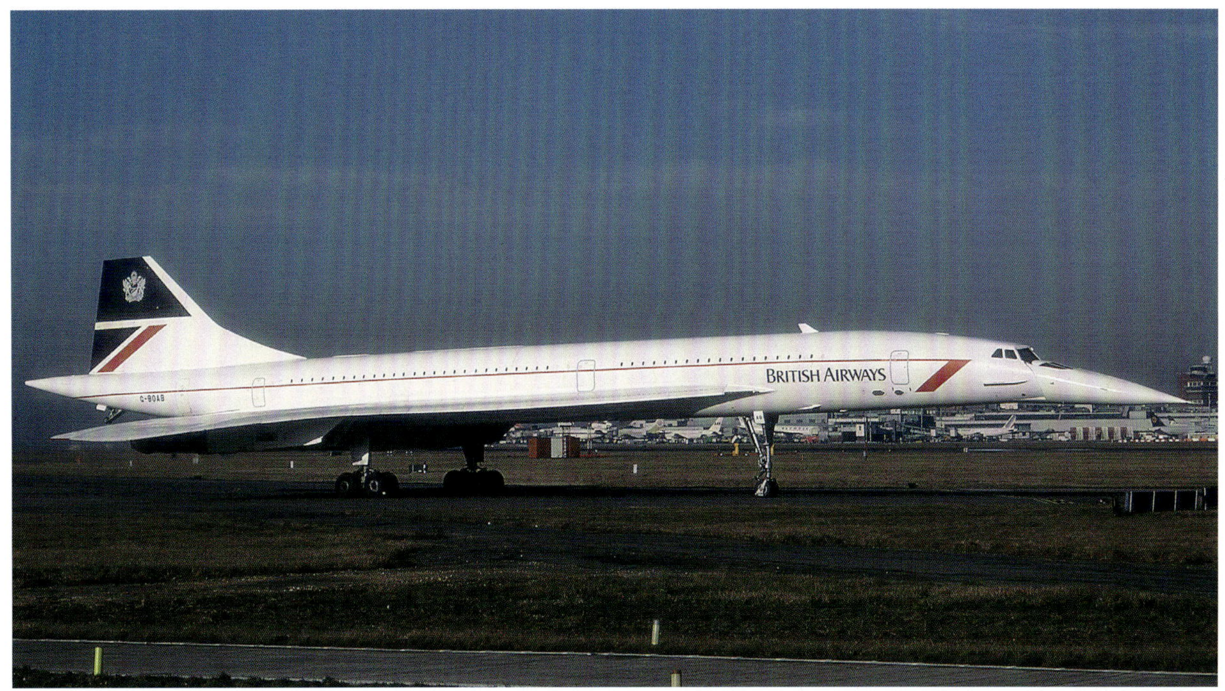

G-BOAB at holding point for runway 27L at Heathrow, ready for another transatlantic journey.

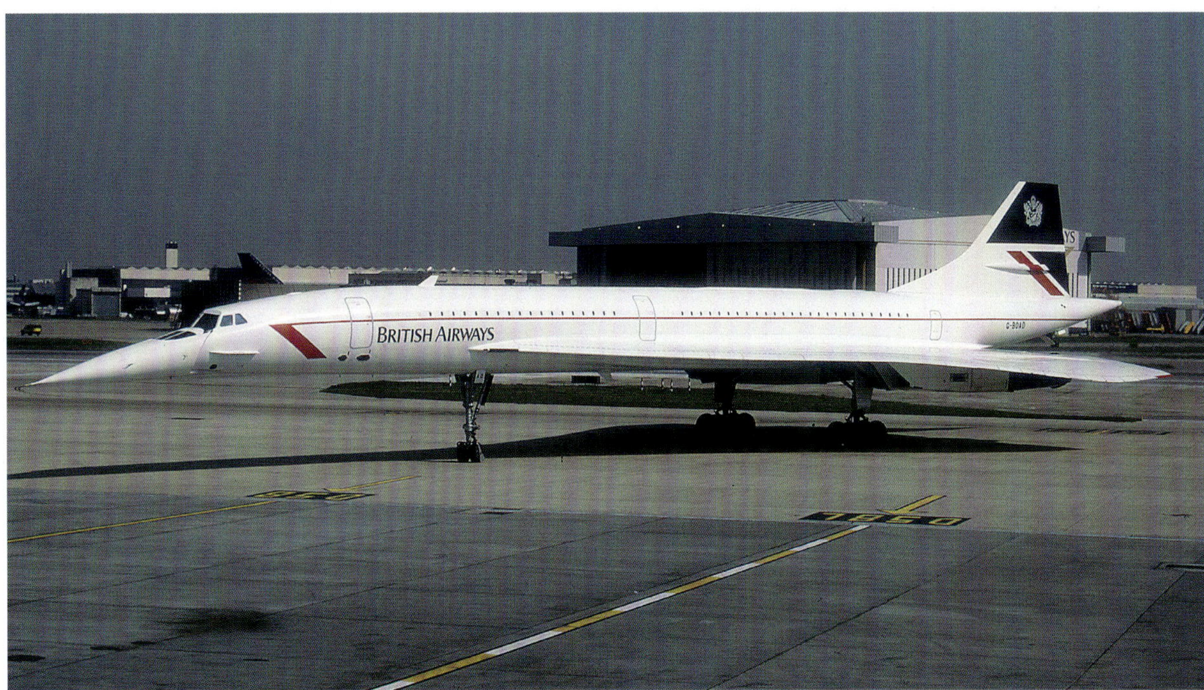

G-BOAD about to park on a gate at Terminal 2 at Heathrow rather than the usual T4 – obviously not returning from a scheduled service.

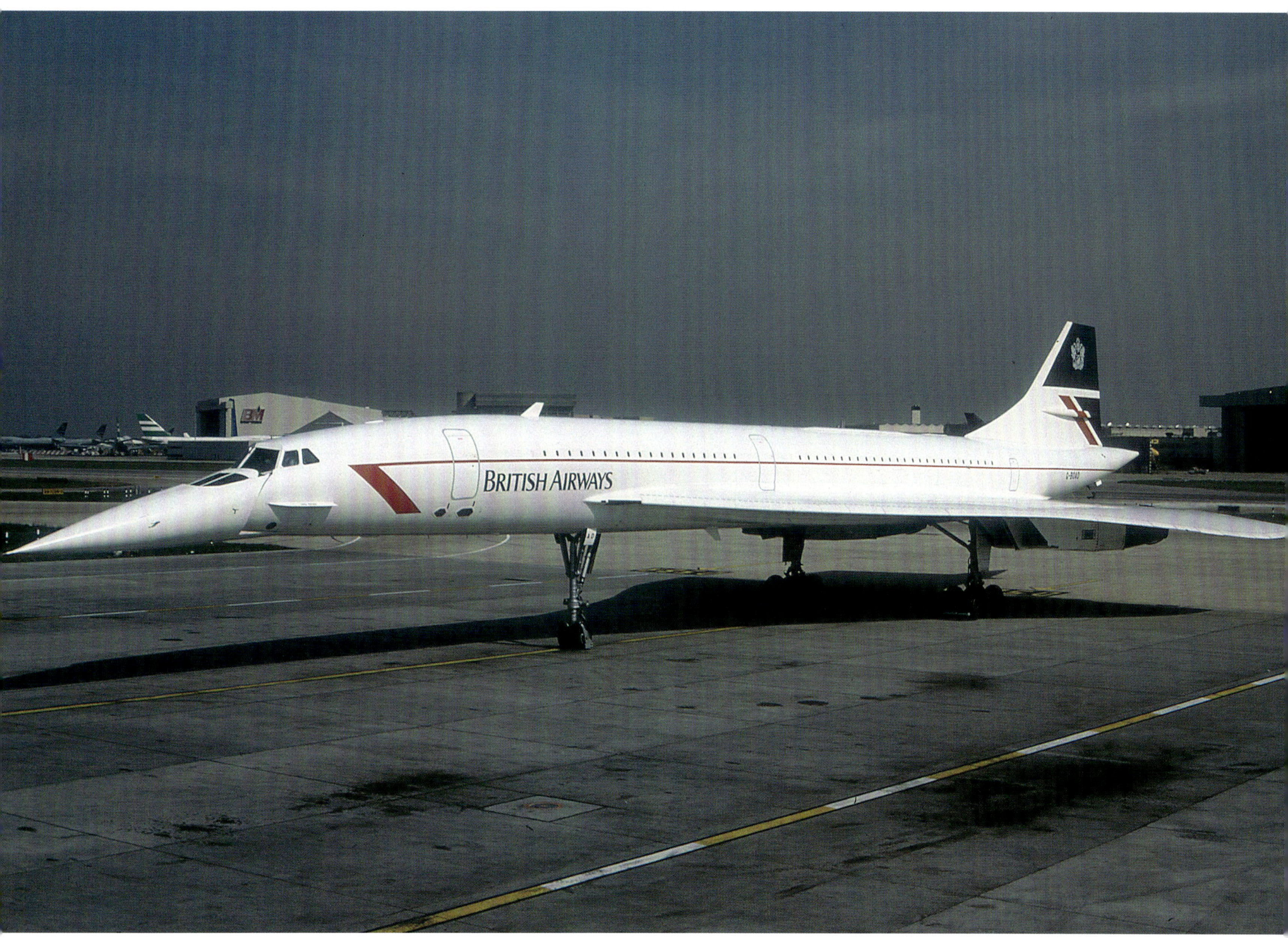

G-BOAD about to park at Heathrow after a charter flight on 9 April 1997.

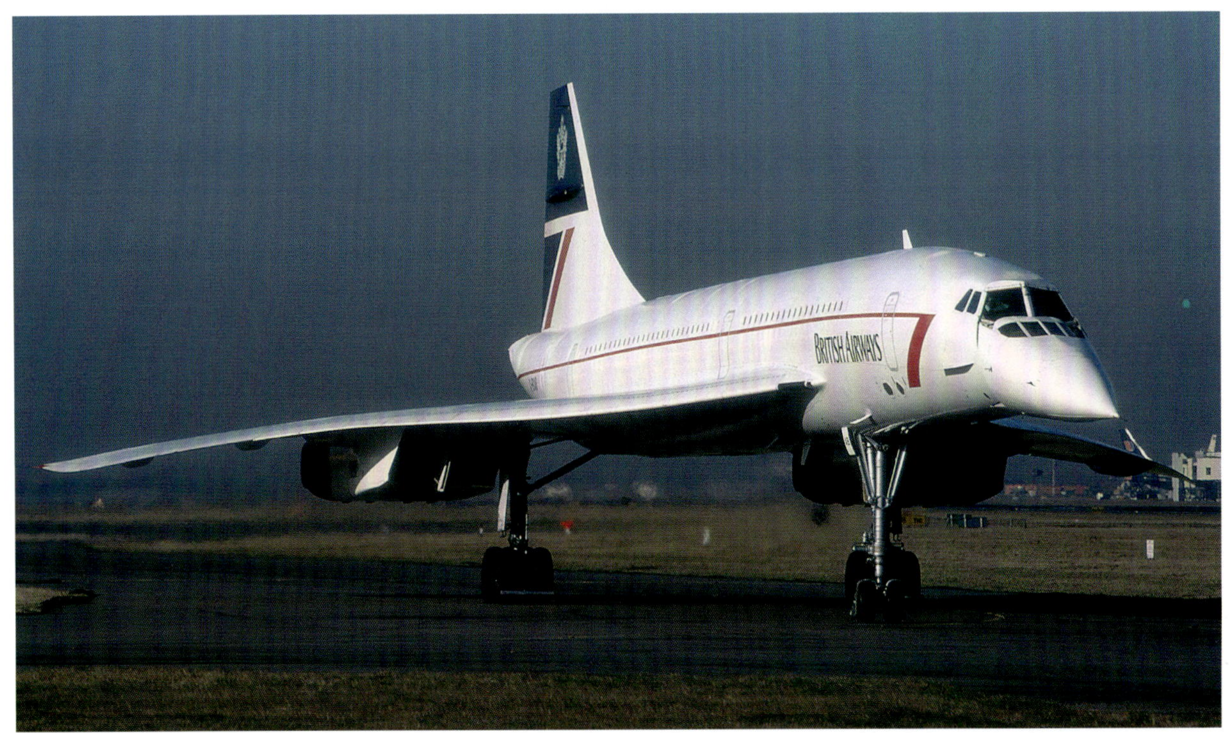

G-BOAB approaching the holding point for runway 27L at Heathrow on 3 February 1997.

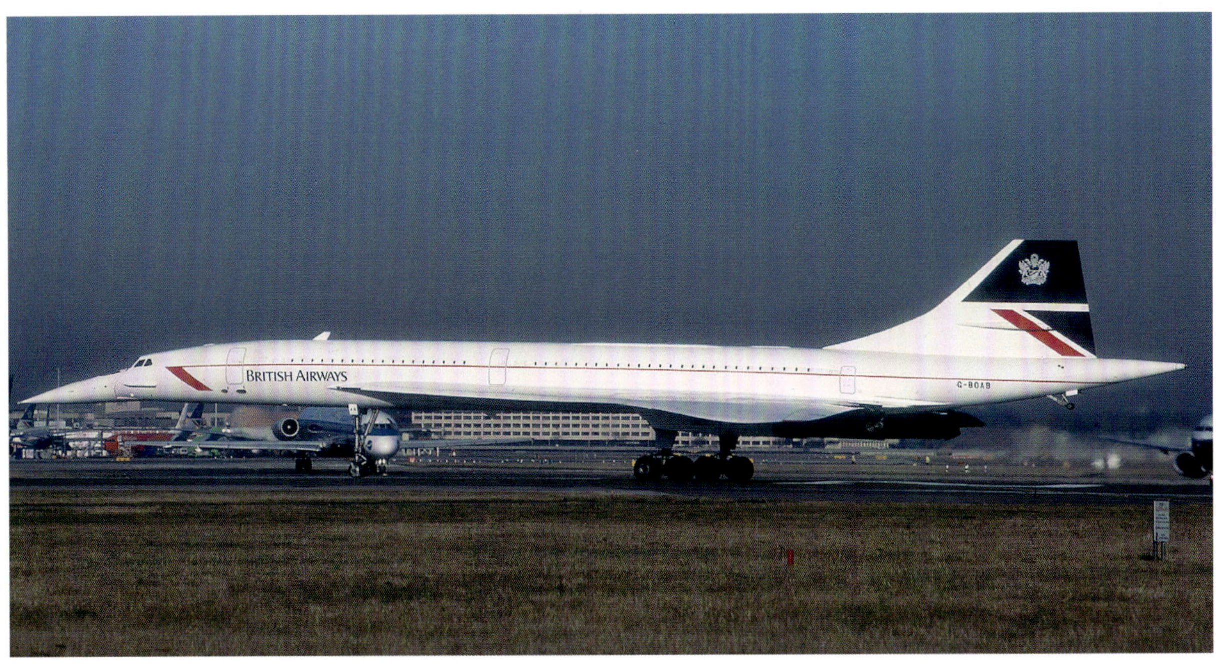

G-BOAB ready to depart off runway 27L at Heathrow on 3 February 1997.

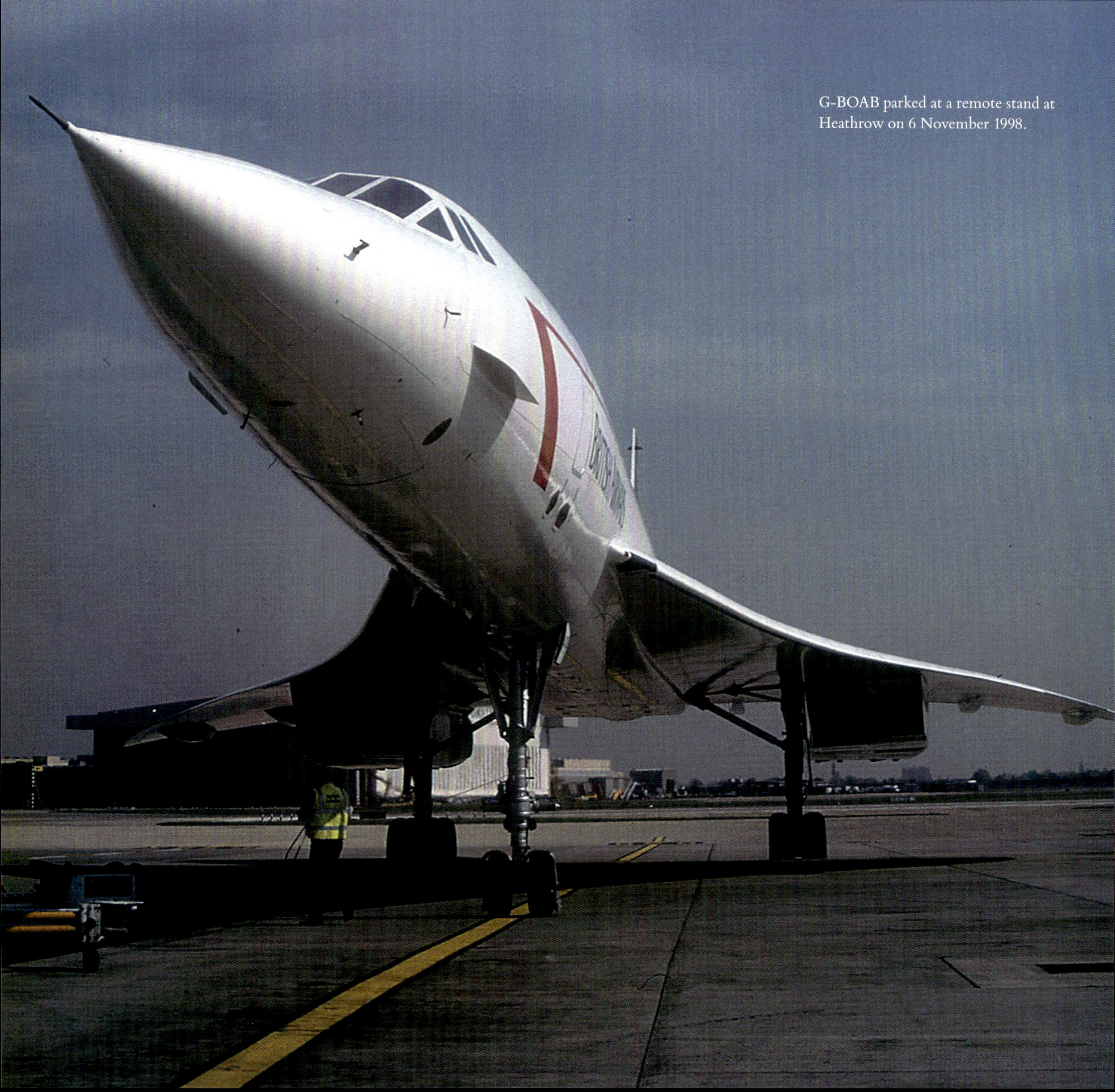

G-BOAB parked at a remote stand at Heathrow on 6 November 1998.

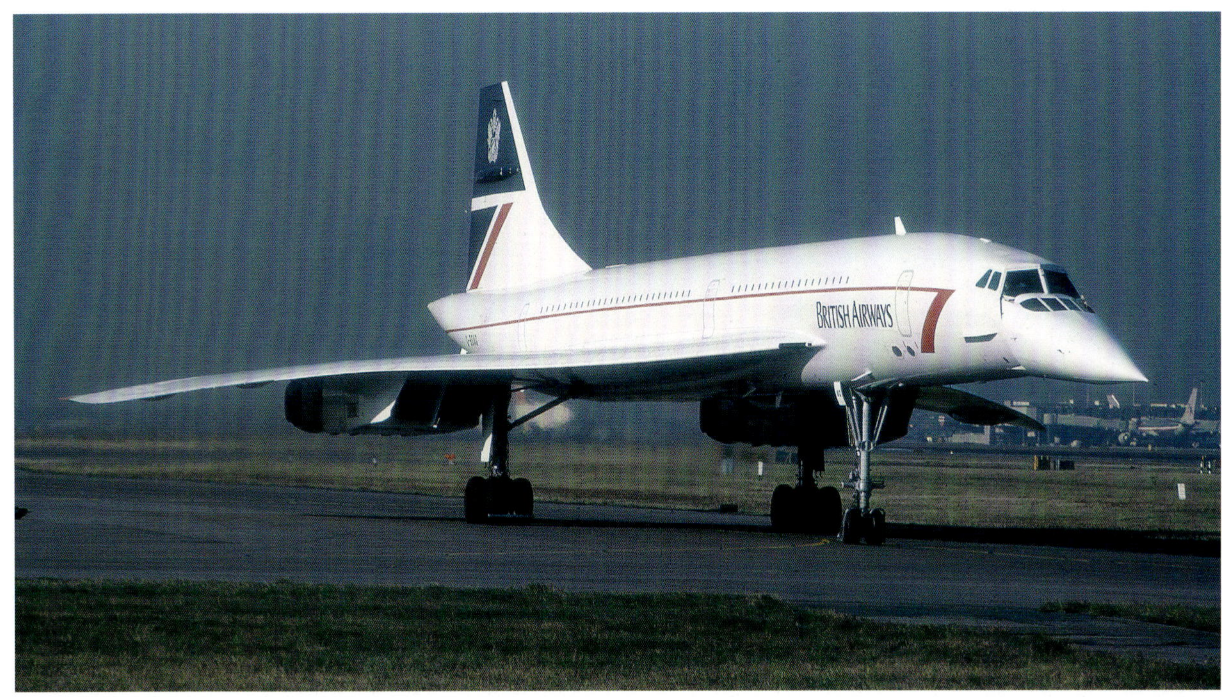

G-BOAG at the holding point for Heathrow's runway 27L after taxiing from Terminal 4 on 30 October 1997.

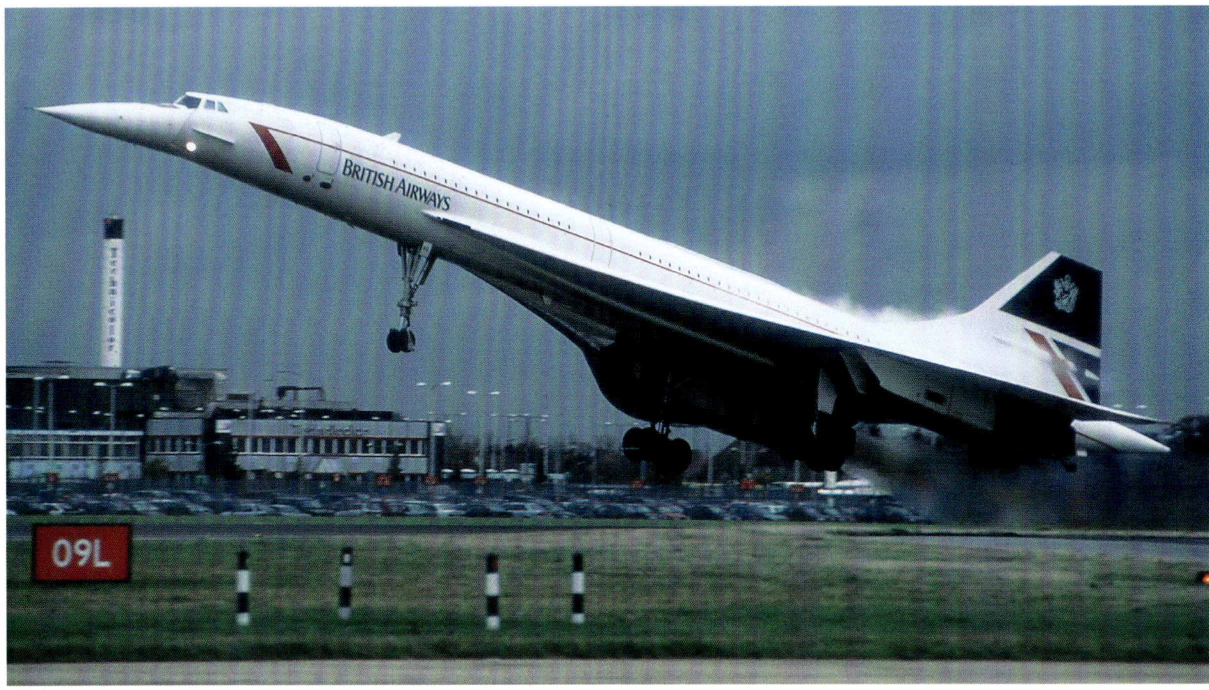

G-BOAG blasting off runway 27R at Heathrow on 6 November 1998.

G-BOAB on
final approach to
runway 27L at
Heathrow on a crisp
winter day on
17 November 1998.

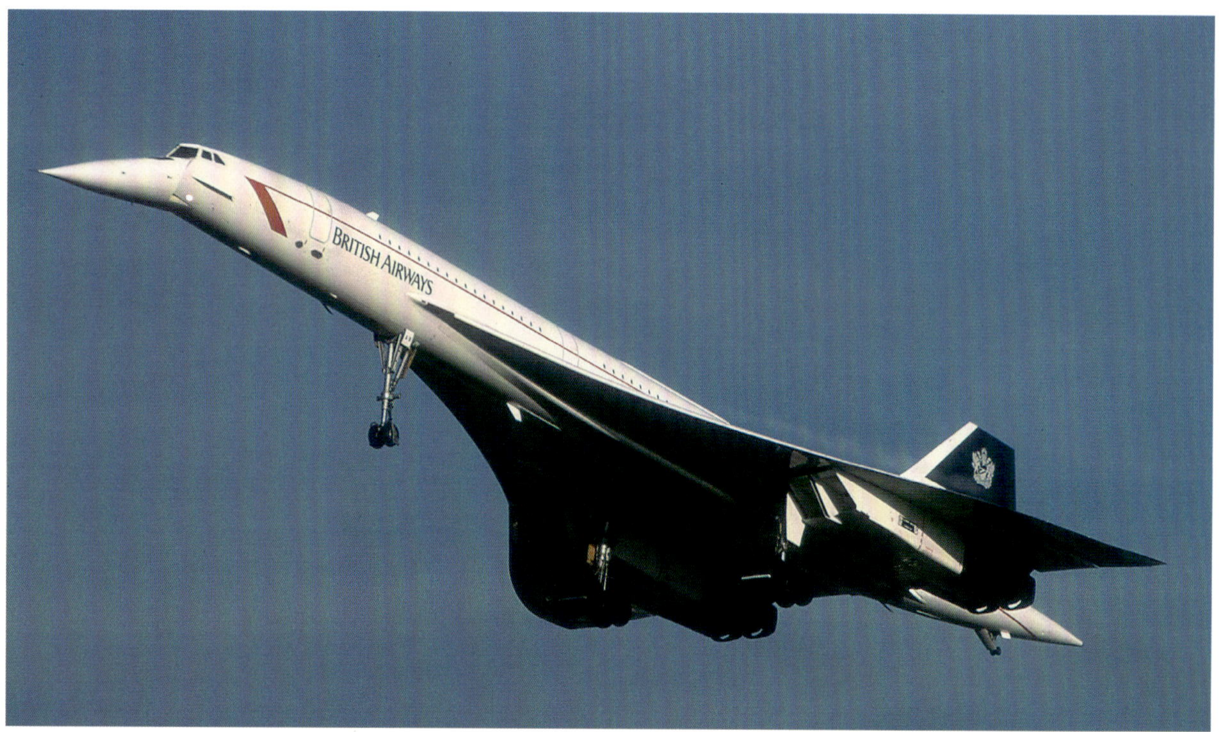

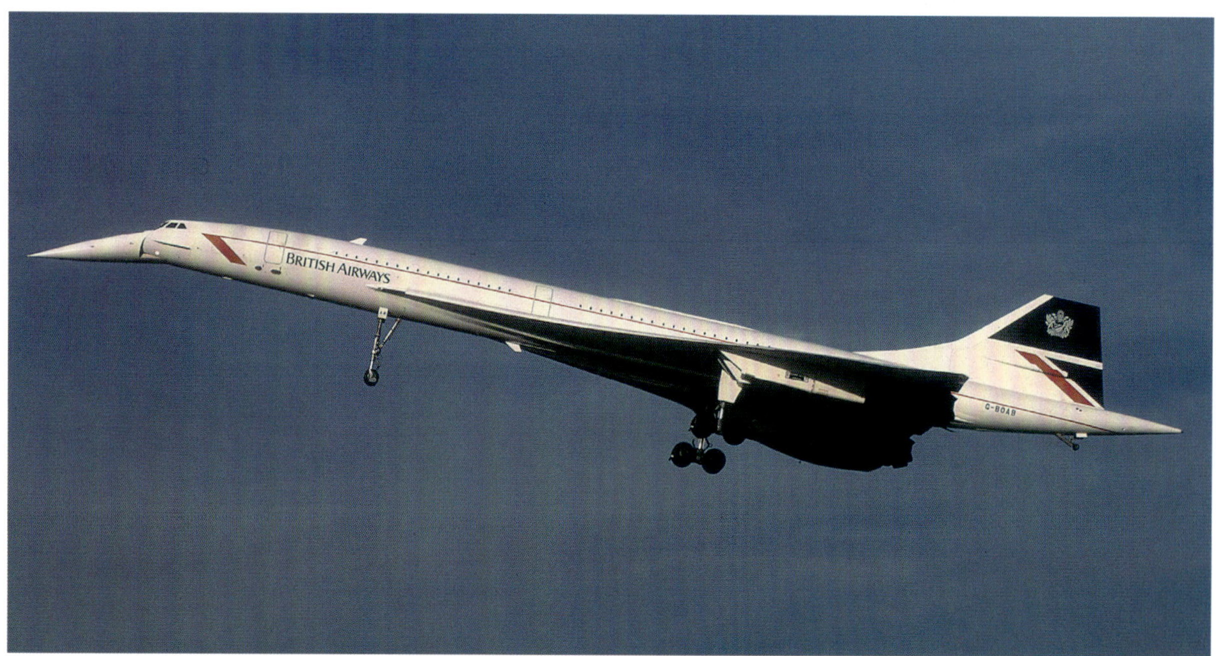

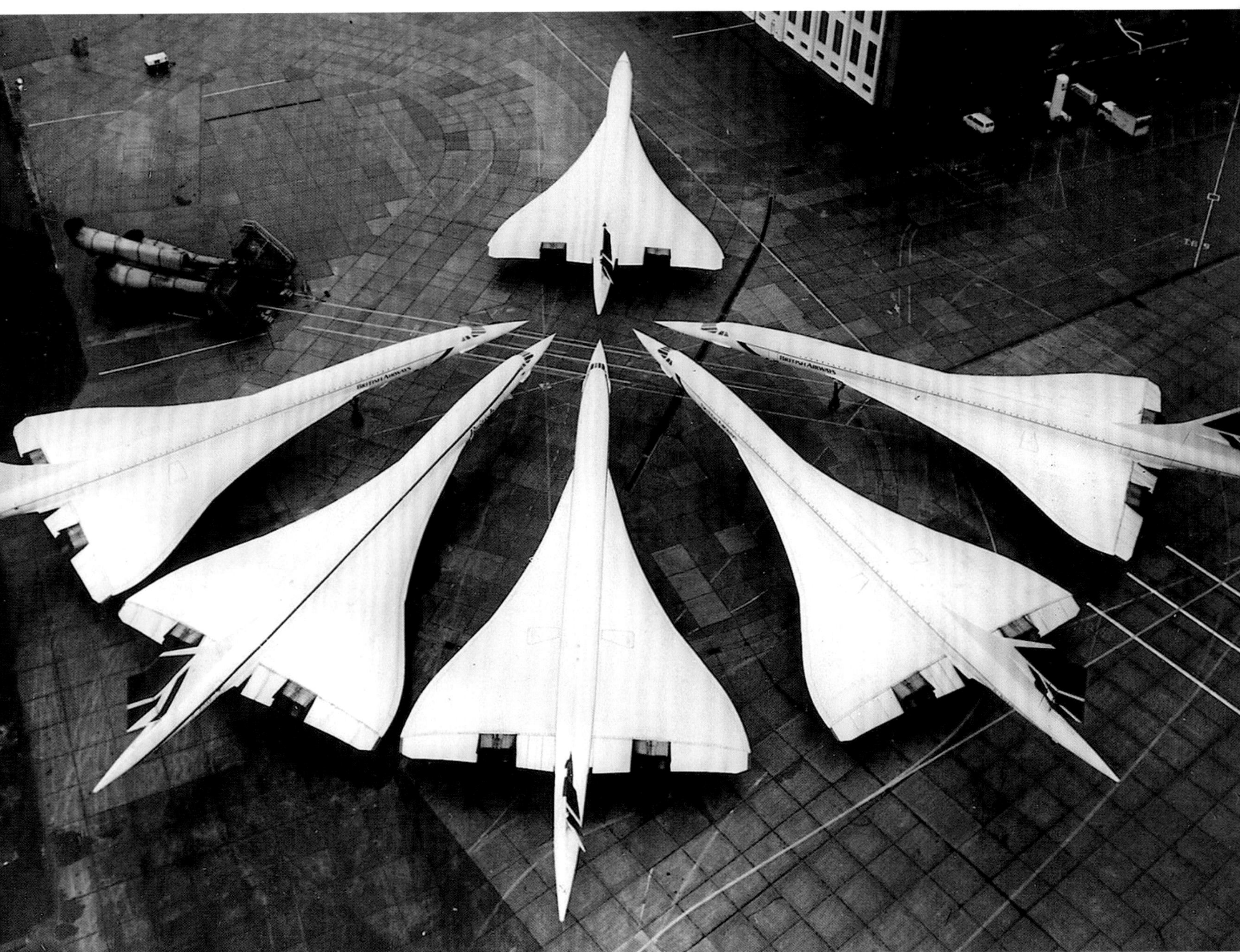

Six of British Airways' Concorde fleet at the airline's Heathrow maintenance base. (Author's collection)

Goodwood Travel brochure for a Concorde trip to the Monaco Grand Prix.

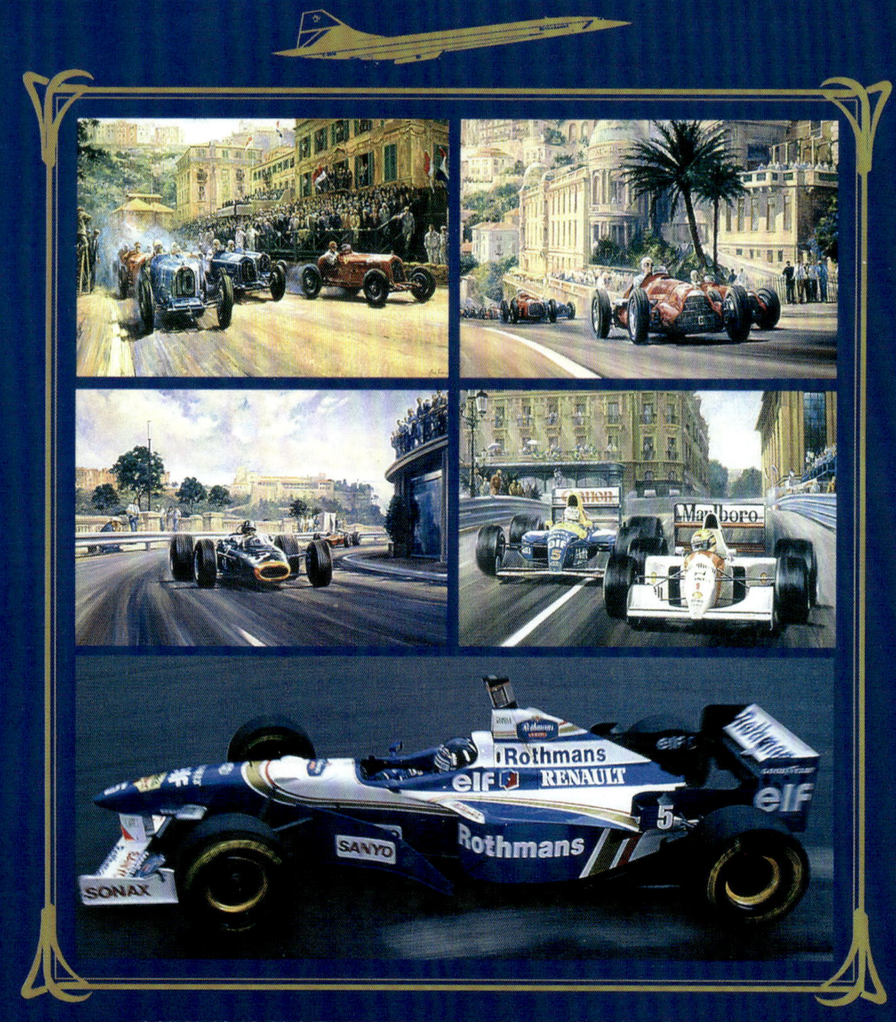

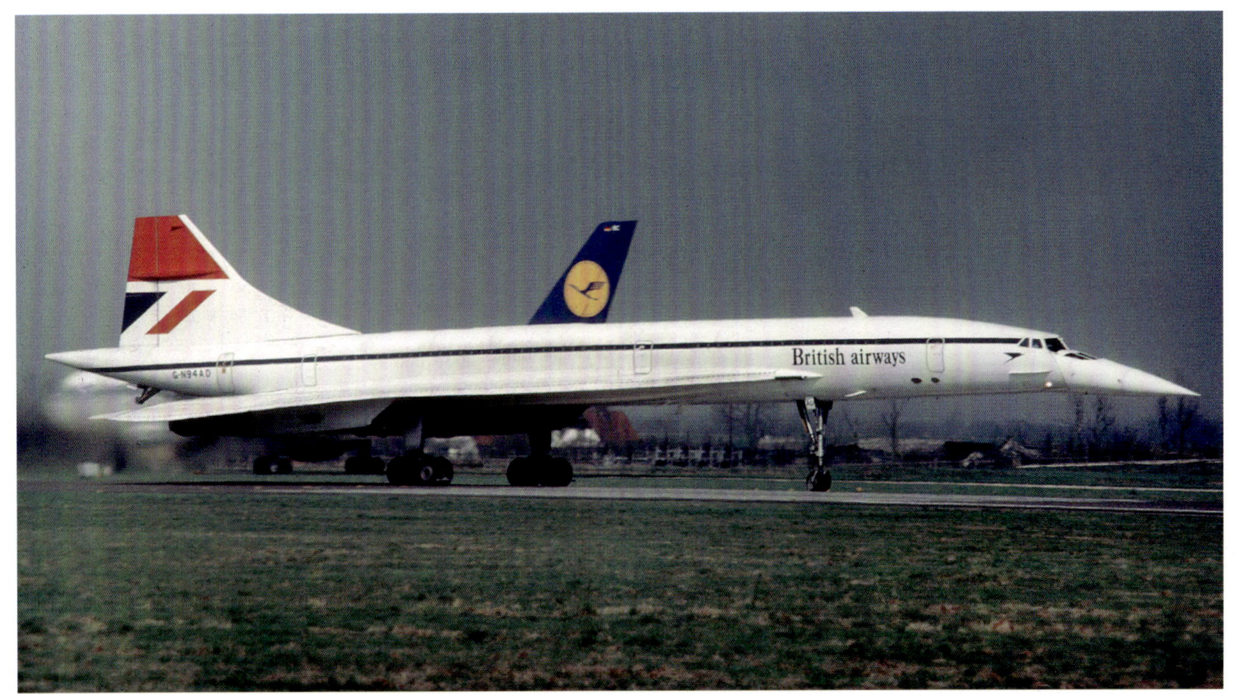

G-N94AD in Negus & Negus BA livery but with a quasi-US registration. When operating for Braniff, the aircraft retained their Air France and British Airways liveries. (Paul Seymour)

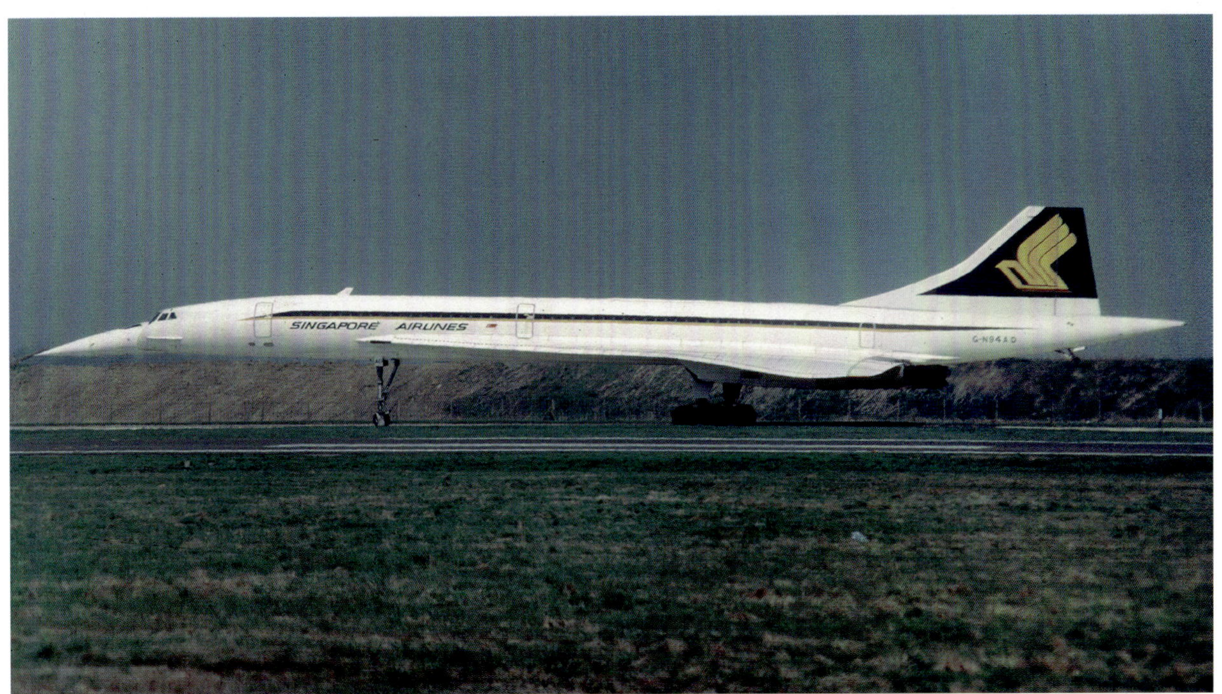

A rare shot of G-BOAD wearing Singapore Airlines livery on the port side but with Braniff registration G-N94AD. (Paul Seymour)

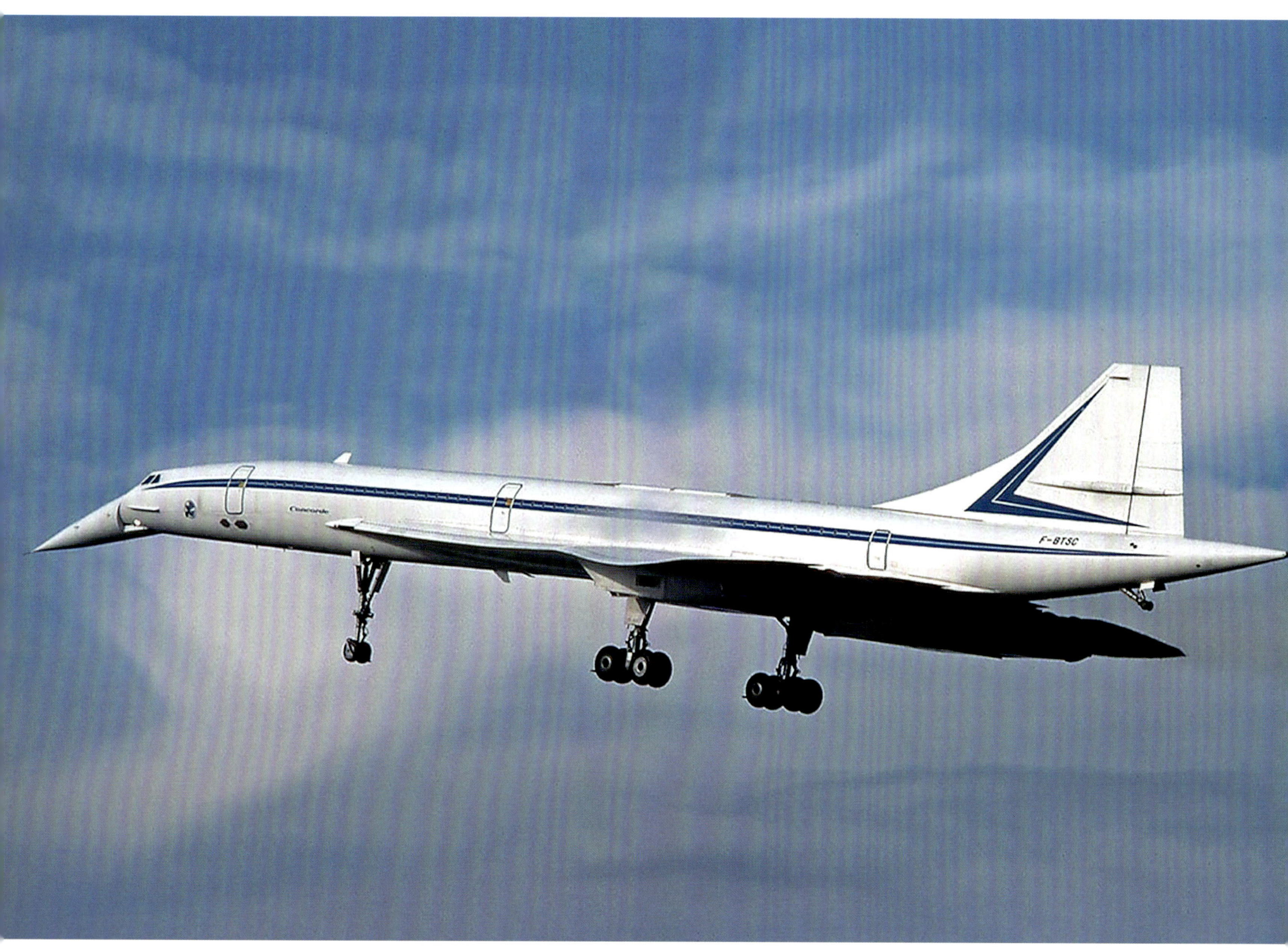

F-BTSC on a rare visit to Heathrow on 11 November 1976. (Tom Singfield collection)

3

AIR FRANCE – CONCORDE 101

The seven-strong Air France Concorde fleet had construction numbers and registrations as follows:

C/N	Series	Customer	Reg.	Delivery date	Currently
203	101	Air France	F-BTSC	24 October 1980	Crashed Gonesse, France, 25 July 2000
205	101	Air France	F-BVFA	19 December 1975	Steven F. Udvar-Hazy Center, Washington Dulles Airport, USA
207	101	Air France	F-BVFB	18 April 1976	Technik Museum Sinsheim, Germany
209	101	Air France	F-BVFC	3 August 1976	Aeroscopia, Toulouse, France
211	101	Air France	F-BVFD	26 March 1977	Scrapped Paris CDG, 1994
213	101	Air France	F-BTSD	18 September 1978	Musée de l'Air et de l'Espace, Paris, France
215	101	Air France	F-BVFF	23 October 1980	On display Paris CDG, France

Like British Airways, Air France commenced commercial Concorde services on 21 January 1976. The first trips were from Paris CDG to Rio de Janeiro in Brazil, with a refuelling stop at Dakar in Senegal on the west coast of Africa, operated by F-BVFA. As Concorde was at the time banned from the US, the supersonic dash across the South Atlantic from Western Africa was ideal. Operating twice weekly, traffic figures on this route were not outstanding but sufficient for Air France to carry on with the service for a period.

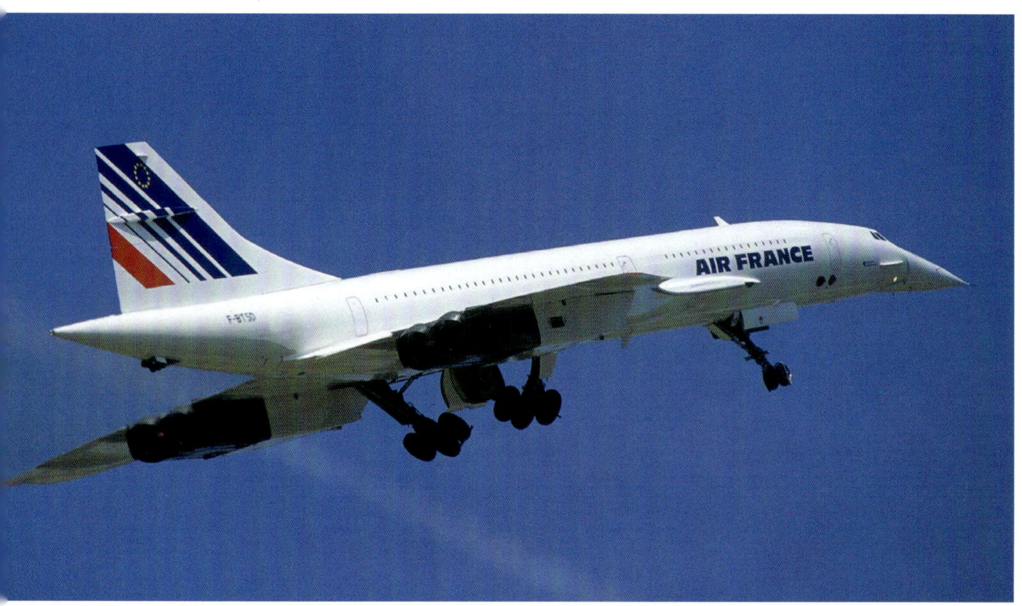

F-BTSD in standard Air France livery in June 2001. (Tom Singfield collection)

After much wrangling, some of it political, the US permitted both Air France and British Airways to operate services to Washington Dulles. Both airlines launched their services to the US capital from Paris and London on 4 May 1976. On the maiden flight both airlines synchronised their arrival at Dulles, landing within a minute of each other, then taxied around the airfield and parked in front of the control tower and terminal building in a staged nose-to-nose encounter. The droop noses were then raised in a mutual salute for the waiting press. This service operated until March 1981.

On 10 April 1977 Air France inaugurated a twice-weekly Paris–Caracas (Venezuela) service with a technical stop at Santa Maria in the Azores, although sometimes, if there was a favourable wind on the eastbound sector, the technical stop at Santa Maria was dispensed with and the flight flown directly to Paris. This service was not a success, due in part to the oil crisis, and was discontinued in April 1982.

New York's Port Authority was determined not to allow Concorde to operate from its JFK airport on noise and pollution grounds. At the time I often visited the US base of Mildenhall in the UK, and I can remember watching noisy KC-135 tankers take off – on a clear day you could see their smoke trail for more than 10 miles. Of course, as they were military aircraft, it was understandable why that was allowed. However, to this day I still think many of the US objections against Concorde were motivated by political protectionism purely because the US did not have its own SST. Again, it is my opinion that the Airbus A380 never sold in the US was because it was NMH (not made here); had it been built by Boeing, I am sure it would have been bought by several US airlines.

In 1977 a federal judge stipulated that the ban on Concorde was 'discriminatory, arbitrary and unreasonable, and that Concorde should be permitted to serve JFK'. The Port of New York Authority appealed against the decision, which was then thrown out by the Supreme Court. On 19 November 1977 a Concorde proving flight was carried out, and the aircraft passed all noise abatement procedures. Three days later, on 22 November, both European airlines commenced a New York JFK service. Air France operated this until the airline ceased all Concorde operations on 31 May 2003, almost five months before British Airways did so. Soon after JFK operations began, Concorde flights were proven to be slightly noisier than a Boeing 707 on departure, but the type was quieter on approach and landing, and soon many of the doubters were won over.

Like British Airways, Air France too had a joint service/lease agreement with Braniff International between October 1978 and May 1980.

Another South American route, this time to Mexico City, was inaugurated on 22 September 1978. This was a twice-weekly service that was a continuation of the airline's New York service. It ceased in November 1982, again due to unsatisfactory loads. Needless to say, Air France's foray into Latin America was not exactly fruitful: three destinations in three different countries, none of which were commercial successes.

The tragic crash of F-BTSC at Gonesse on 25 July 2000 meant Concorde was immediately grounded until safety modifications had been carried out. On the same day, F-BVFC was performing the Paris–New York service; upon landing at JFK it was grounded until early September. After being checked over by Air France engineers, the aircraft was permitted to fly back to Paris without passengers. After the prescribed maintenance work was carried out, Concorde was permitted to carry passengers again. On 7 November 2001 commercial services to New York JFK were resumed, and the passengers were met on arrival by the then Mayor of New York, Rudy Giuliani.

Alongside F-BTSC, two other Air France Concordes did not fulfil their expected lifespans:

- **F-BVFD**, which was delivered to Air France on 26 March 1977, was involved in a heavy landing at Dakar, and the tailwheels were badly damaged. After repair it was returned to service. However, this aircraft had a short service life of just five years. It became corroded after twelve years of being stored outside, during which time it was frequently used for parts to keep the rest of the Air France fleet flyable. It was finally scrapped at Paris CDG Airport in 1994.

- **F-BVFF** was being modified in 2002 for return to service when the retirement decision was made. It is now on permanent display next to a taxiway near Terminal 9 at CDG airport.

CHARTERS

Like British Airways, Air France was also involved in Concorde charters, though not to the same extent. Air Loisirs Services in France flew regular Saturday Air France charters with round trips from its Paris Charles de Gaulle airport base that included a supersonic dash around the Bay of Biscay. To mark the opening of the Disney Epcot Centre in Florida in 1982, both Air France and British Airways undertook charters to Orlando, and the event was staged so that both aircraft landed simultaneously on Orlando's parallel runways: a unique event. To mark the 500th anniversary of Christopher Columbus landing in the New World, a chartered Air France Concorde circumnavigated the world in thirty-two hours forty-nine minutes and three seconds. During this flight the aircraft visited Lisbon, Santo

F-BVFB at Paris Charles de Gaulle Airport in October 1986. (Tom Singfield collection)

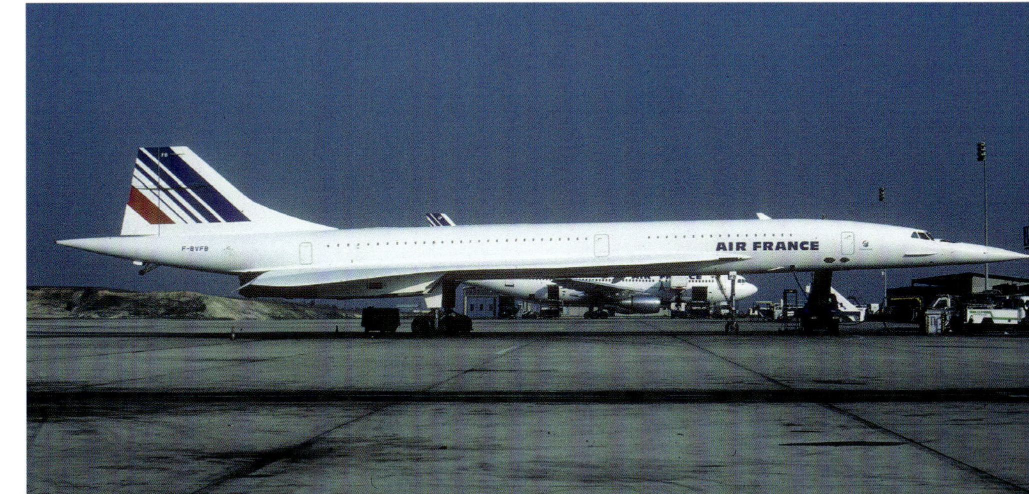

Domingo, Acapulco, Honolulu, Guam, Bangkok and Bahrain.

Concorde was also used regularly by French President François Mitterand for official travel.

F-BTSC CRASH

F-BTSC's crash on 25 July 2000 at Paris CDG had a major effect on subsequent Concorde operations. All 100 passengers and 9 crew on board were killed, as well as 4 people on the ground. The aircraft was carrying out charter flight AFR4590 to New York and was full of German tourists.

Like many accidents, the cause of this crash was because of a series of incidents, and ultimately could have been avoided. Having read the official report, there were several noticeable occurrences. The aircraft was running late for the service. It was a hot day and the aircraft's tanks were completely full of fuel – some say almost over-fuelled. There were bags in the rear hold that had not been weighed, and afterwards it was calculated that the aircraft was above its maximum structural weight. For taxi out, 2,000kg of fuel was expected to be used, but on this occasion only 800kg was used, so the aircraft was very heavy and slightly overweight.

The accident was caused by a piece of titanium strip falling on to the runway from a Continental Airlines DC-10 aircraft that had departed five minutes ahead of the Concorde. As F-BTSC accelerated down the runway and came close to rotation point, one of the tyres on the aircraft's left main bogie ran over this piece of metal and was sliced open. The tyre was not punctured, but a large part was literally scalped off and flew upwards, penetrating the number five fuel tank and setting off a shock wave inside the tank. Because of the amount of fuel in it, there was not enough air to absorb the shock wave, thereby causing a mini explosion. This ejected a significant amount of burning fuel, some of which was sucked into the number two engine, setting off the fire warning in the cockpit. The flight engineer immediately carried out the fire drill and shut down the number two engine. Heavy and now underpowered, the aircraft staggered into the air, hitting a runway light in doing so. Another factor was that the crew were unable to retract the landing gear, so this was also probably damaged. The loss of fuel from a forward tank meant the aircraft's centre of gravity changed and it was now tail heavy. With the aircraft engulfed by fire and losing height, the crew told CDG Air Traffic Control they were going to try for Le Bourget Airport. But with the engines losing power, the aircraft only could only attain a speed of 200 knots and flew for one minute before crashing in flames into a hotel at La Patte d'Oie in Gonesse. Afterwards pieces of the fuel tank wall were found on the runway, as was part of a burning tyre.[*] Coincidentally, this site is close to the

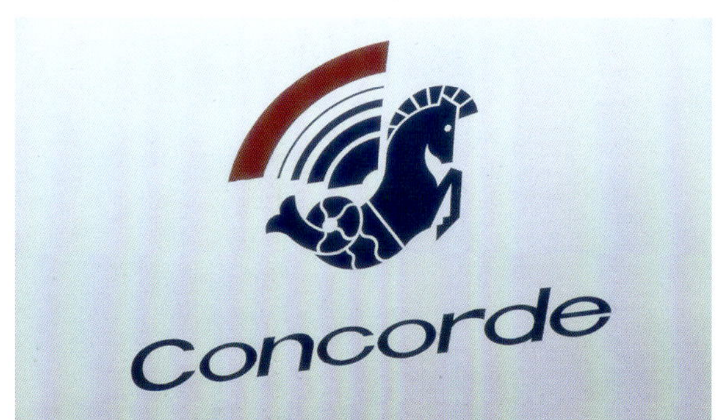

Air France's Seahorse logo on Concorde F-BTSC.

---

* The accident report into the crash of F-BTSC by BEA – d'Enquetes et d'Analyses (French Civil Aviation Investigation Bureau); BBC4 documentary *Concorde: A Supersonic Story* aired on 29 August 2024.

location of the Tu-144 crash during the 1973 Paris Air Show.

Prior to the crash this aircraft had flown 11,989 hours during 4,873 cycles (flights), and had in fact just completed a major service only four days earlier. This aircraft's early career was mostly with Aérospatiale and it was actually stored from 1982 until 1986. It was then brought up to production standard and leased to Air France in June 1979, with the airline purchasing it in October 1980.

Air France's final JFK–Paris service was on the morning of 31 May 2003, operated by F-BTSD. This was intended to be the airline's last commercial Concorde service; however, a trip around the Bay of Biscay flight F-BVFB was actually the last because it ran late. The last of the airline's Concordes to fly was F-BVFC on 27 June 2003, when it was flown 'home' to Toulouse to join the excellent Aeroscopia museum.

Air France operated Concorde for twenty-seven years. Proof that British Airways' commercial Concorde operations were more successful perhaps comes from the statistic that the Air France Concorde with the highest total number of hours flown had fewer hours 'on the clock' than the British Airways Concorde that had flown the least. It is still my opinion that, had the Air France fleet been as successful as that of British Airways, then Aérospatiale (by then Airbus) would not have withdrawn spares support of the aircraft.

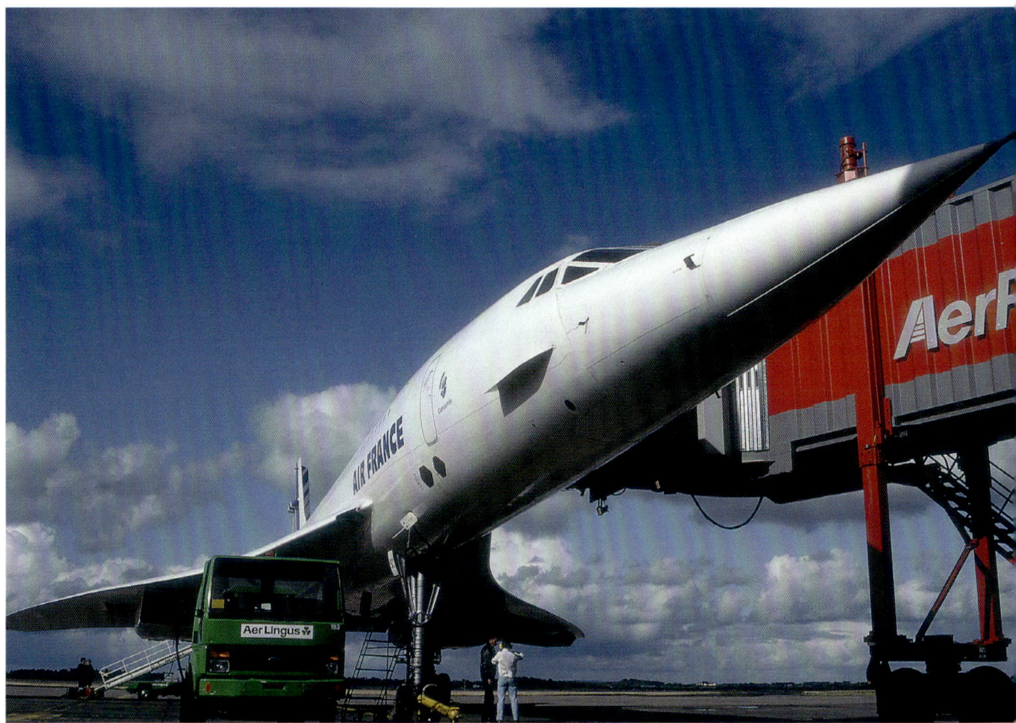

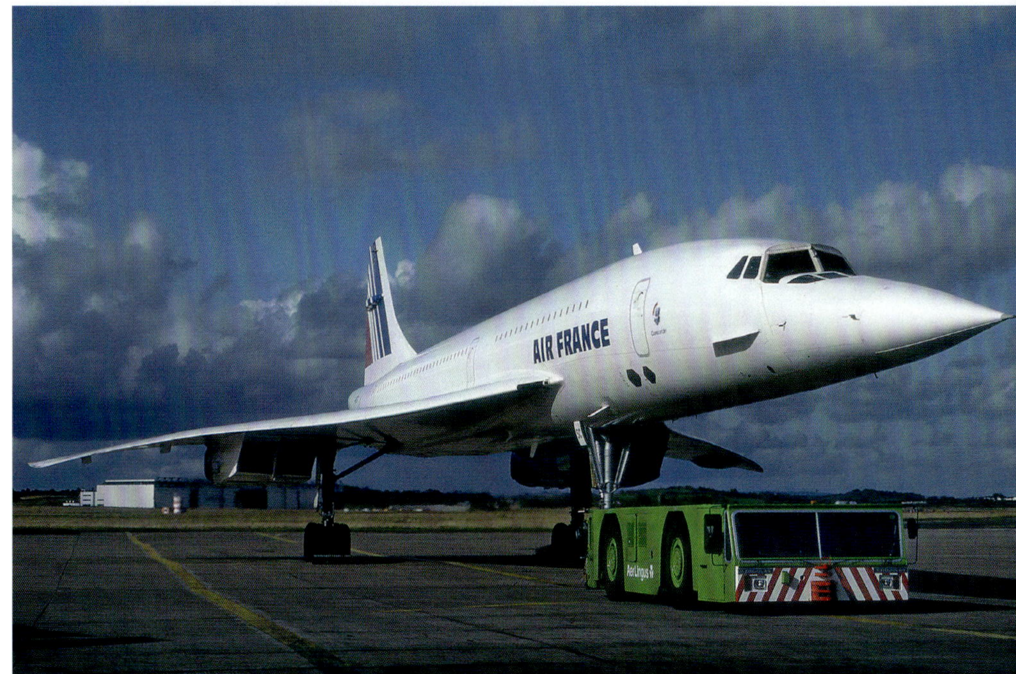

Top: F-BTSC head-on at the gate at Shannon Airport, Ireland, on 30 August 1982.

Bottom: F-BTSC on push back at Shannon, ready for a crew training exercise.

Storm clouds approaching as F-BTSC starts up at Shannon. Concordes of both Air France and British Airways regularly used Shannon for crew training.

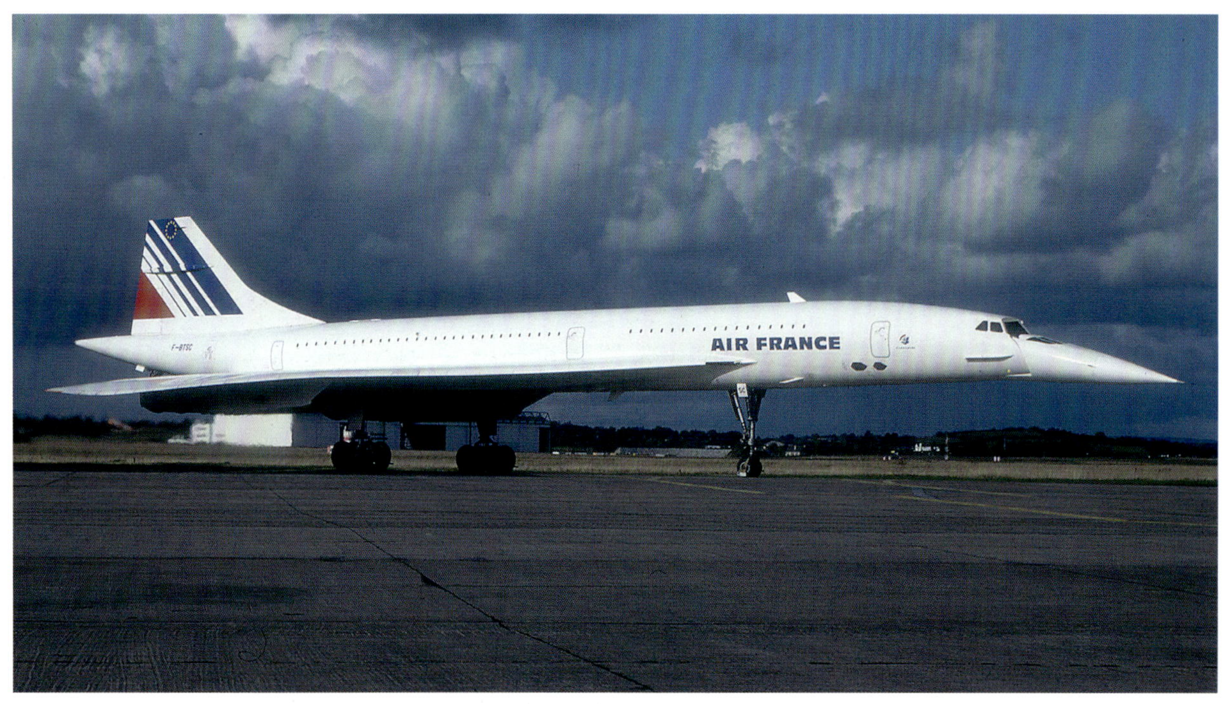

F-BTSC ready to taxi at Shannon on 30 August 1982.

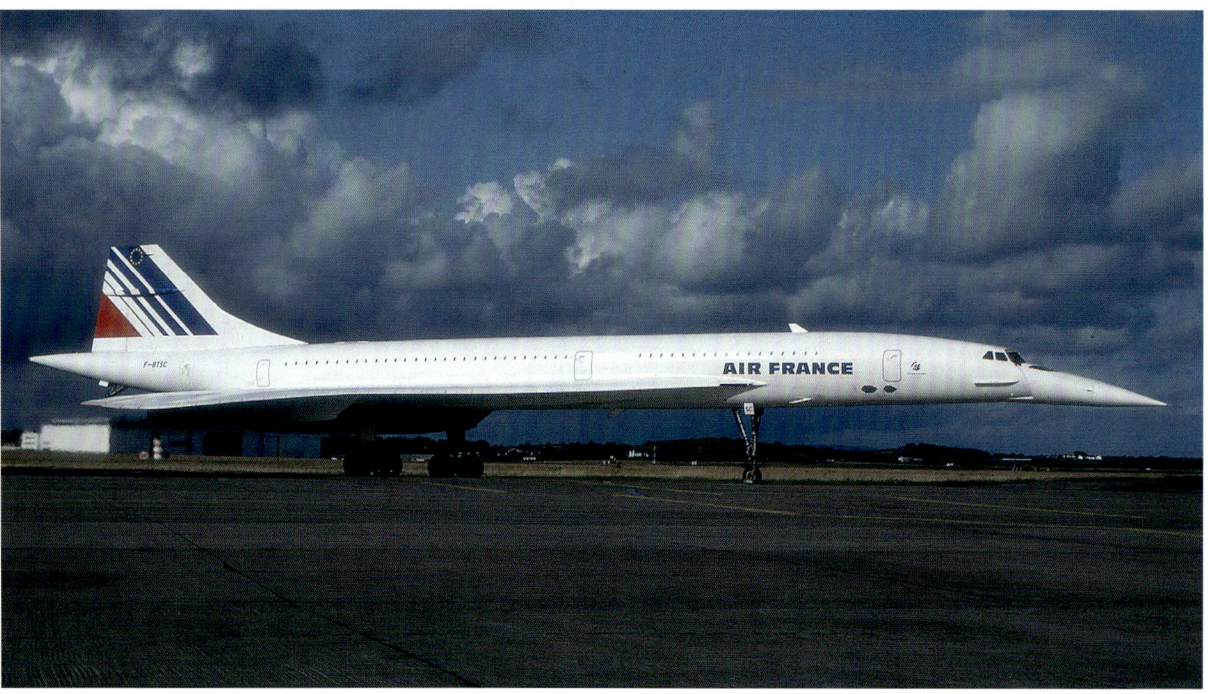

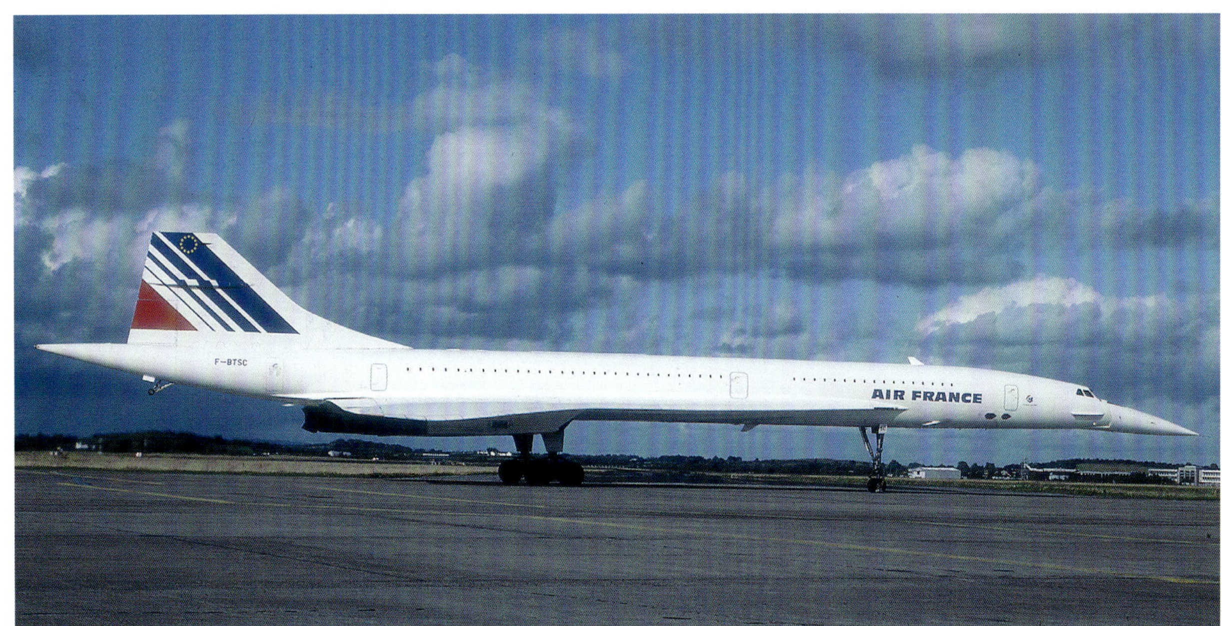

F-BTSC taxies at Shannon on 30 August 1982 for a period of 'circuit bashing' on a crew training sortie.

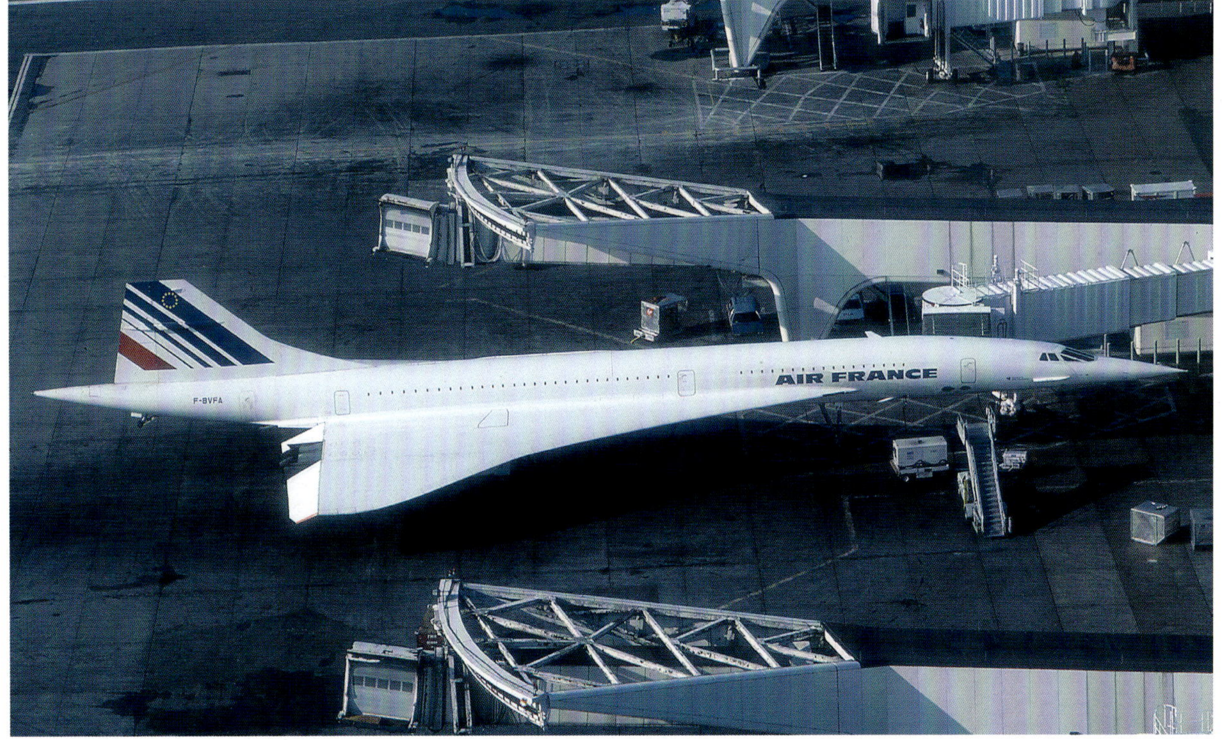

F-BVFA of Air France on the gate at JFK Airport in October 1994.

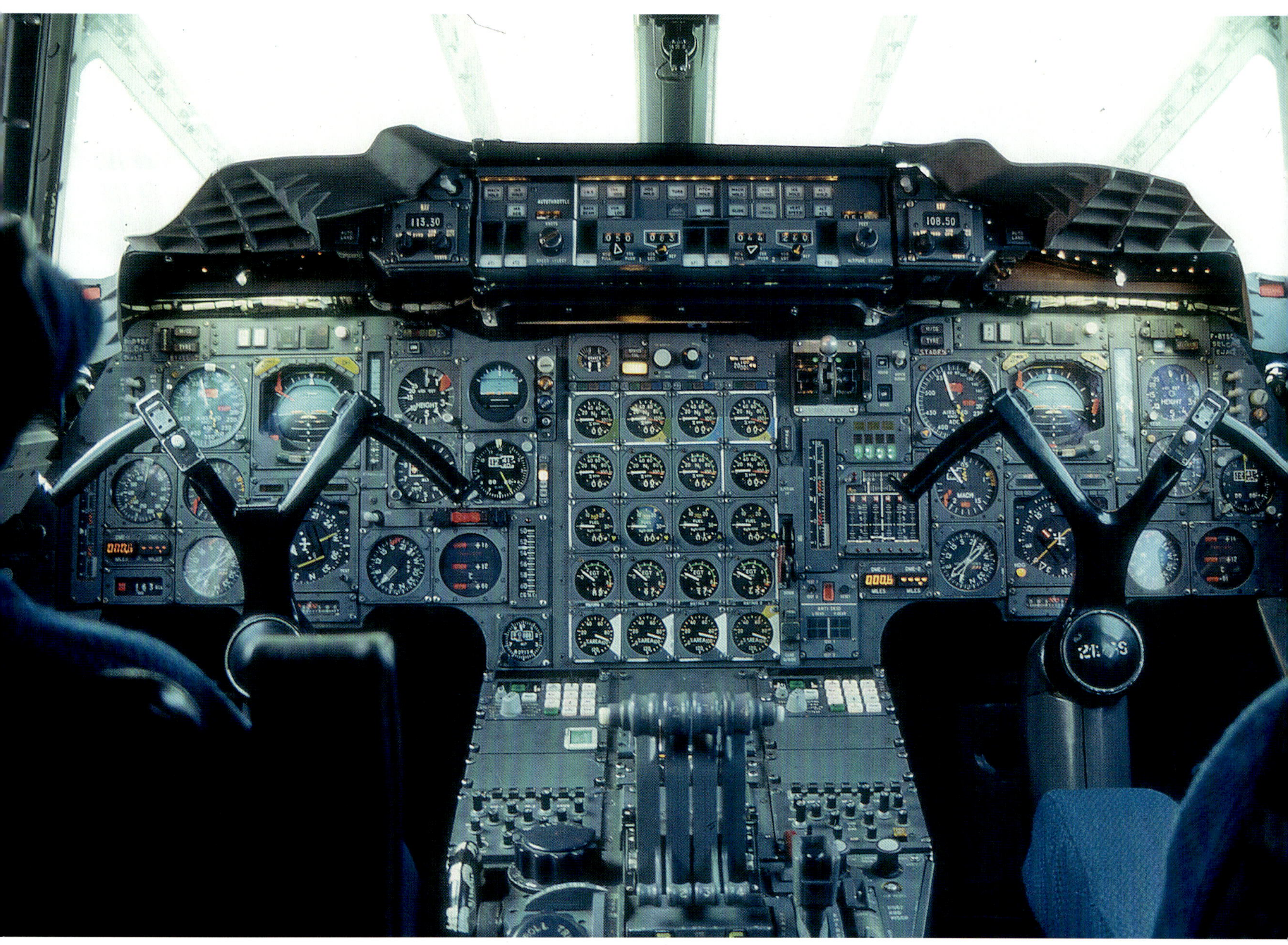

A cockpit view of F-BTSC at Shannon.

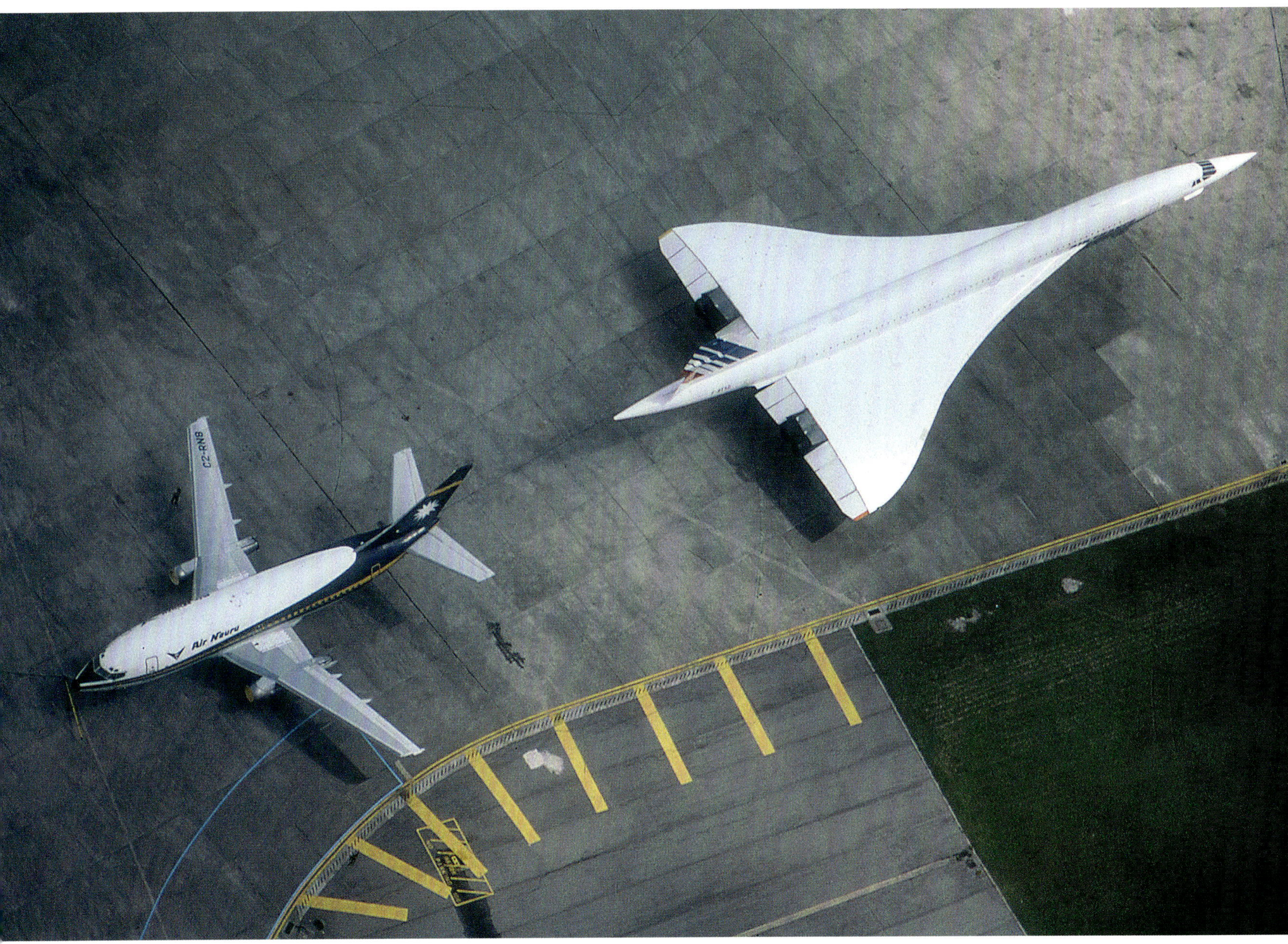

An interesting size comparison of Air France Concorde F-BTSD and an Air Nauru Boeing 737-200 on the ramp at Hong Kong's
Kai Tak Airport on 24 August 1987.

F-BTSC on its take-off
roll at JFK's runway 31L on
21 October 1994.

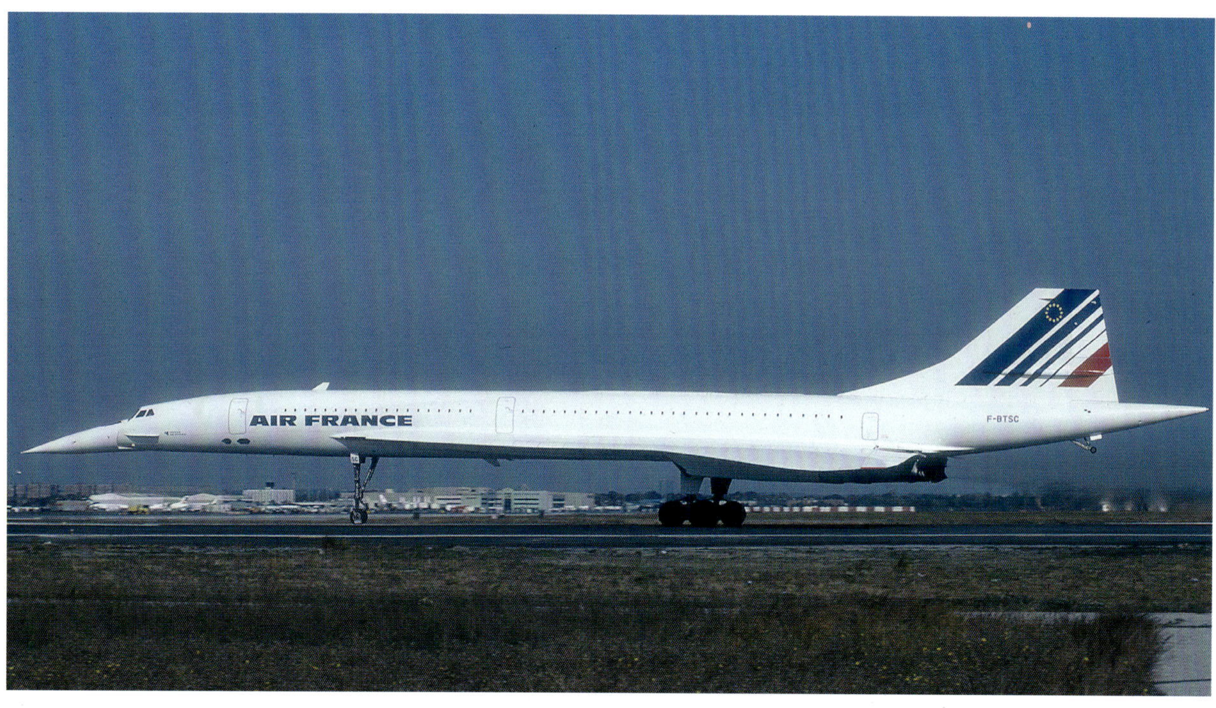

F-BTSC close to rotation
on runway 31L at JFK on
21 October 1994.

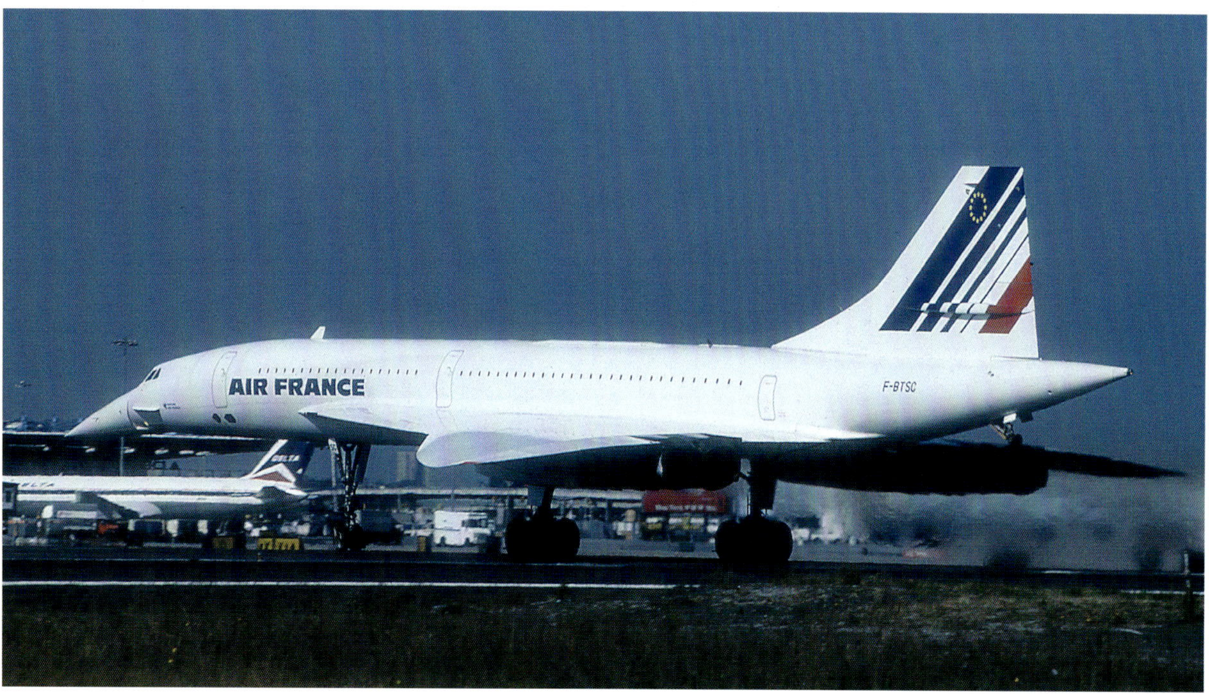

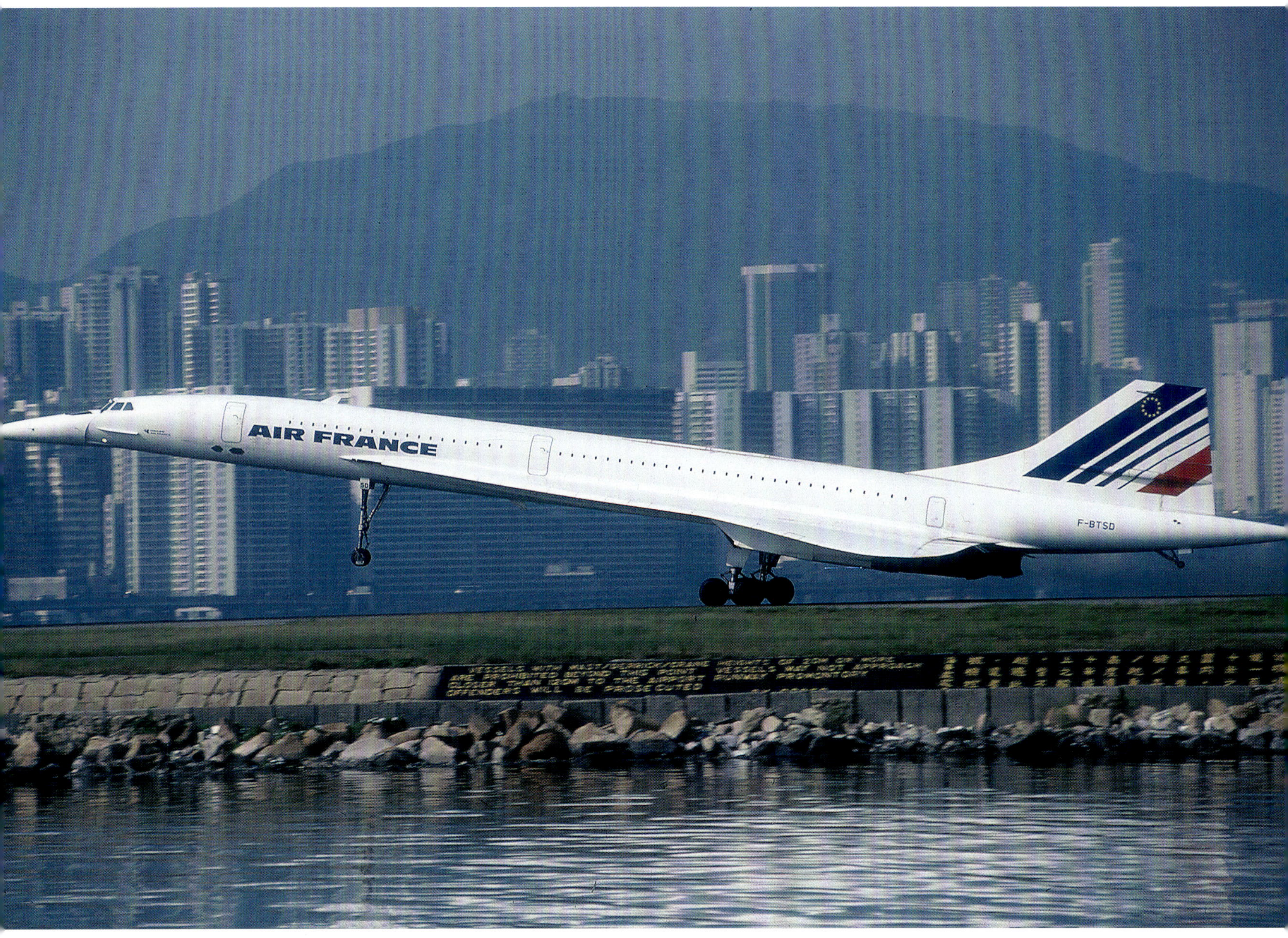

F-BTSD starts to rotate off runway 13 at Hong Kong's Kai Tak International Airport on 24 September 1995. Hong Kong Island is visible in the background. This will have been on one of the airline's special charters, perhaps even a round-the-world trip.

F-BTSD on its take-off
roll on runway 13
at Kai Tak on
24 September 1995.

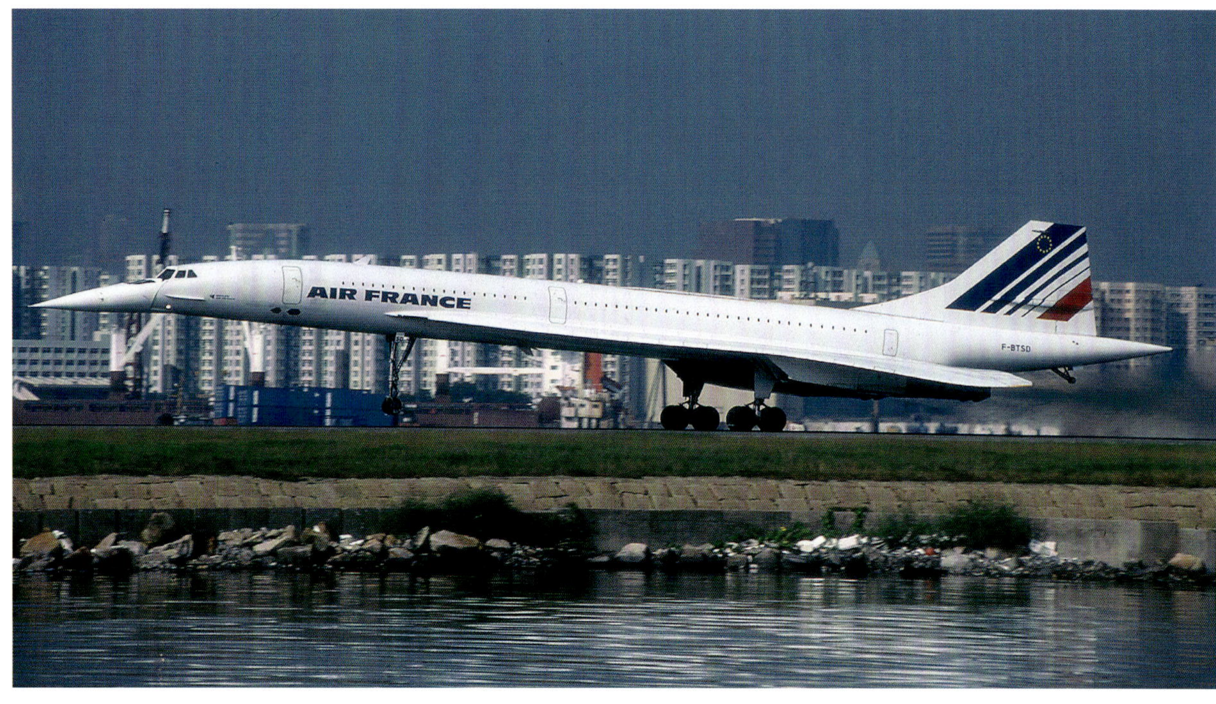

F-BVFF on a rare visit to
Heathrow in October 1987.
(SPA Photography)

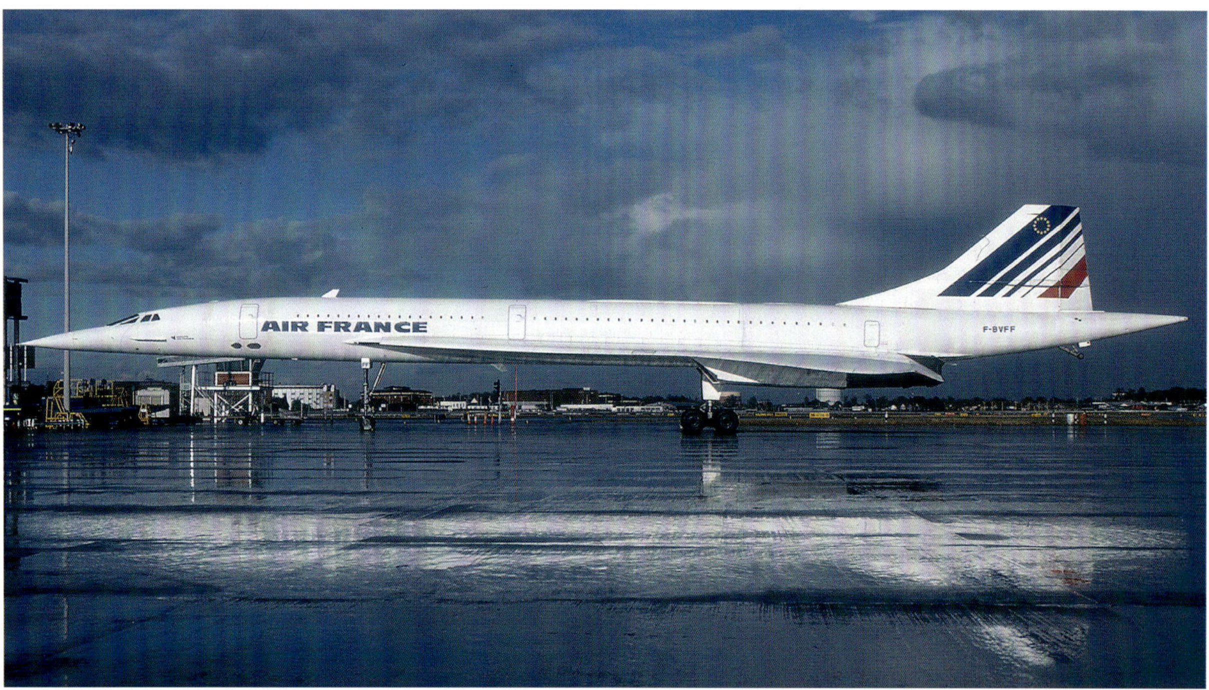

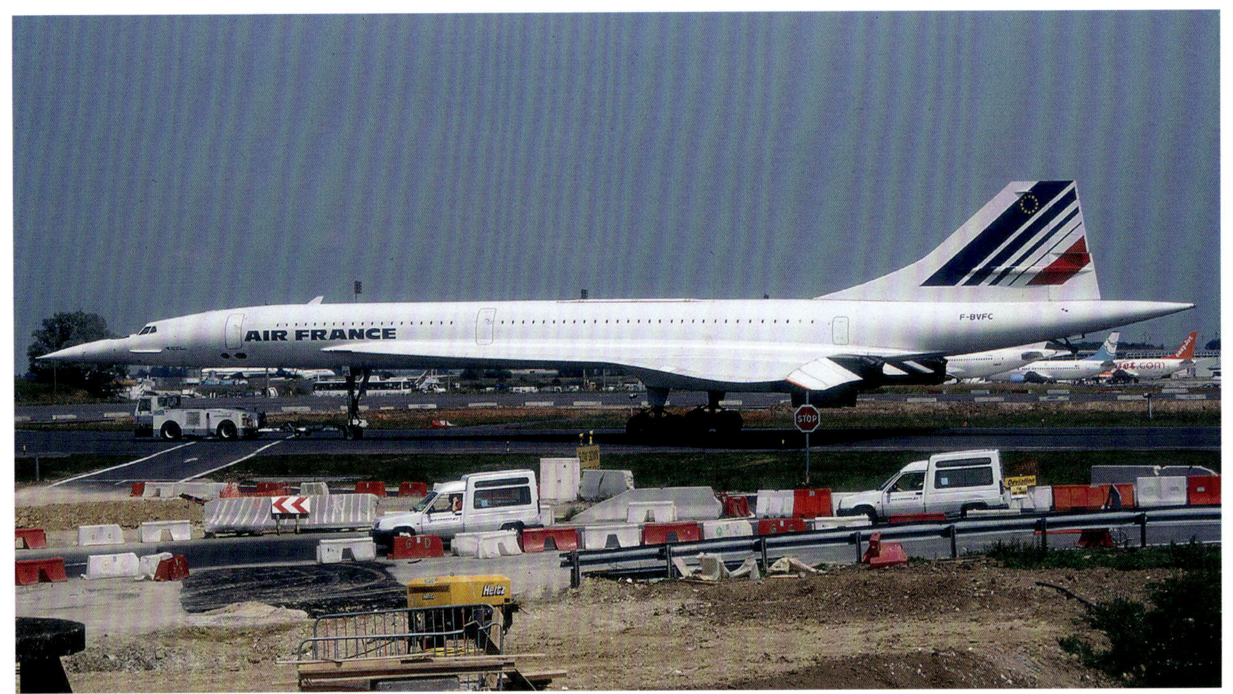

F-BVFC under tow at Paris CDG on 12 June 2003. I was lucky to get this shot: Air France had ceased Concorde operations less than two weeks earlier and, only two weeks later, this aircraft would fly to Toulouse. It is still there now, preserved at the Aeroscopia museum.

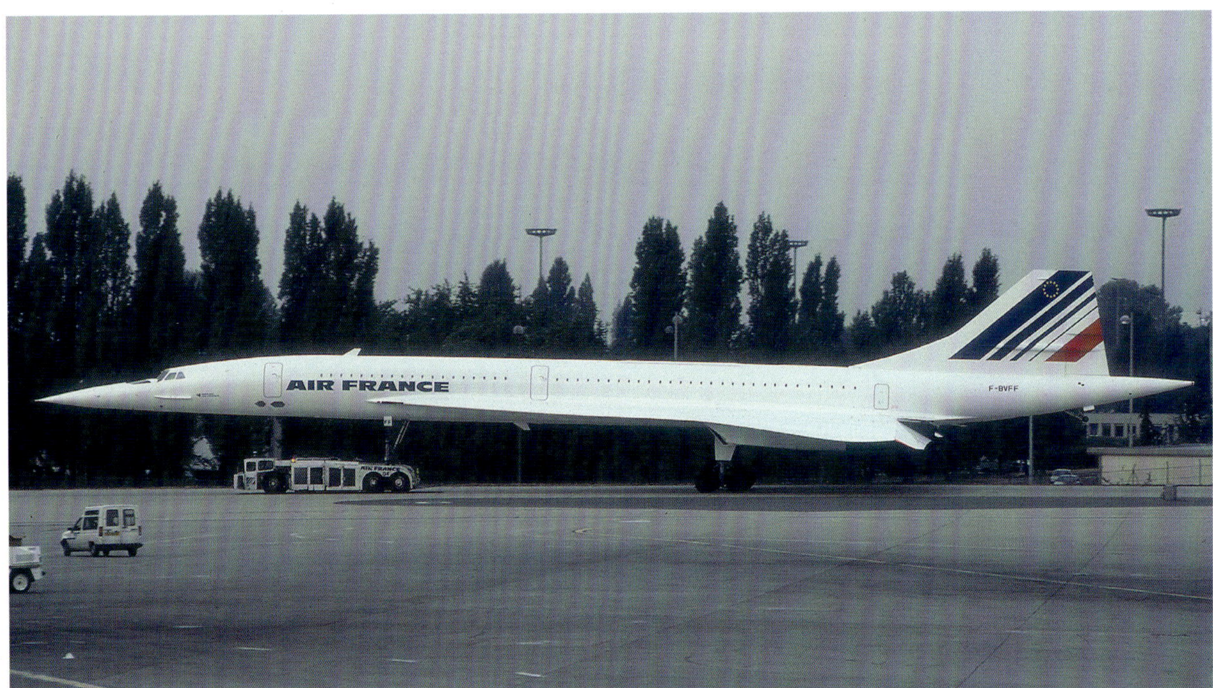

F-BVFF under tow at Paris CDG on 11 August 1992.

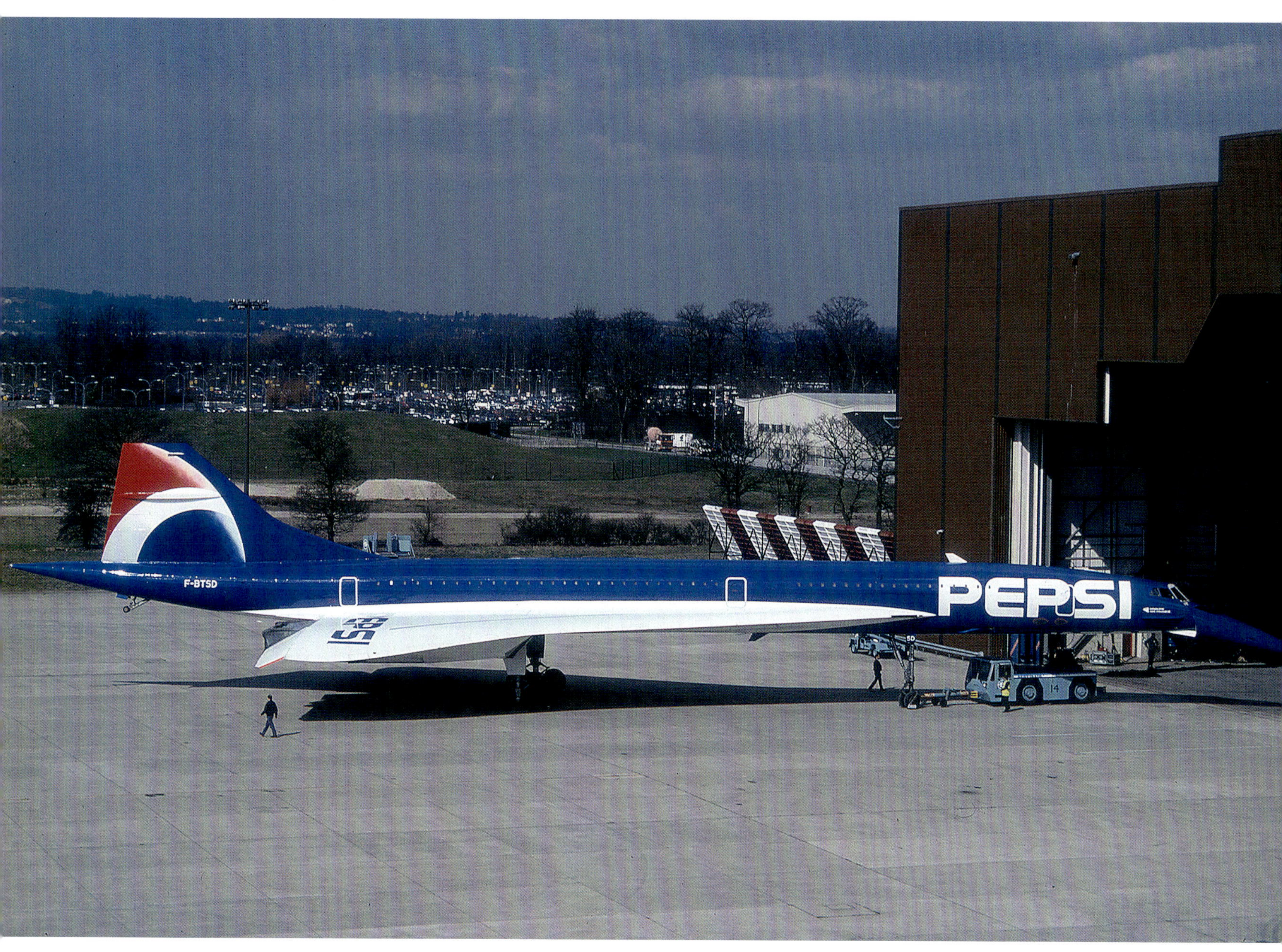

Having been unveiled to the press inside the hangar at Gatwick on 2 April 1996, Air France machine F-BTSD is pushed outside so that it can take its lucky passengers on a flight.

4

THE PEPSI BLUE CONCORDE

Over the years a number of airliners have appeared wearing distinctive advertising schemes for a variety of customers. One of my favourites was the all-red McDonalds livery that adorned a Danish Air Transport McDonnell Douglas MD-80. However, without doubt one of the best, and one which is relevant to this book, is the Pepsi Blue Concorde.

Apparently, due to falling market share, the Pepsi Cola company in the USA undertook a reported $500 million rebranding in 1996. Part of this spending involved the painting of a stunning blue scheme on Air France Concorde F-BTSD.

This was a promotional event like no other, and was aimed at the introduction of the Pepsi Blue soft drink. It was decided that the event would see celebrities, sports stars and Pepsi executives on board several flights in both Europe and the Middle East in a specially painted Concorde. As the only Concorde operators were Air France and British Airways, both airlines were invited to bid to host the event, and Air France was the selected winner. The design involved the body of the aircraft being painted blue overall with the large Pepsi logo on the tail. The wings, however, were painted white to avoid any heat issues around the fuel tanks. In case of heat issues elsewhere due to the blue paint, the aircraft's supersonic speed was limited to Mach 1.7. The repainting at the Air France Paris Orly engineering base took 2,000 man-hours and 200 litres of paint. The whole event was covered in secrecy, and after painting the aircraft remained hidden in a hangar, reportedly wrapped in brown paper.

Surprisingly, the aircraft was unveiled not in France, but at London Gatwick airport on 2 April 1996. Prior to the unveiling, the aircraft quietly and under cover of darkness flew into Gatwick on the evening of 31 March and was quickly hidden away out of sight in a hangar. Two days later it was unveiled at a major media event in front of the press, celebrities, sports stars and Pepsi executives, including Andre Agassi, Cindy Crawford and Claudia Schiffer.

After the event the aircraft was towed out of the hangar and a number guests boarded the aircraft, which was parked at a remote gate. It then departed Gatwick for a demonstration flight, where no doubt Pepsi Blue was on offer as well as champagne.

This was the start of a tour taking in ten cities across Europe and the Middle East. The next day, Concorde departed Gatwick to begin the tour in earnest. These promotional flights were as follows:

2 April 1996 Gatwick–Gatwick
3 April 1996 Gatwick–Dublin
3 April 1996 Dublin–Dublin
4 April 1996 Dublin–Stockholm
4 April 1996 Stockholm–Stockholm
4 April 1996 Stockholm–Paris CDG
6 April 1996 Paris CDG–Beirut

7 April 1996 Beirut–Dubai
7 April 1996 Dubai–Dubai
7 April 1996 Dubai–Jeddah
8 April 1996 Jeddah–Cairo
8 April 1996 Cairo–Milan Linate
9 April 1996 Milan Linate–Madrid
9 April 1996 Madrid–Madrid
9 April 1996 Madrid–Paris ORY

On arrival back at Orly, the aircraft was restored to its usual Air France livery. Just the painting work alone must have cost Pepsi a lot of money.

Pepsi colours on the tail of F-BTSD. A very impressive livery indeed, which I think looks stunning on Concorde.

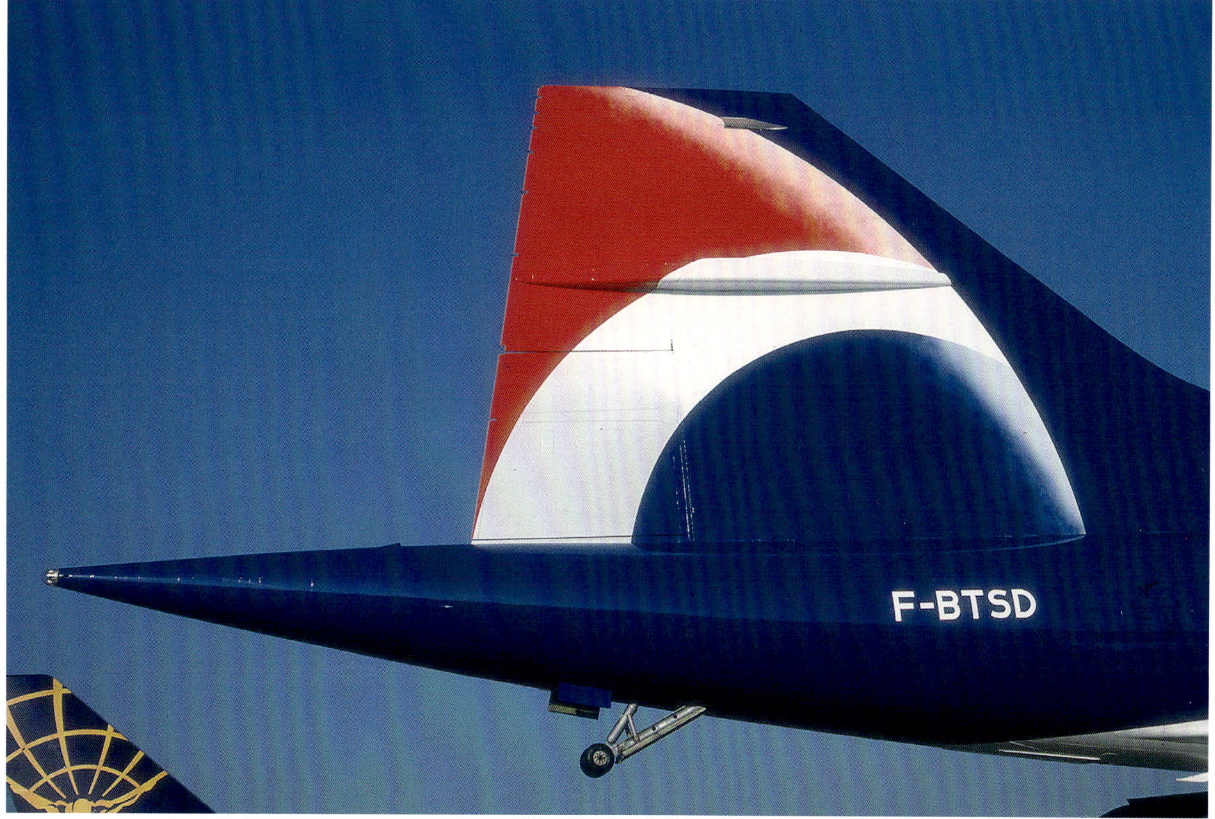

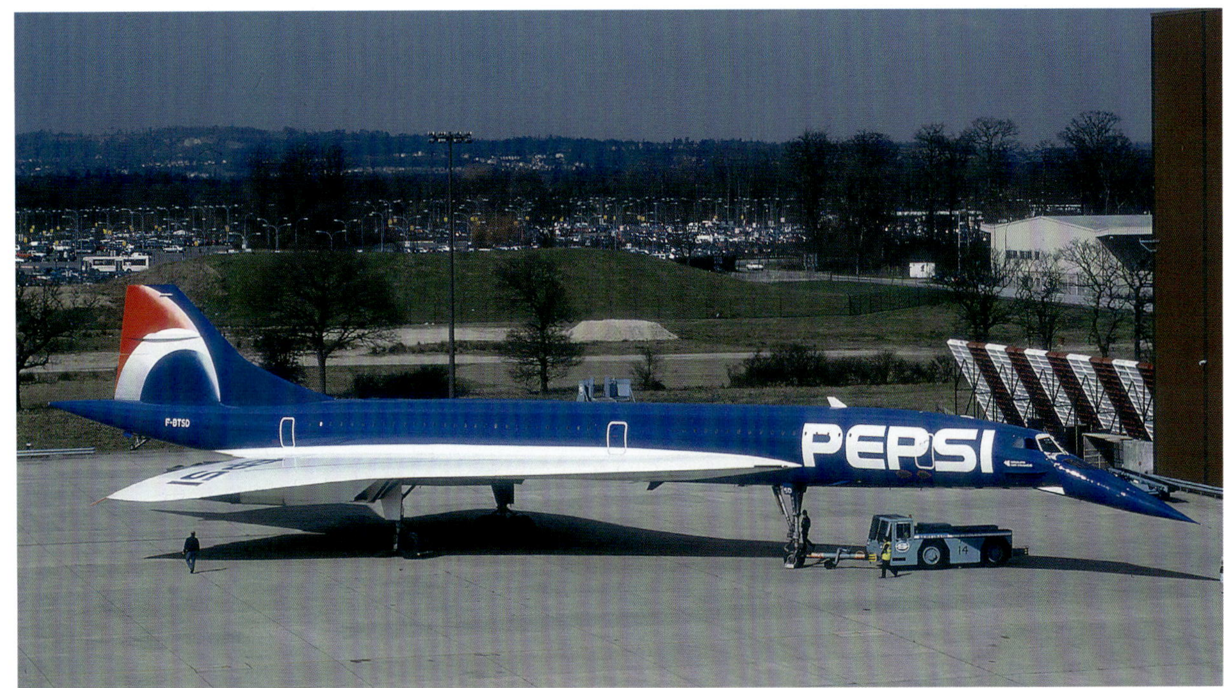

The Pepsi Concorde being pushed back out of the hangar.

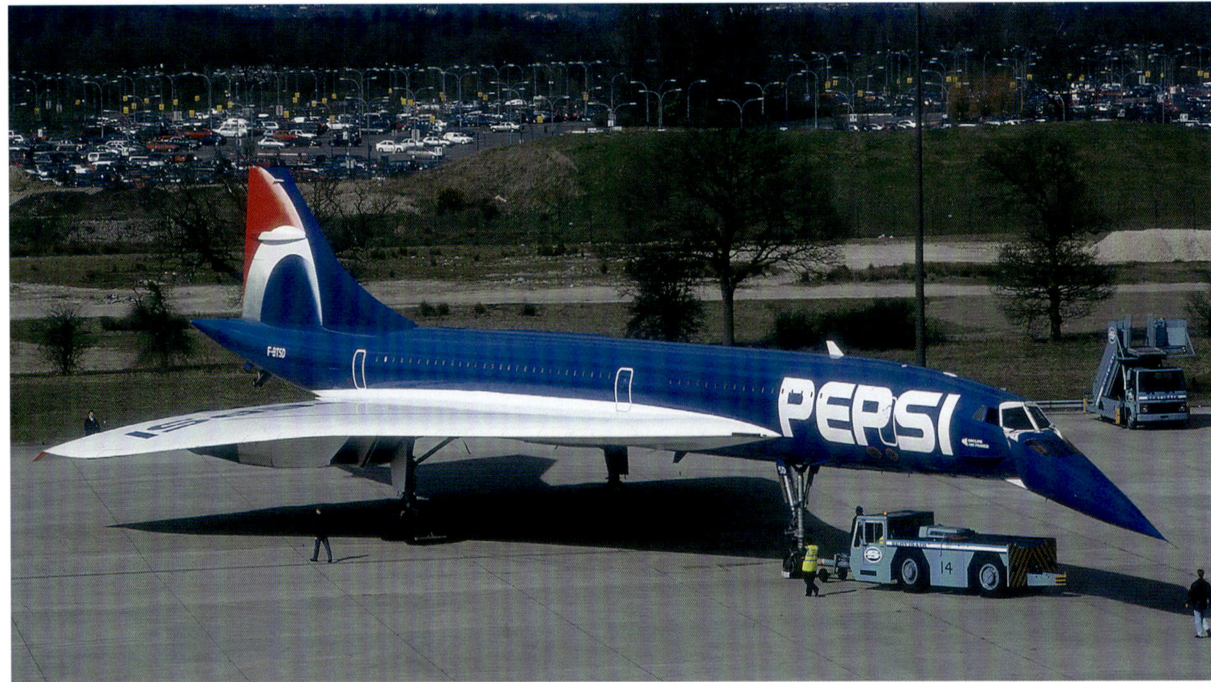

F-BTSD awaits towing into position for its passengers. Note the nose droop.

This head-on shot shows the
droop nose to good effect.

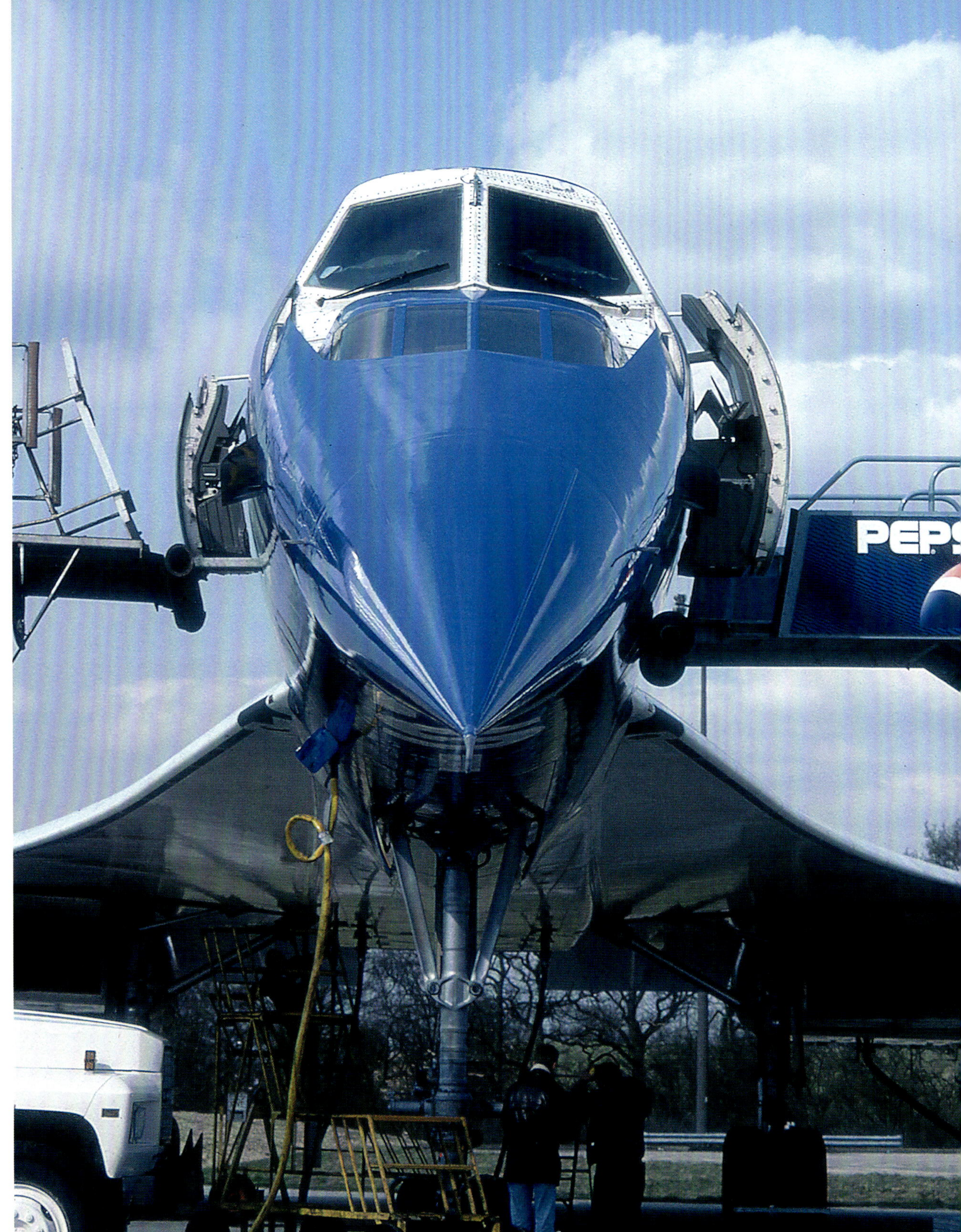

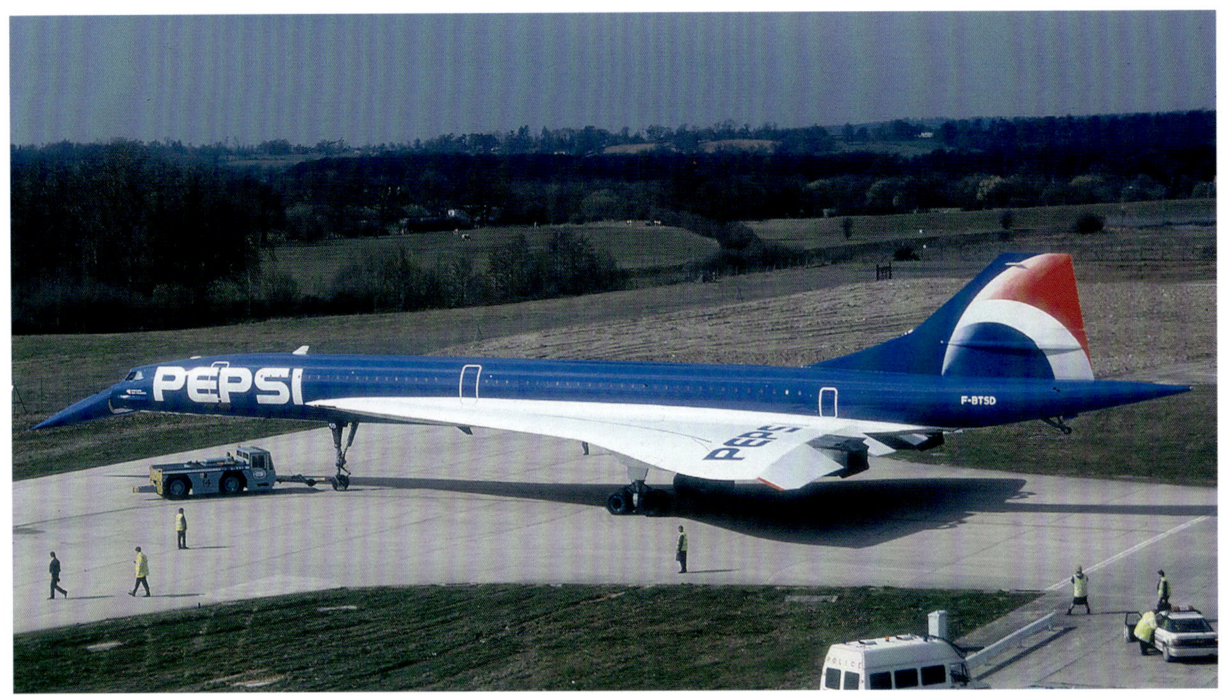

F-BTSD being towed at Gatwick for its first passenger flight in this stunning livery. Note the Pepsi titling on the top of the wings.

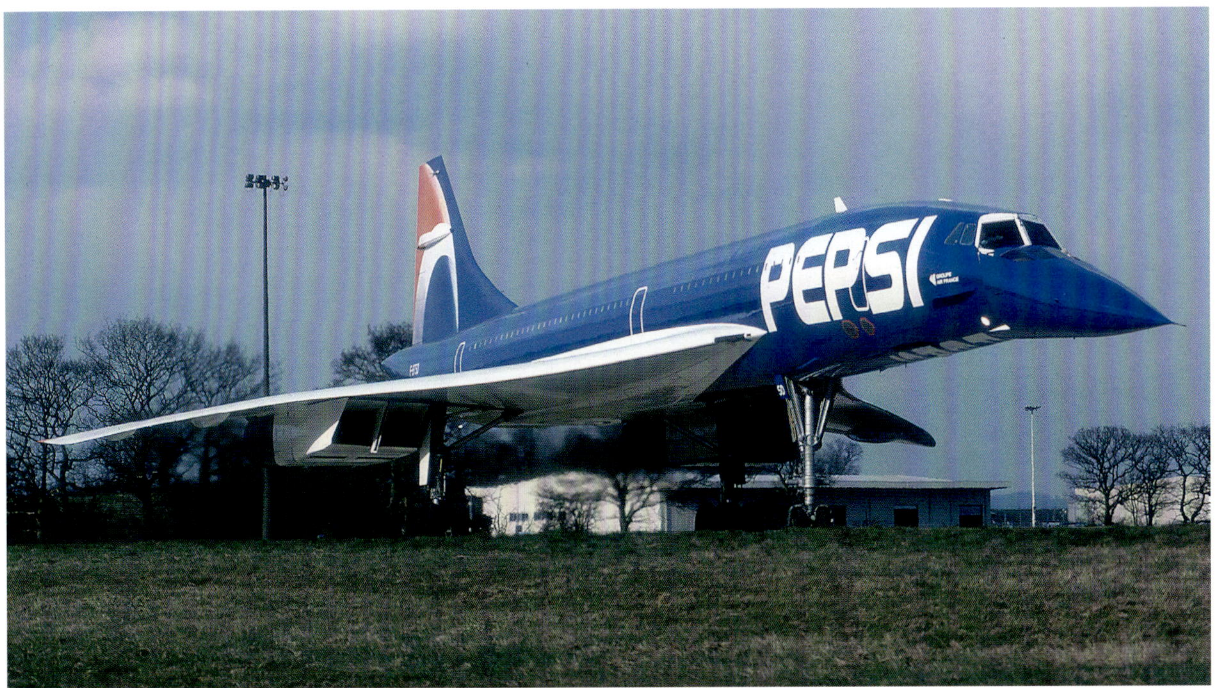

The sleek lines of F-BTSD in the Pepsi Blue colours at Gatwick on 2 April 1996.

The Pepsi Blue Concorde taxies out at Gatwick on 2 April 1996 with a full load of passengers.

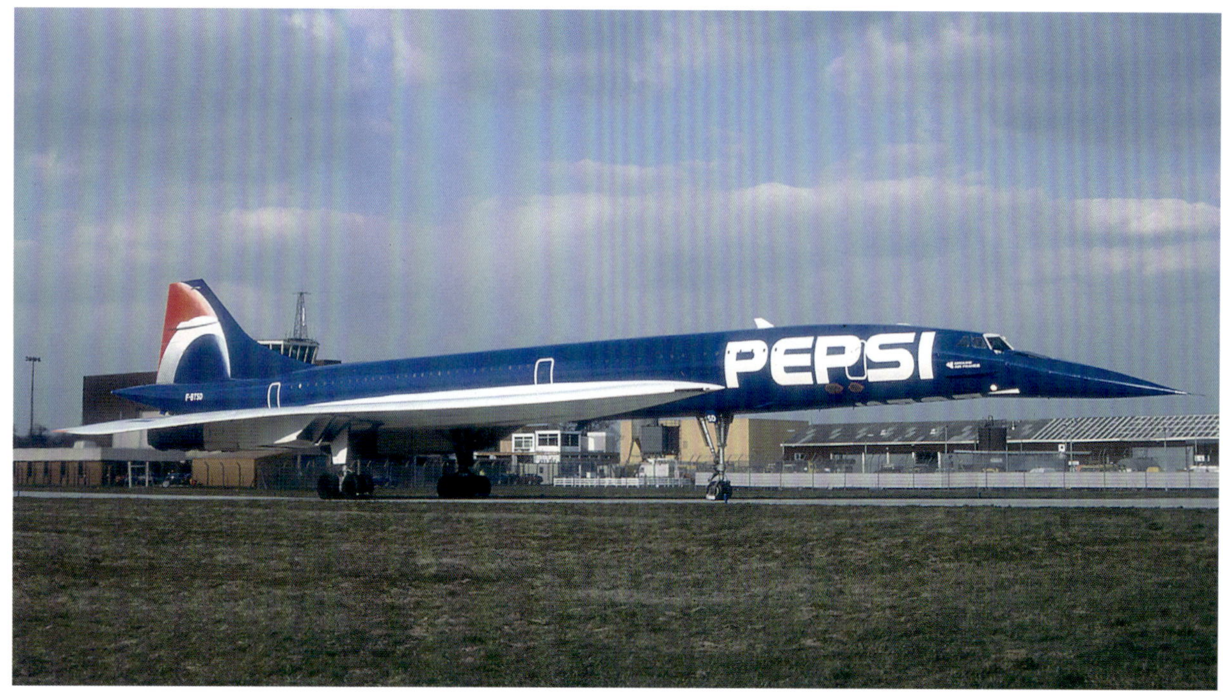

F-BTSD taxiing to a remote stand upon its return to Gatwick.

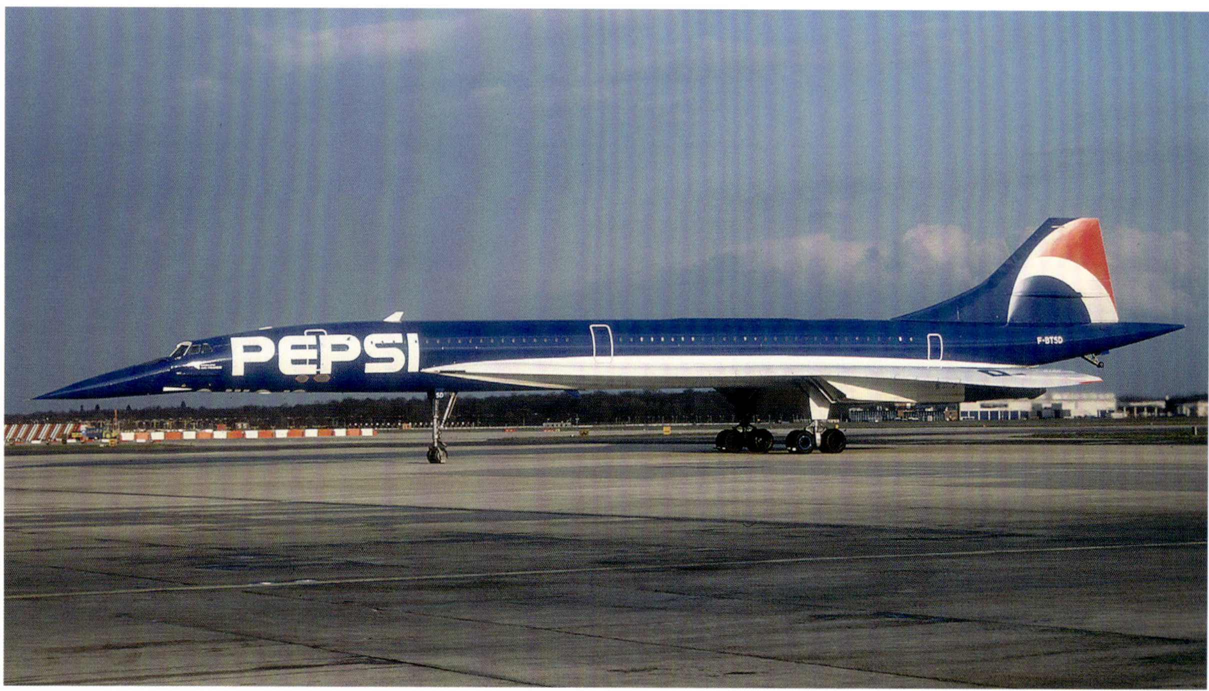

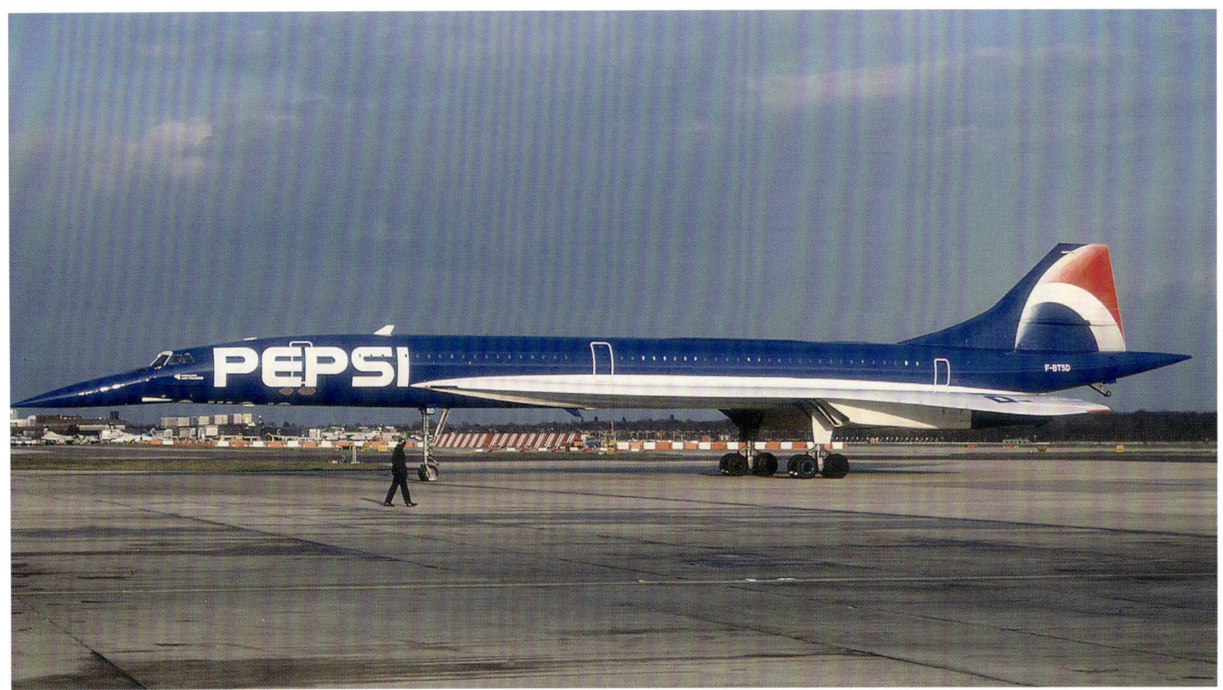

F-BTSD taxies to a remote stand at Gatwick after its first passenger flight on the tour.

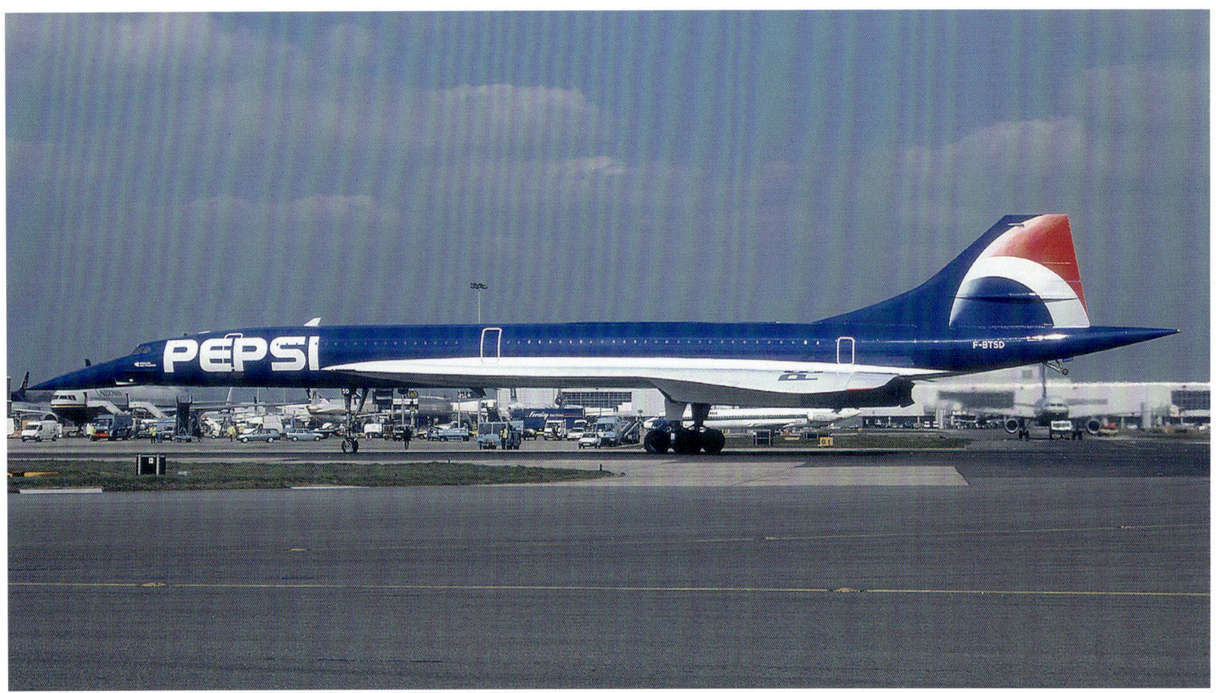

Taxiing out at Gatwick the next day for a positioning flight to Dublin.

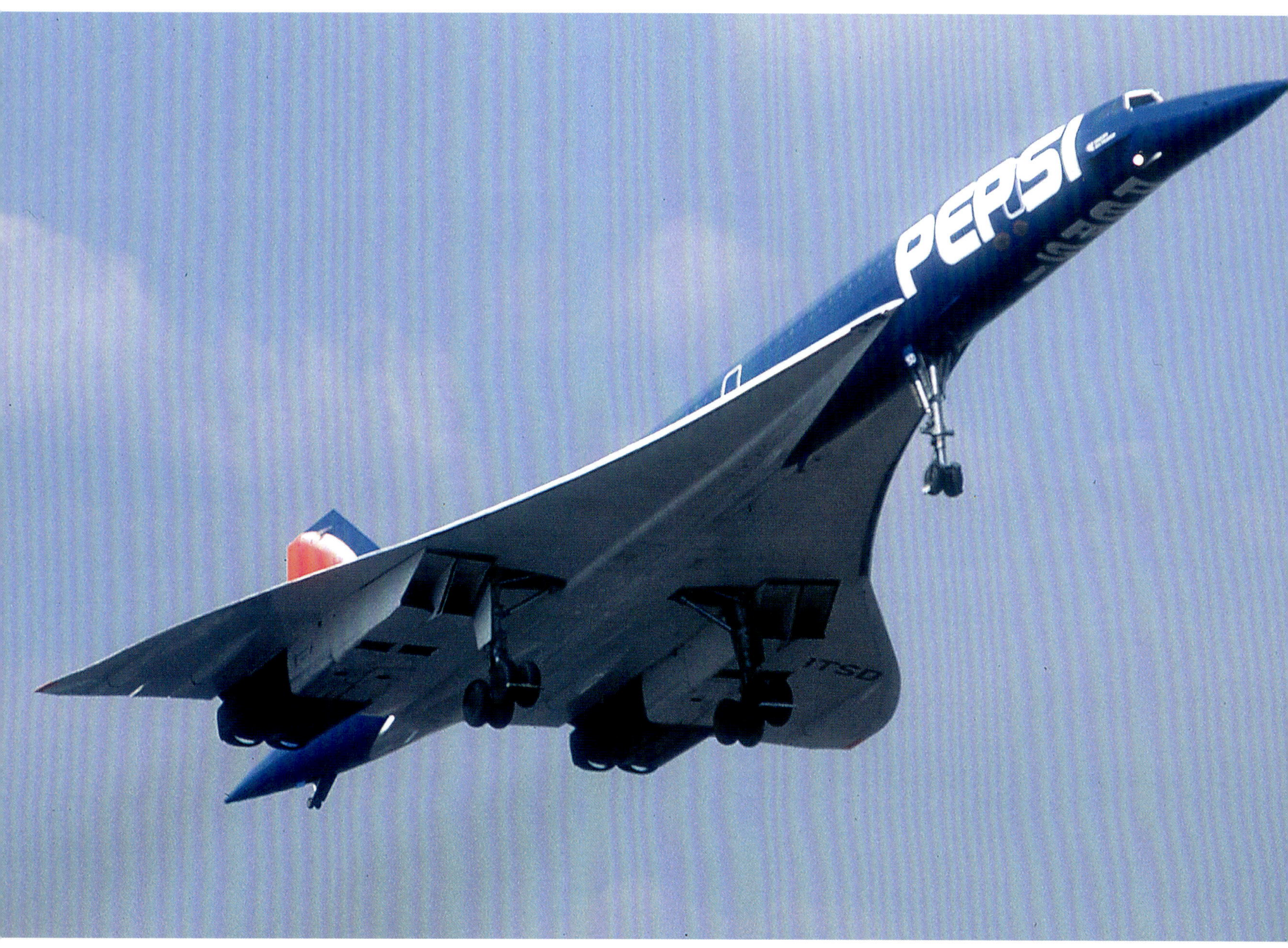

Airborne off runway 08R at Gatwick on 3 April 1996, bound for Dublin.

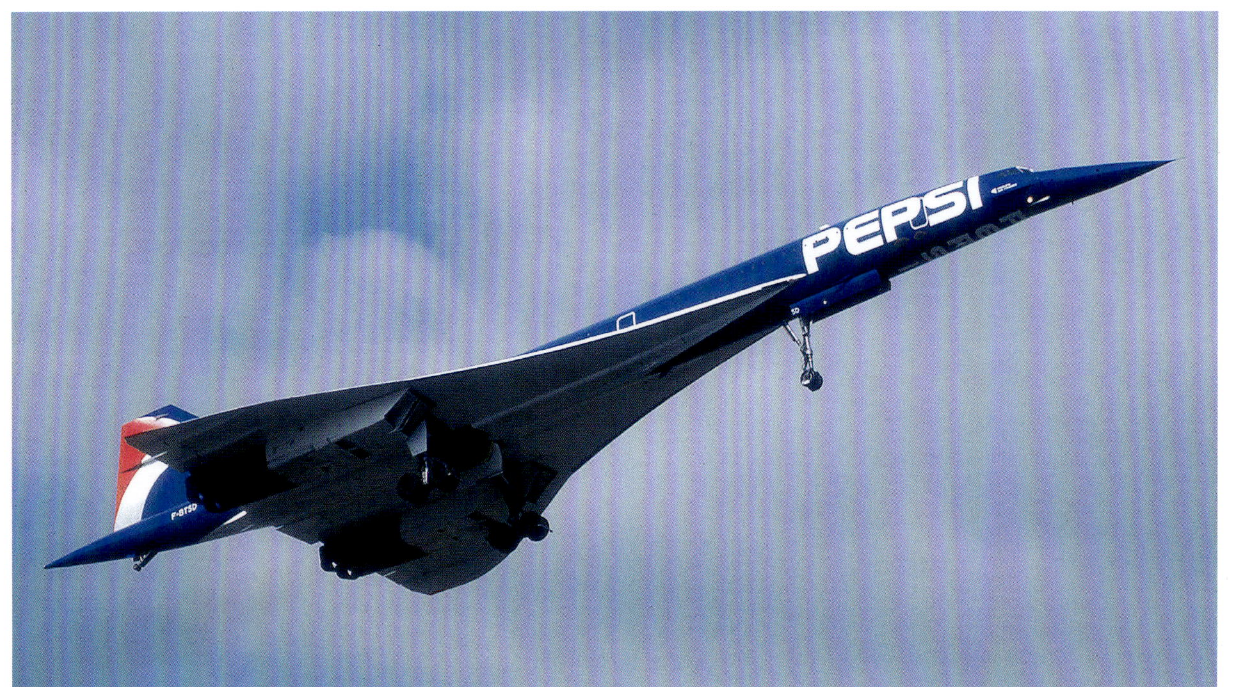

Airborne from runway 08R bound for Dublin. This was a positioning flight for the next stage of the tour. Note the large 'Pepsi' painted on the belly near the nose.

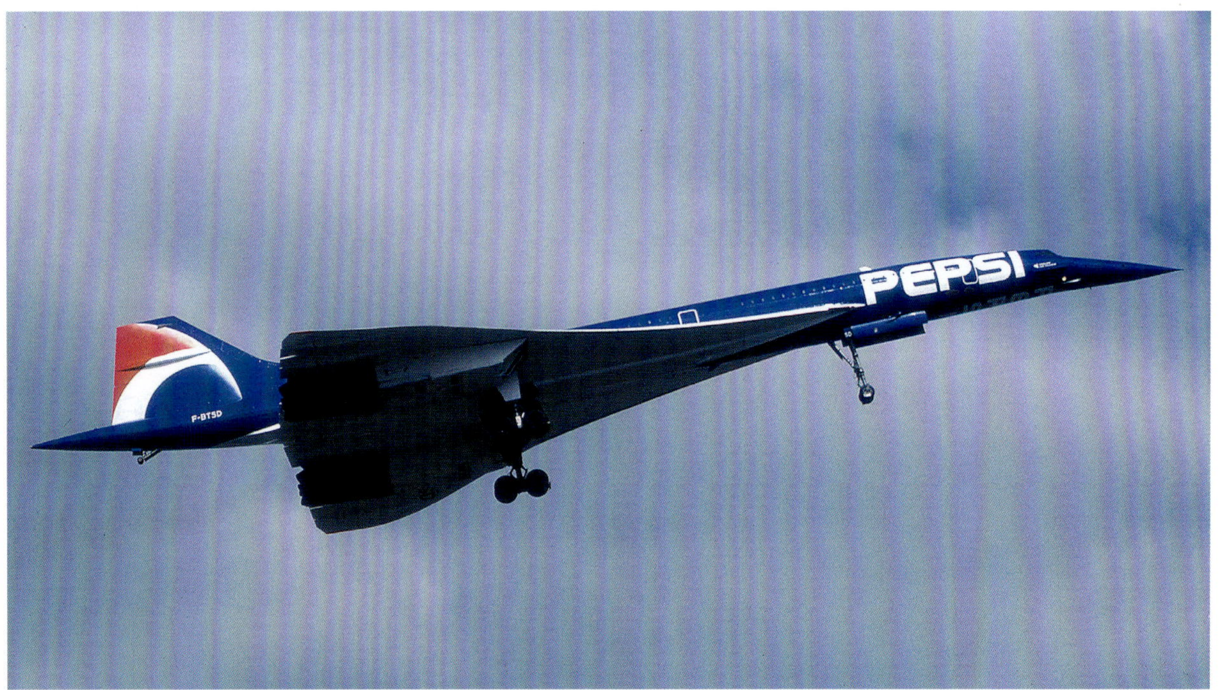

Airborne bound for Dublin on 3 April 1996. This view shows the clean lines of the Concorde design.

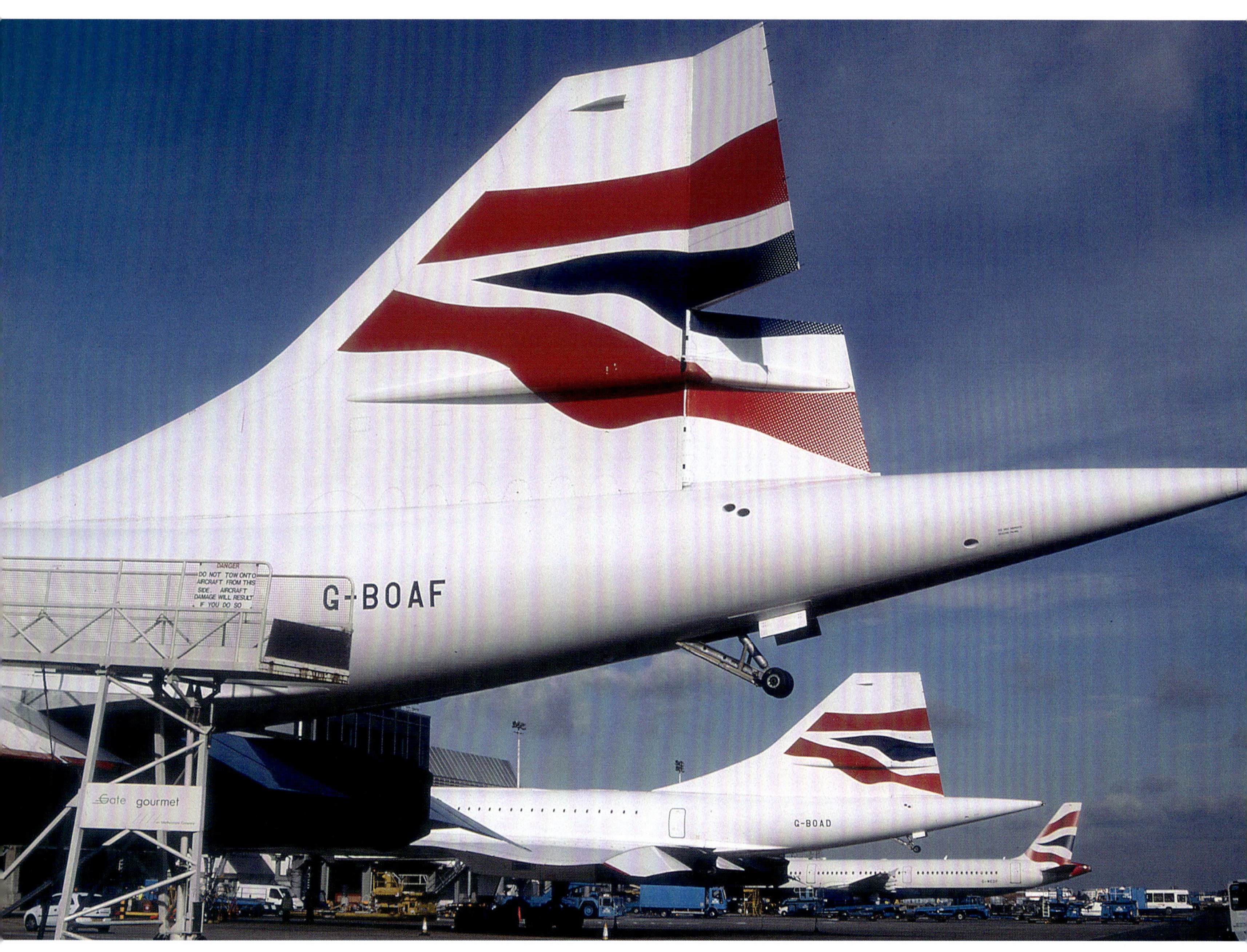

G-BOAF and G-BOAD at Heathrow's Terminal 4 on retirement day, 24 October 2003.

5

BRITISH AIRWAYS RETIREMENT DAY

During the week of the retirement day, British Airways' Concorde fleet was kept busy flying to regional airports such as Belfast, Birmingham, Cardiff and Edinburgh, in some cases flying low over those cities. On 22 October a Concorde charter from Manchester and the scheduled BA002 from JFK landed simultaneously on Heathrow's parallel runways.

British Airways' Concorde operations had been an unqualified success, particularly their charter services. Therefore, Friday, 24 October 2003 was a really sad day when the airline and the nation said farewell to a wonderful aircraft. I was fortunate enough to be inside at Heathrow on the day in question, while many hundreds, or indeed thousands, lined the perimeter fence to watch the events. The morning started bright and sunny with clear skies, but then the clouds rolled over for most of the afternoon, and was far from ideal from a photographer's point of view. However, it was a day not to be missed. There was the unforgettable sight of three Concordes flying low over London, having been given special permission by the Civil Aviation Authority. These aircraft were G-BOAG, operating the scheduled BA002 from JFK; G-BOAF, on a Bay of Biscay round trip carrying VIPs and former Concorde pilots; and G-BOAE, on an Edinburgh charter. All three aircraft then landed at Heathrow one after the other, then taxied around in front of the many British Airways and airport workers. A sight never to be forgotten.

There were two final BA Concorde flights in November. The first was G-BOAG from New York JFK to Boeing Field in Seattle, where it joined the Museum of Flight. The Canadians allowed the aircraft to go supersonic over parts of its territory on this flight on 5 November. On 26 November 2003 it was the turn of G-BOAF, which carried BA staff supersonic over the Bay of Biscay one last time before landing at Bristol's Filton airport, where it was built. It then joined the museum on site.

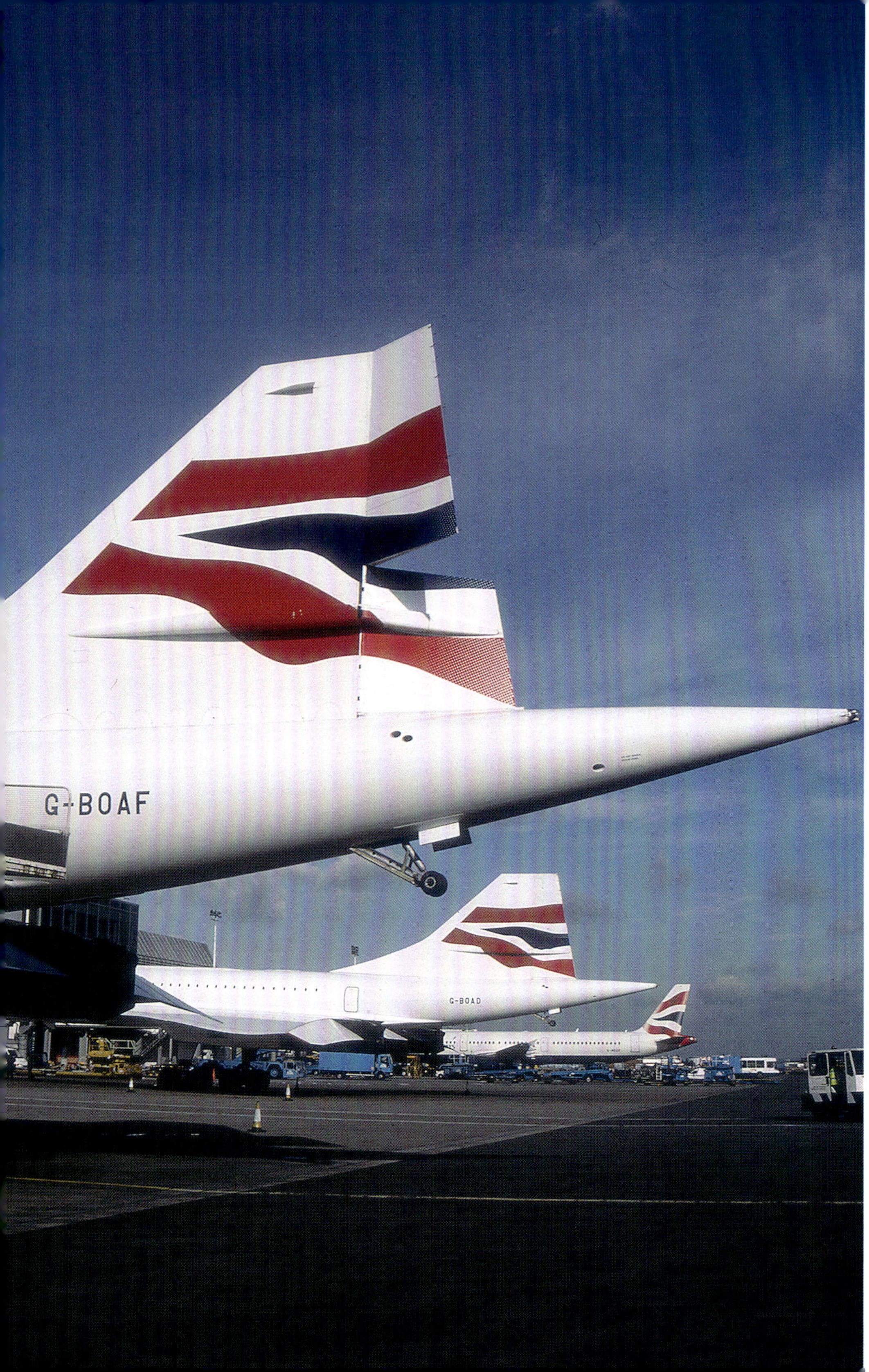

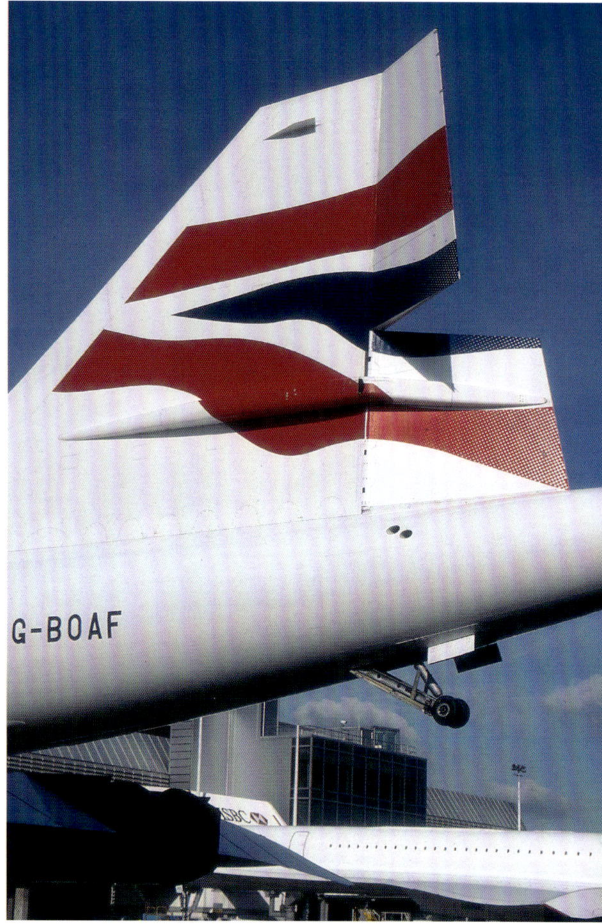

G-BOAF in Union Flag livery at Terminal 4 on 24 October 2003.

G-BOAF and G-BOAD on the lovely sunny morning of retirement day.

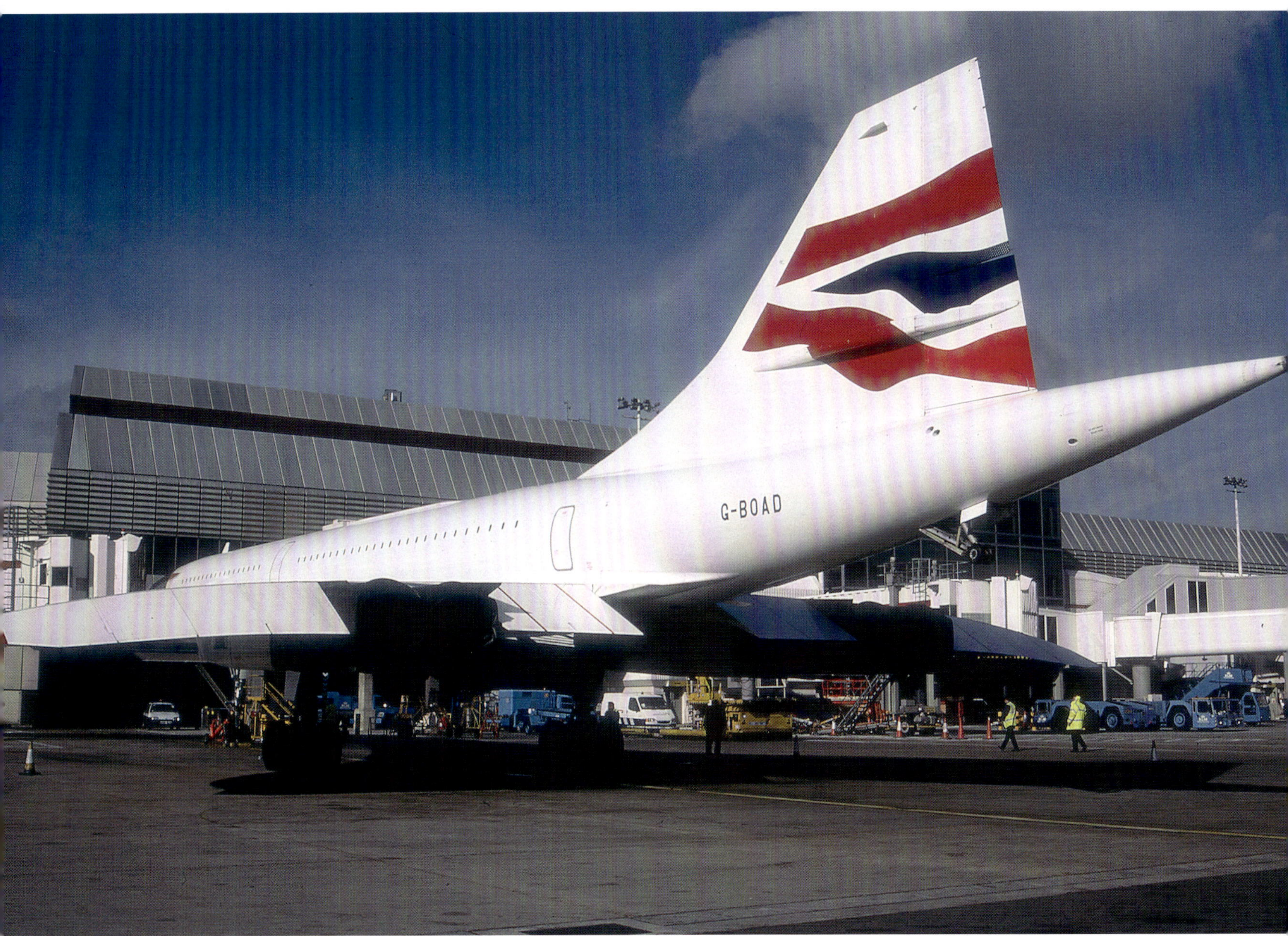

G-BOAD at Terminal 4 on the morning of retirement day.

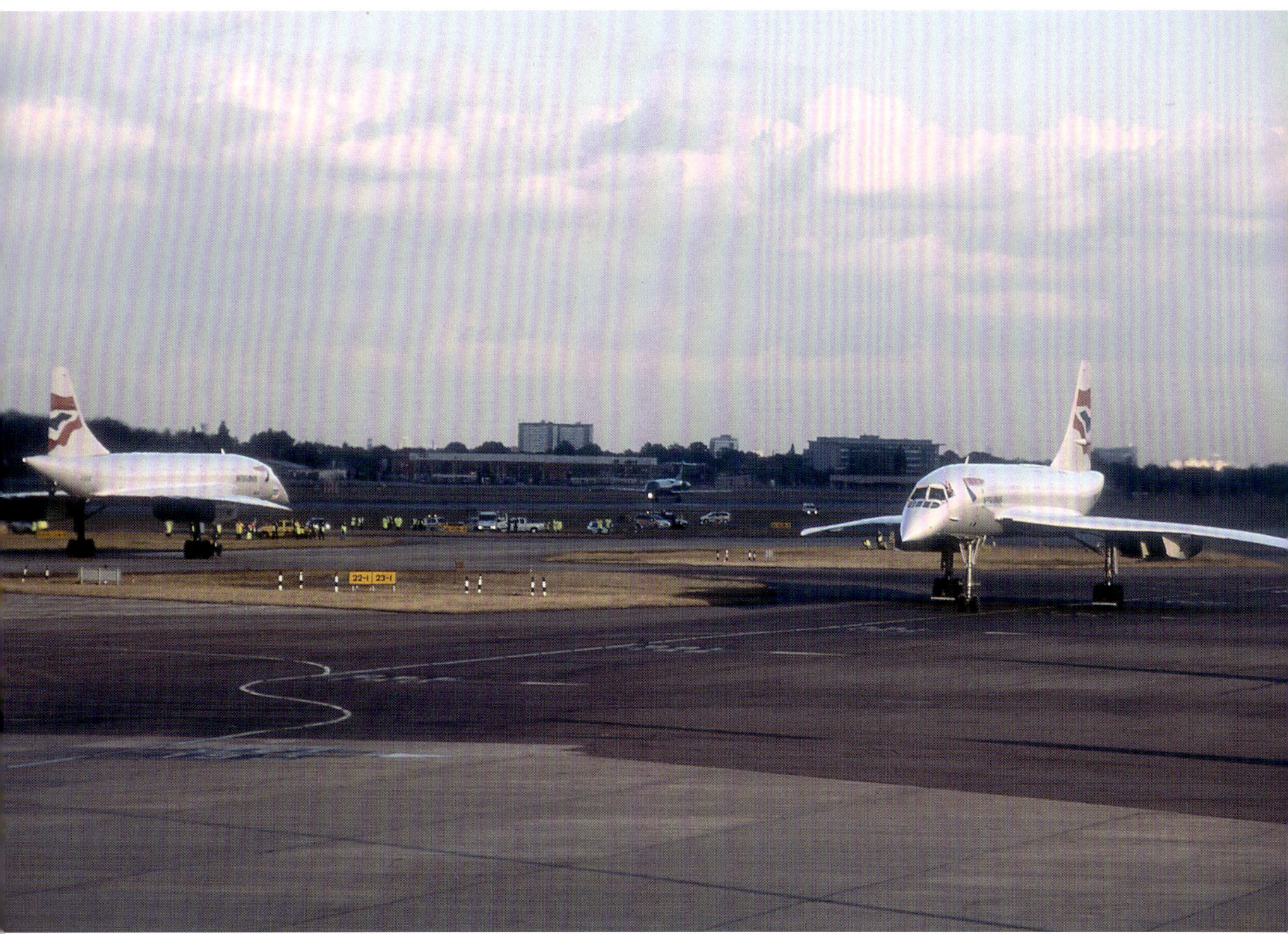

'Hello Concorde.' Two aircraft taxi past each other on retirement day at Heathrow.

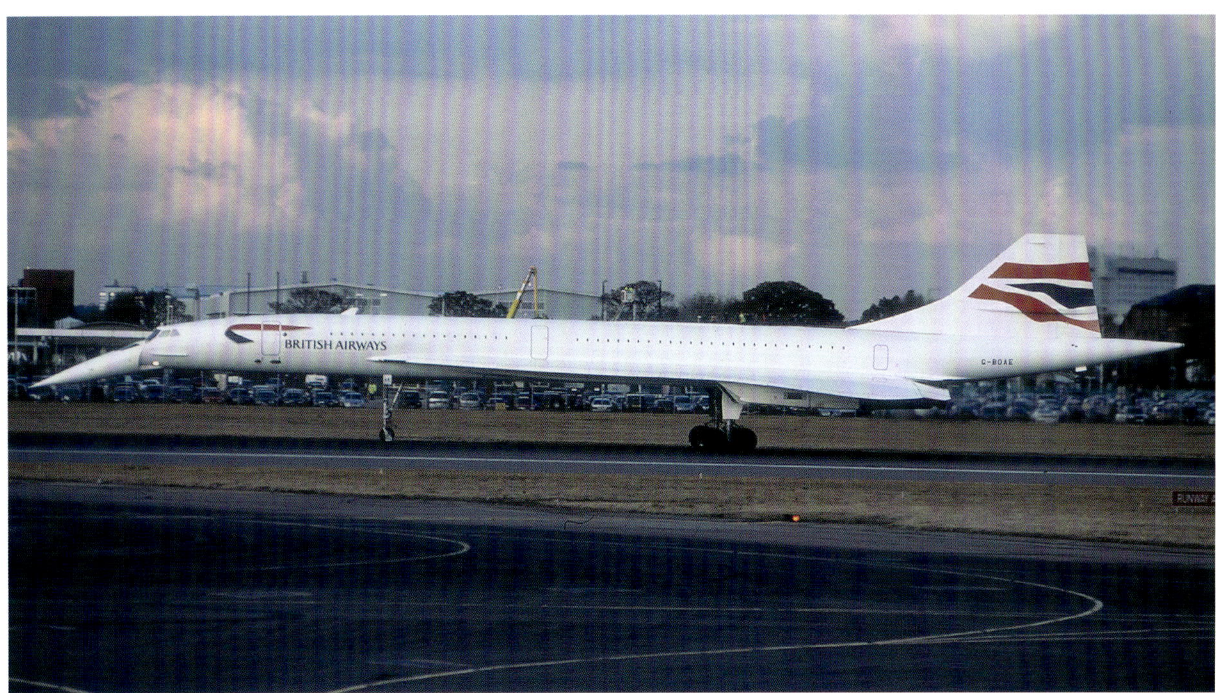

G-BOAE lands
from Edinburgh.

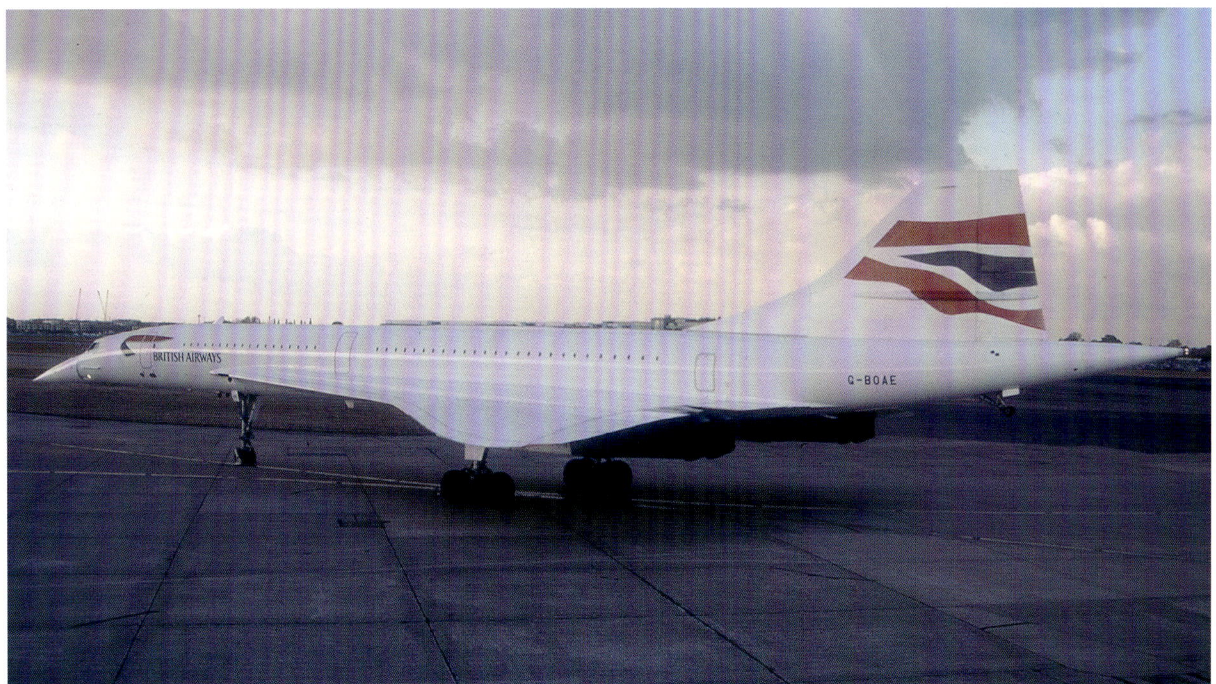

G-BOAE taxiing around
Heathrow after a flight
from Edinburgh.

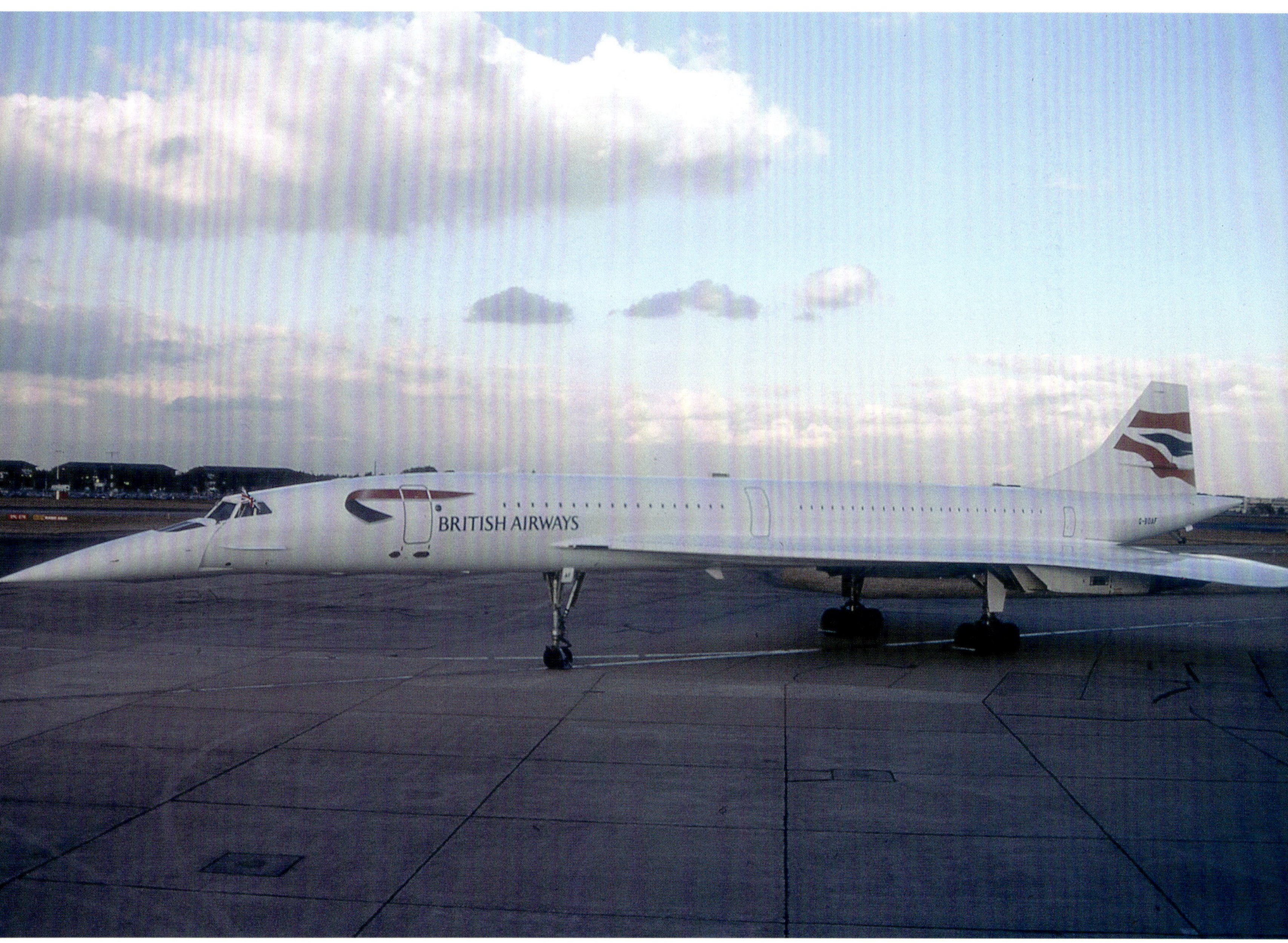

G-BOAF taxies in after a Bay of Biscay supersonic run.

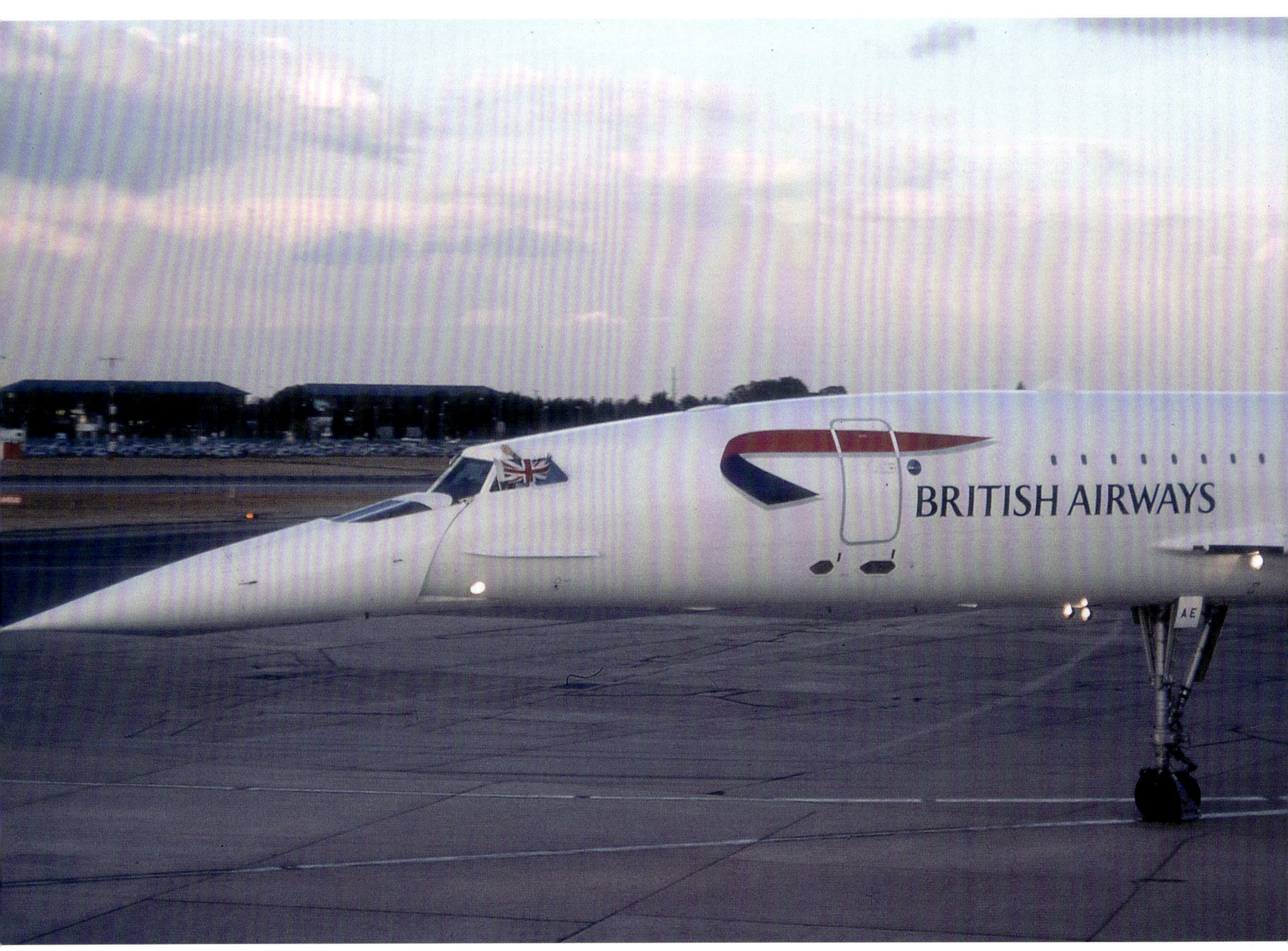

G-BOAE taxies in with a Union Flag flying from the cockpit window.

G-BOAF lifts off runway 27R with an audience of airport workers.

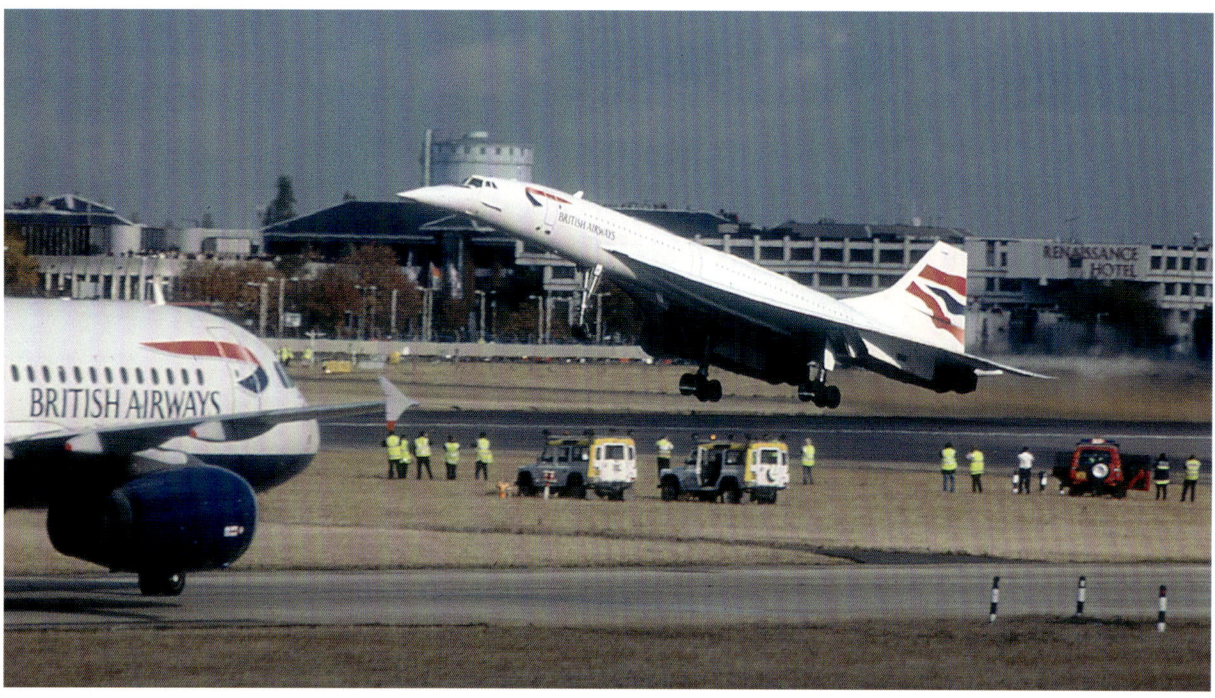

G-BOAF powering off runway 27R for a final Bay of Biscay supersonic run.

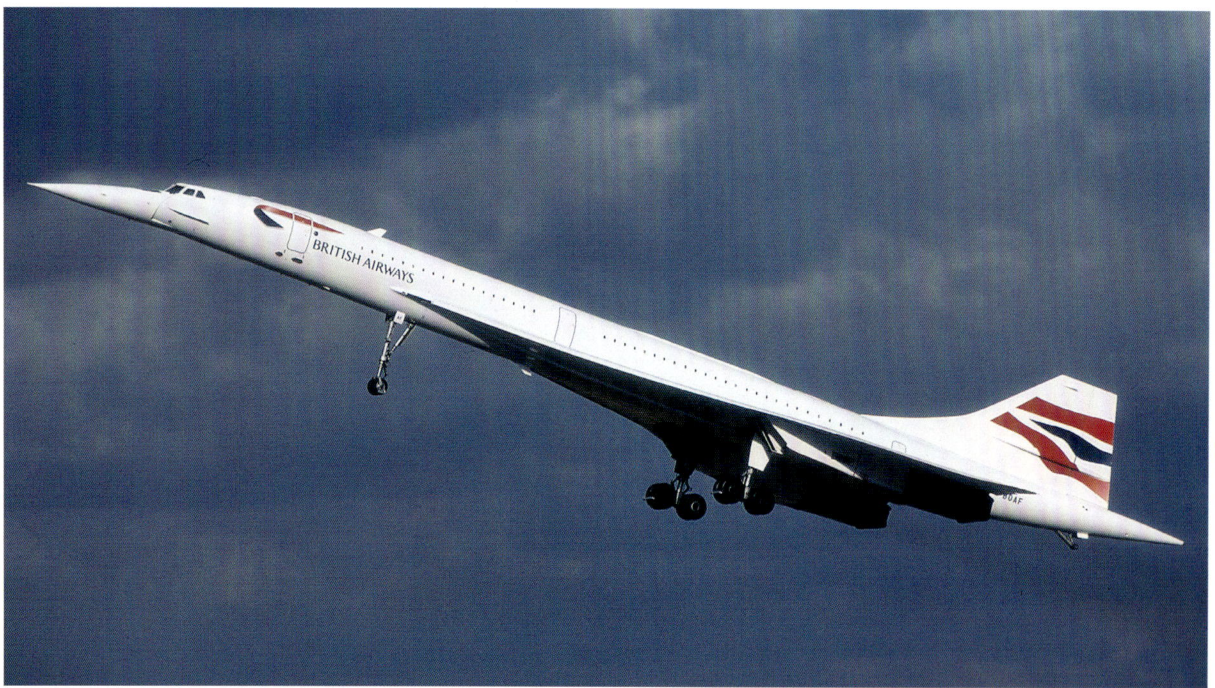

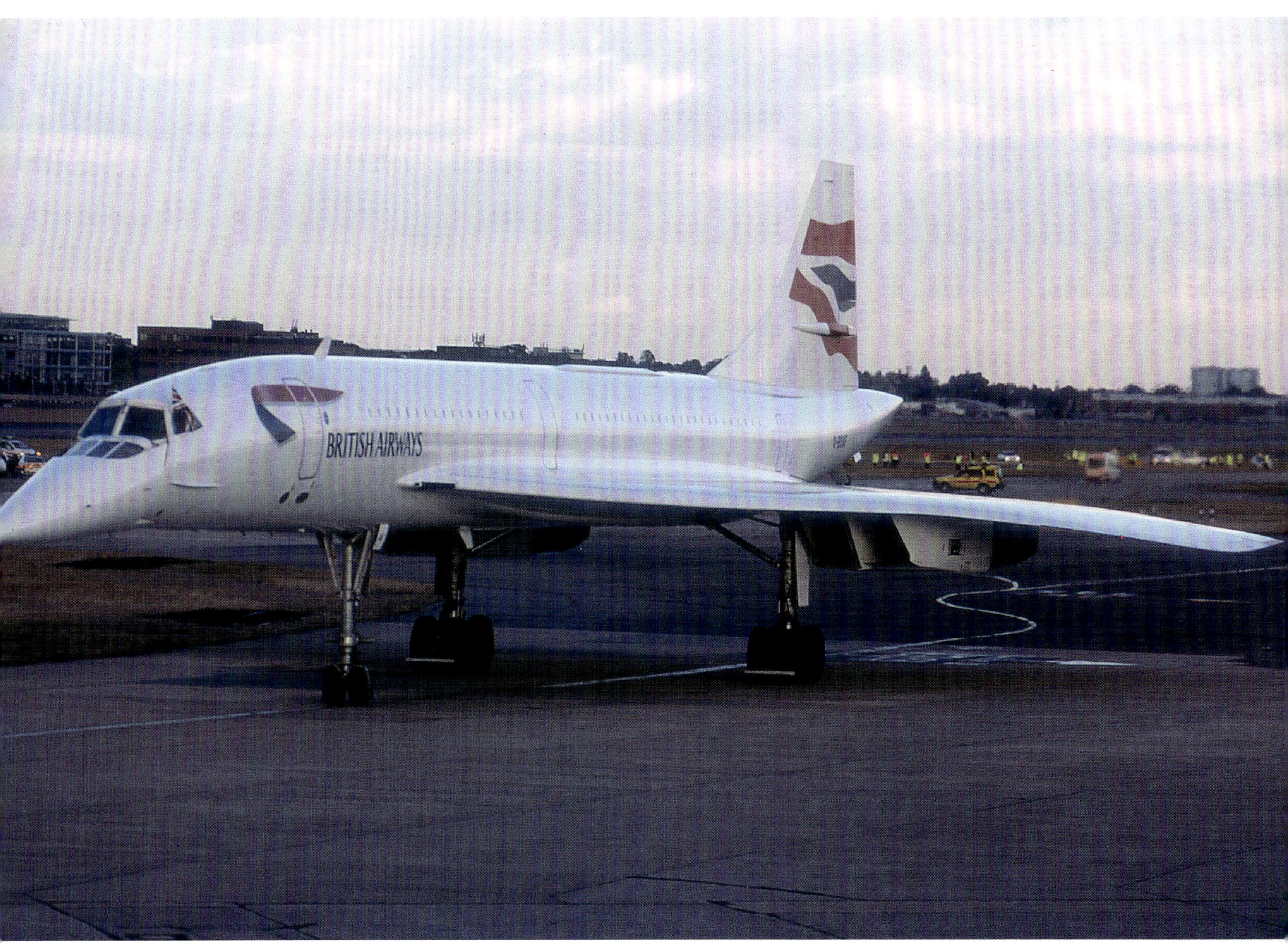

G-BOAF taxies in after a Bay of Biscay round trip.

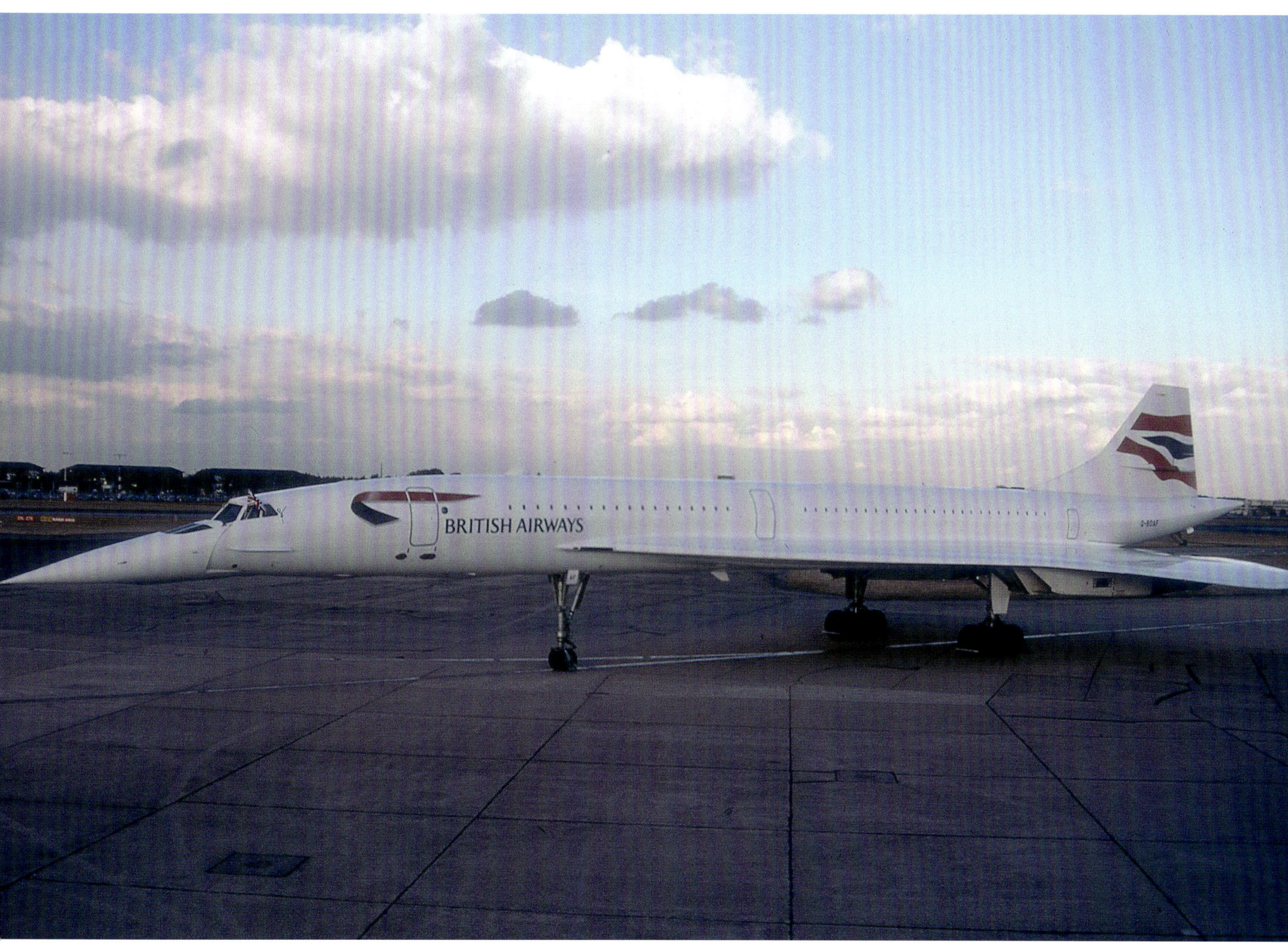

G-BOAF taxiing in at Heathrow after a supersonic dash around the Bay of Biscay.

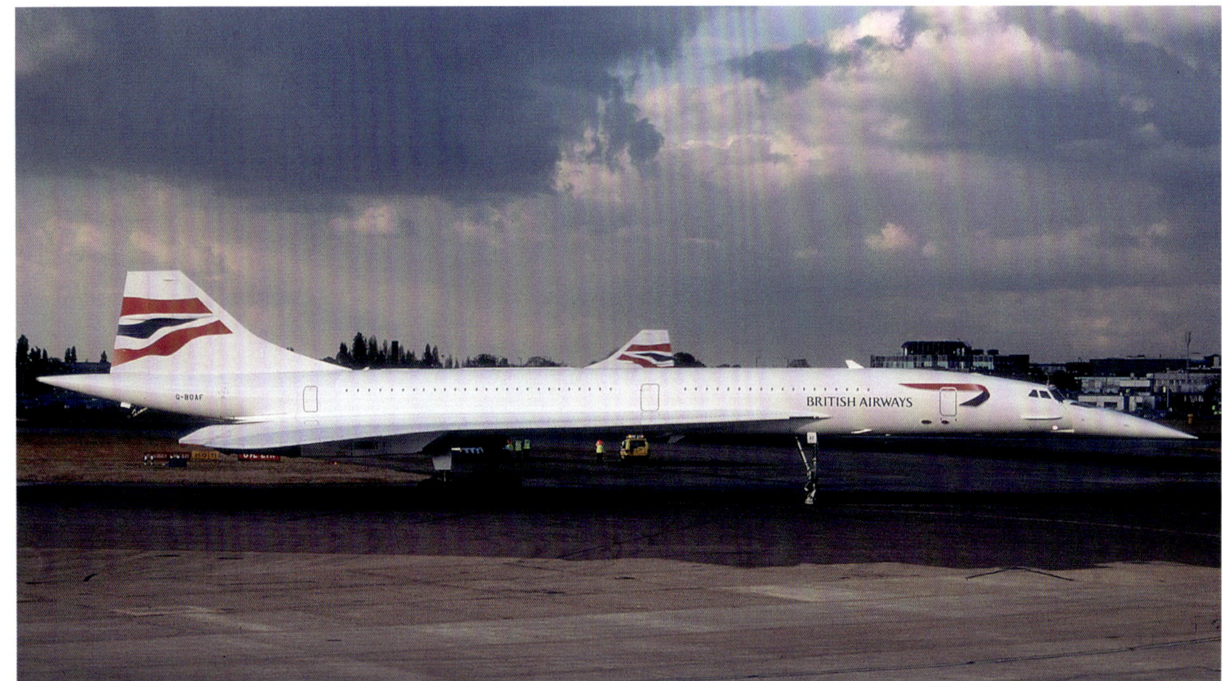

G-BOAF taxies in at Heathrow for the last time.

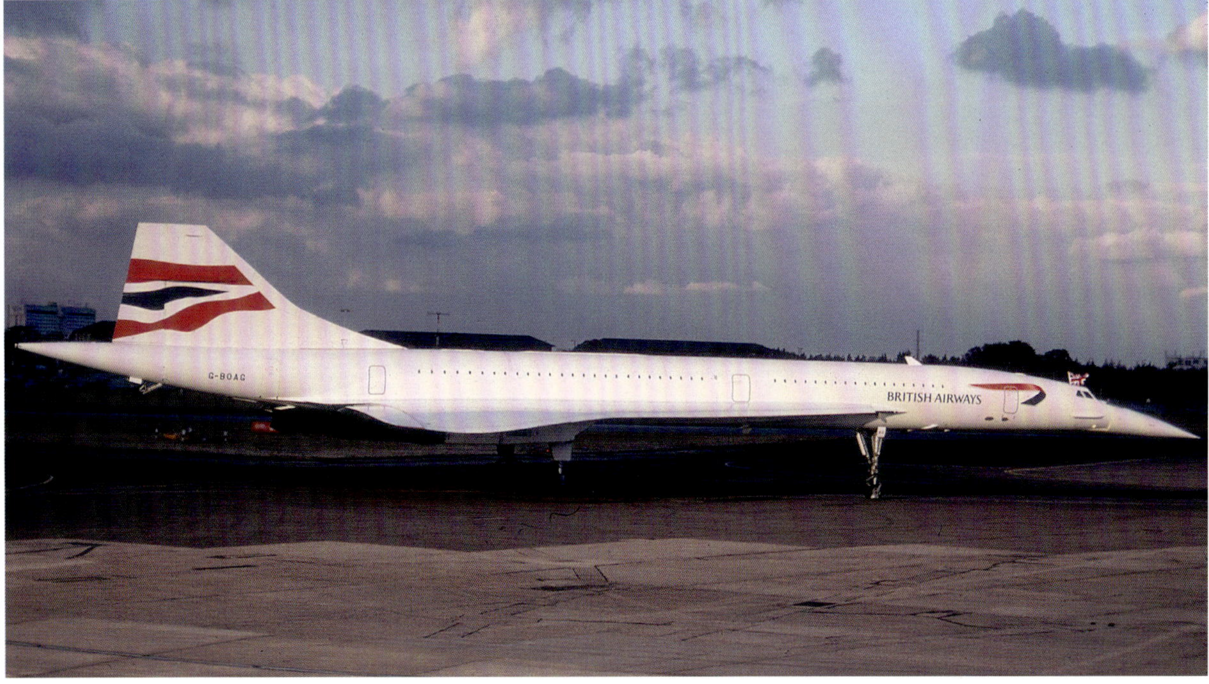

G-BOAG after landing from JFK for the last time as flight BA002.

Gate 6 in Terminal 5 at New York's JFK airport shows that my flight on BA002 (G-BOAE) will soon be leaving from here.

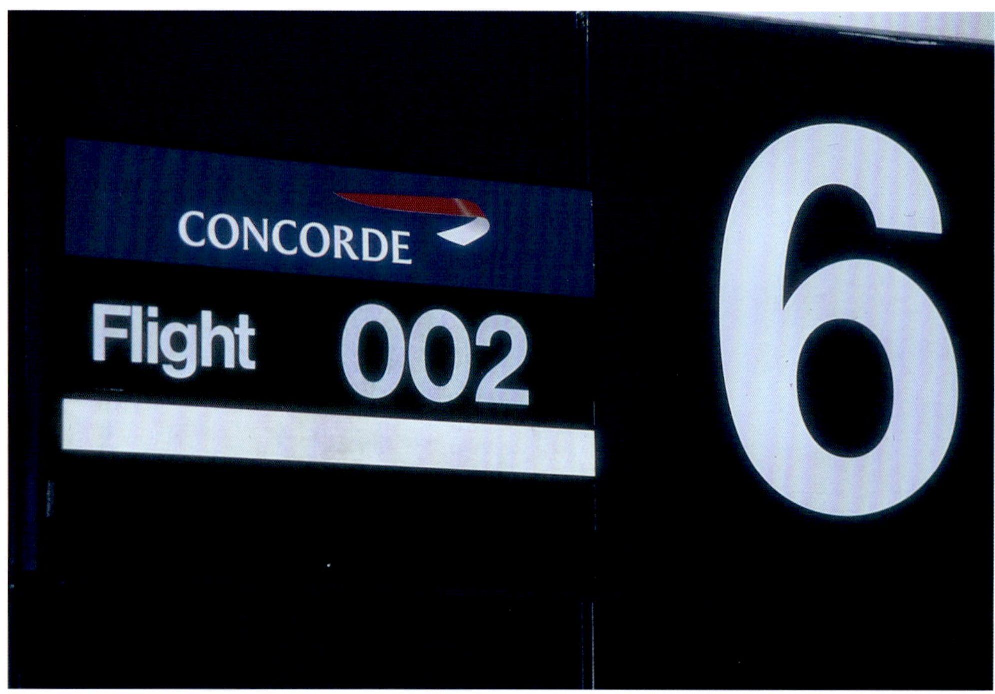

The Machmeter on G-BOAE showing that we are at Mach 2.00 and 54,500ft.

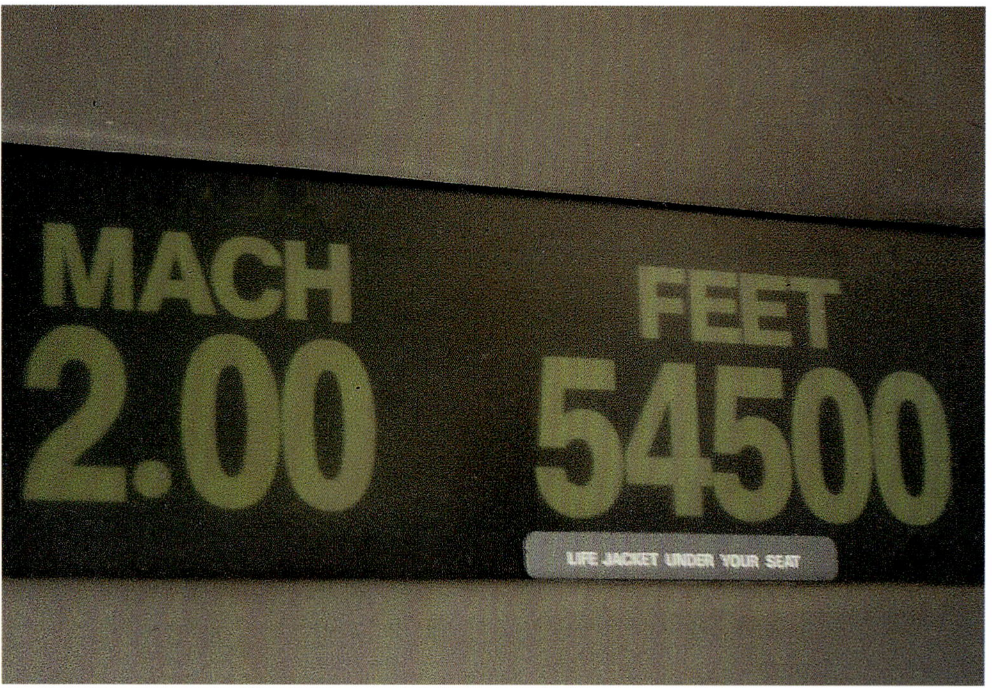

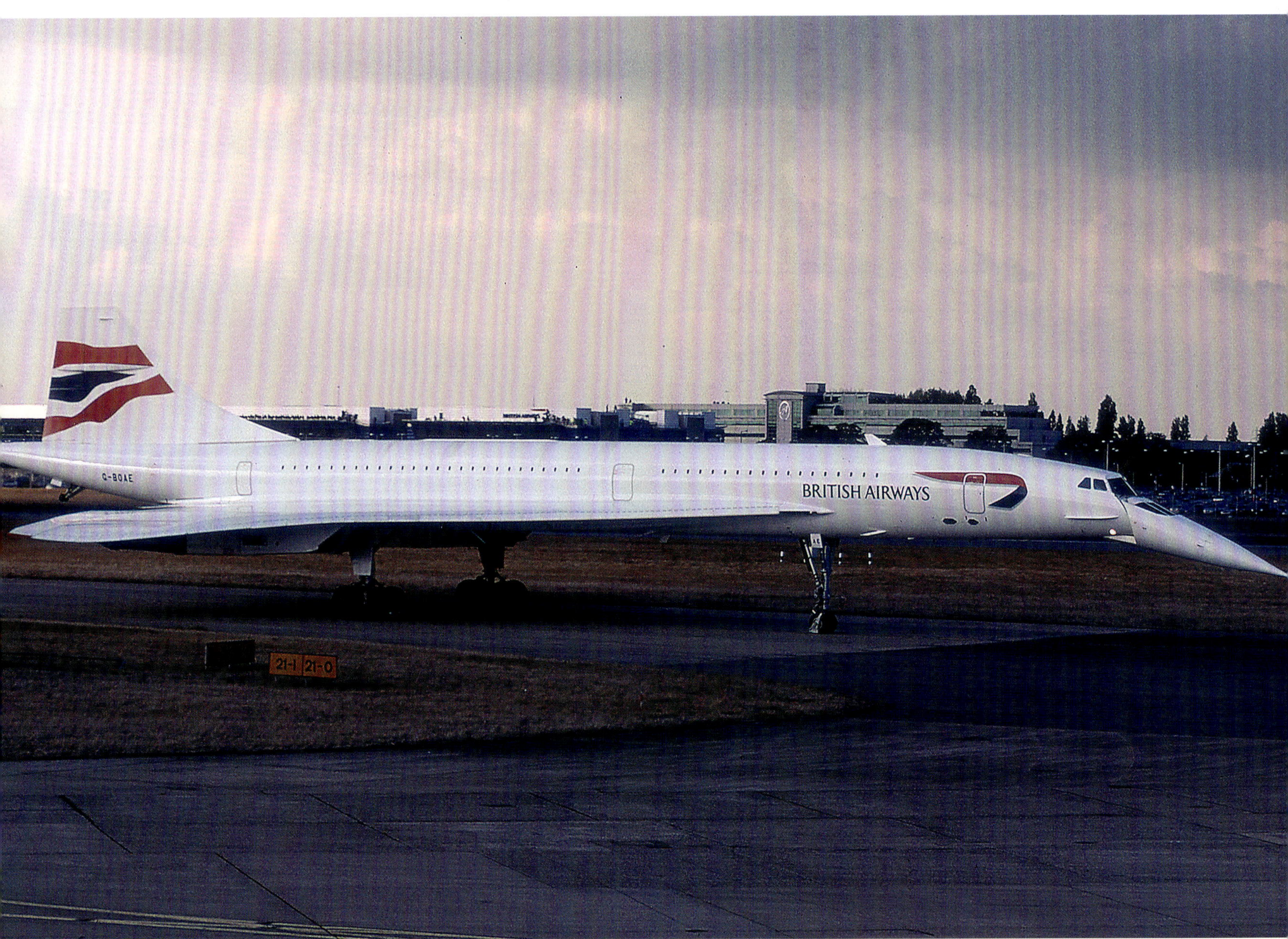

'My Concorde' (G-BOAE) seen at Heathrow on retirement day.

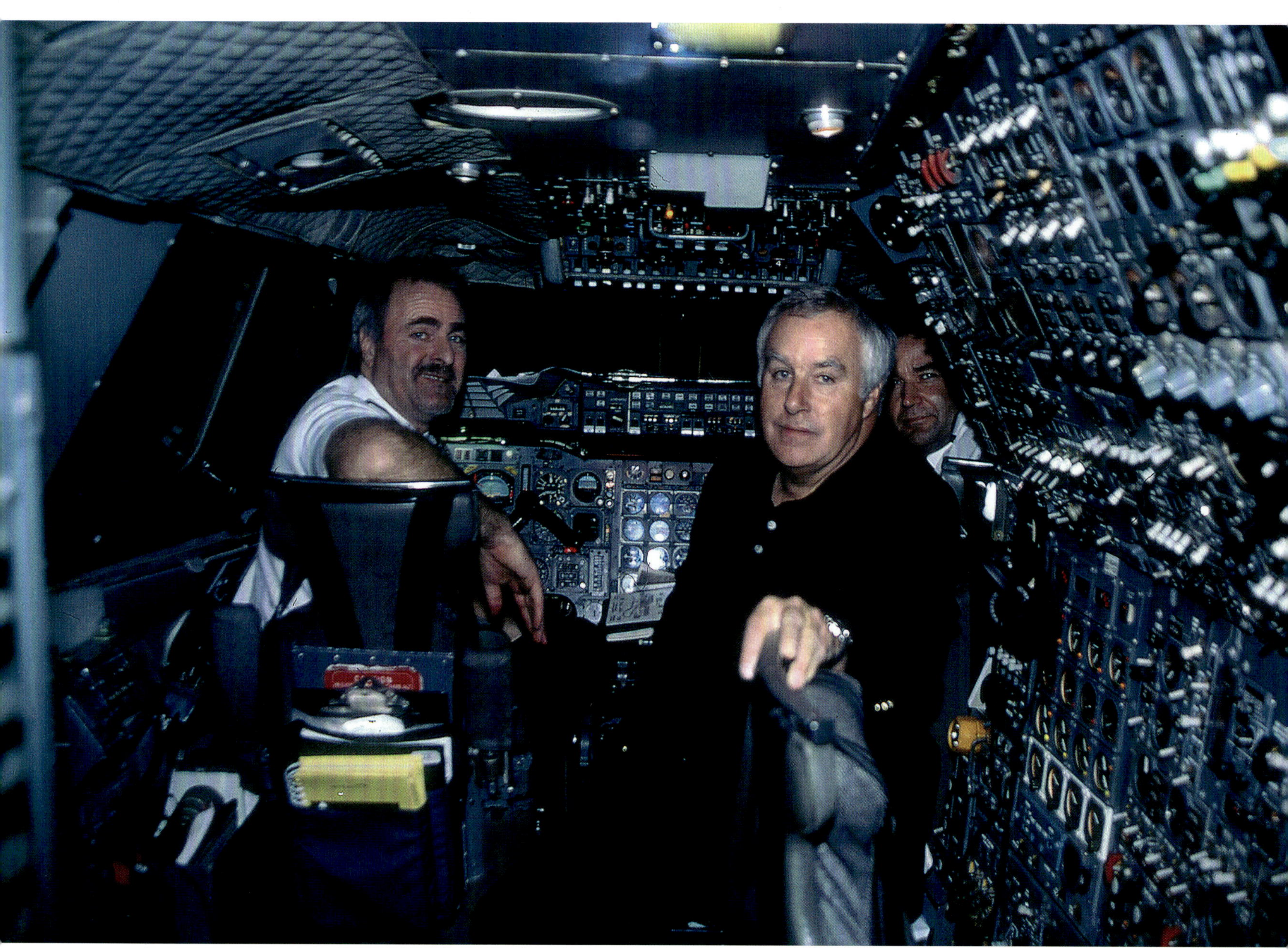

Me in the cockpit after my flight on G-BOAE from New York.

MY CONCORDE FLIGHT

I have to say that, having flown supersonic three times in military jets, initially I was not that fussed about flying in Concorde. I always thought I would have a chance of a cockpit ride on a positioning flight between Gatwick and Heathrow but the opportunity never arose. With only weeks before Concorde operations ceased, my wife then convinced me that, if I did not fly in the type, I would forever regret it. Therefore, only a few weeks before that date, I bit the bullet and booked a trip. It was a Boeing 747 flight from Heathrow to New York's JFK airport but returning on Concorde. So, on 19 October 2003, I presented myself at Terminal 5, the British Airways terminal at JFK.

I boarded flight BA002 from gate six on to G-BOAE under the command of Captain Adrian Thompson. With a surge of power from the Olympus engines, we sped down runway 31L and departed on the Canarsie Standard Instrument Departure (SID), which involved a sharp left turn after take-off. Next stop Heathrow. Soon we were climbing steeply, eyes regularly straying to the Machmeter. At Mach 0.93 the captain restarted the afterburners, injecting raw fuel into the jet pipe to provide extra thrust. Soon we were passing Mach 1 – the speed of sound. Then the Machmeter flickered upwards through Mach 1.98 … 1.99 … 2.00. We were travelling at twice the speed of sound, an amazing 1,350 miles an hour – or 23 miles a minute. With a full complement of 100 passengers, the flight was completed in three hours and twenty-five minutes. Yes, during the transit we flew high enough that, through the small windows, the skies got gradually darker, and yes, at 60,000ft you can actually see the curvature of the Earth. Think about it, other than those who have flown high enough in Concorde or some military jets, the only people who have seen this vista are astronauts. Concorde fuselages were painted white to reflect the sun and help keep the cabin cooler. One result of this heating process was that during a flight Concorde could stretch up to 10in.

I do have to inform readers, however, that I nearly choked on my drink when the American passenger next to me turned to me and said, 'Nice aircraft this, built by Boeing right?'

ACKNOWLEDGEMENTS

I have to thank friends Tom Singfield, Jon West and Paul Seymour for their photographic assistance. Unless otherwise stated, all photographs were taken by the author. Thanks also to Wikipedia, where some of my research was clarified. For the photographers, it should be noted that not one of the images in this book is digital. All of my photographs reproduced here are from 35mm colour slides on the excellent Kodachrome film, which unfortunately the manufacturer stopped making several years ago.

SOURCES AND FURTHER READING

In writing this book, much of the information came from my own memory (my wife tells me my head is full of useless information!), but other sources I used for research deserve a mention:

British Airways News, 23 October 2003.
Goodwood Travel Flights of Fantasy brochure, 1997.
Mach 2: a magazine for Concorde enthusiasts.
BBC4 documentary *Concorde: A Supersonic Story*, aired on 29 August 2024.
The accident report into the crash of F-BTSC by Bureau d'Enquetes et d'Analyses (BEA), the French civil aviation investigation bureau.
Wikipedia.

BOOKS

Bannister, Mike (former BA Concorde captain), *Concorde*, Penguin, 2023.
Falconer, Jonathan, *Concorde: A Photographic History*, JH Haynes & Co., 2008
Gaskell, Keith, *British Airways: Its History, Aircraft and Liveries*, Airlife Publishing, 1999.
Glancey, Jonathan, *Concorde: The Rise and Fall of a Supersonic Airliner*, Atlantic Books, 2016.
Leney, David, and McDonald, David, *Concorde: Owners' Workshop Manual*, JH Haynes & Co., 2018.
March, Peter R., *The Concorde Story*, The History Press, 2005.
Meredith, Adrian, *Concorde: A Photographic Tribute*, The History Press, 2013.
Orlebar, Christopher, *The Concorde Story*, Osprey Publishing, 2011.
Trubshaw, Brian (former test pilot), *Concorde: The Complete Inside Story*, The History Press, 2004.

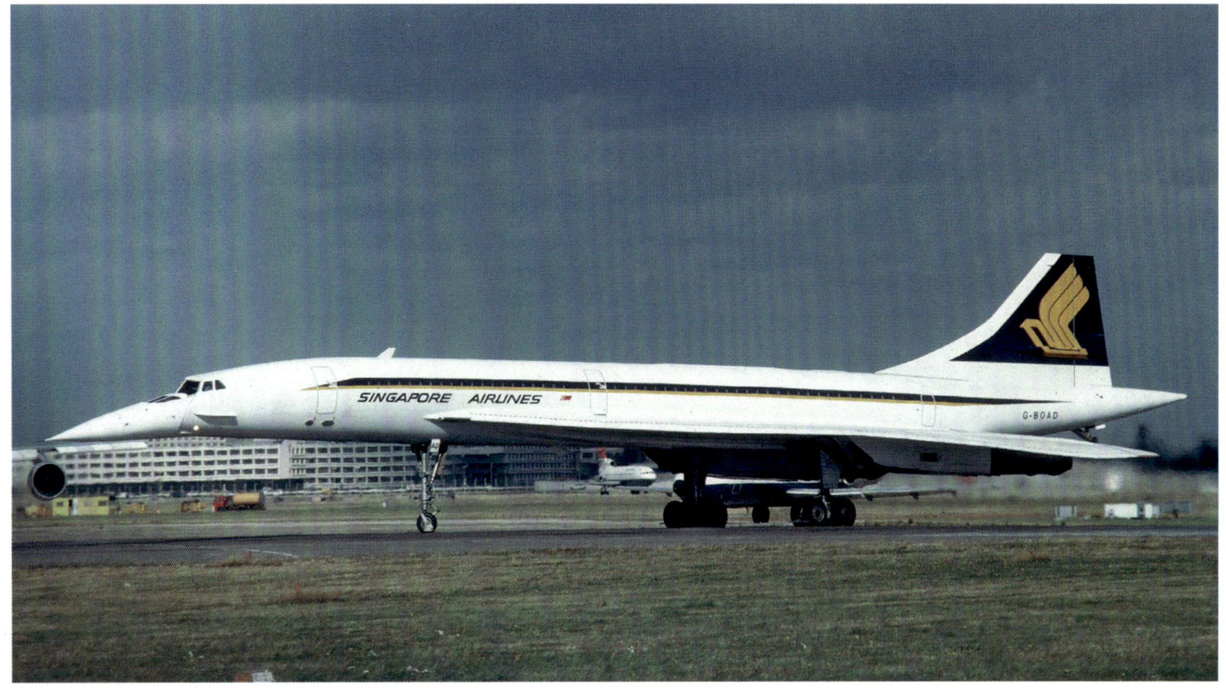

G-BOAD with Singapore Airlines livery on the port side about to depart Heathrow for Singapore's Paya Lebar Airport. (Paul Seymour)

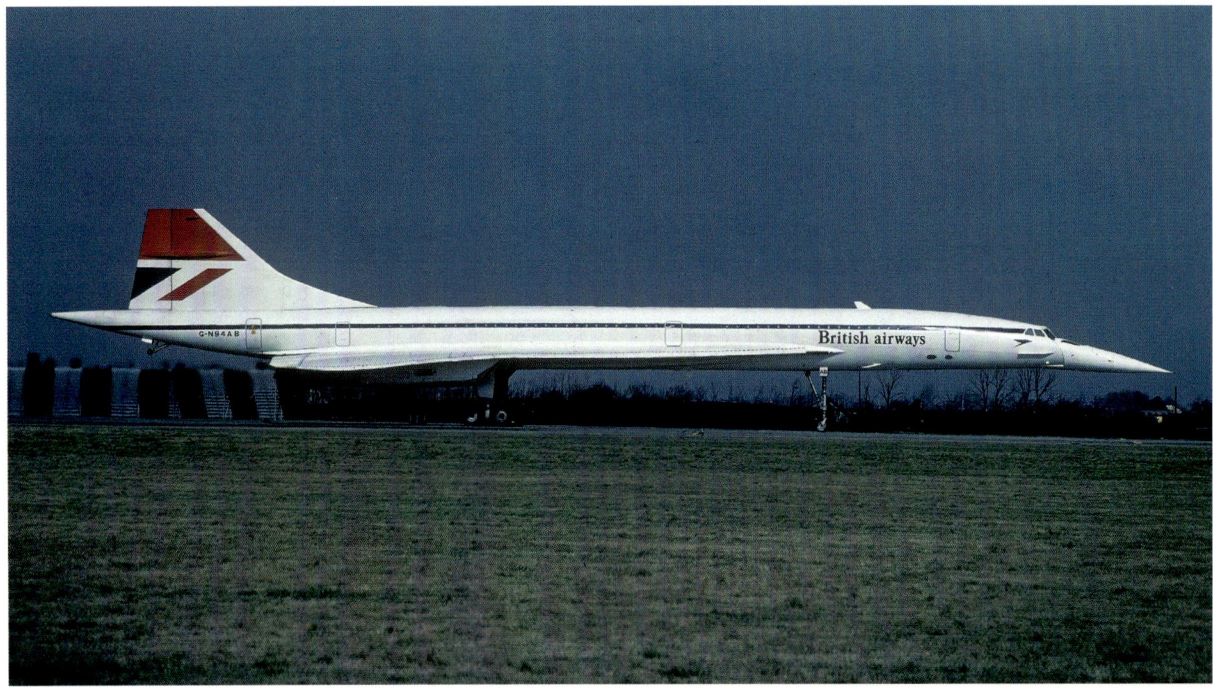

G-N94AB in Negus & Negus BA livery but US registration. (Tom Singfield collection)